What To Believe Now

For my parents, Margaret and Tony, with love and gratitude

What To Believe Now

*Applying Epistemology to
Contemporary Issues*

David Coady

WILEY-BLACKWELL

A John Wiley & Sons, Ltd., Publication

Blackwell Publishing was acquired by John Wiley & Sons in February 2007. Blackwell's publishing program has been merged with Wiley's global Scientific, Technical, and Medical business to form Wiley-Blackwell.

Registered Office
John Wiley & Sons, Ltd, The Atrium, Southern Gate, Chichester, West Sussex, PO19 8SQ, UK

Editorial Offices
350 Main Street, Malden, MA 02148-5020, USA
9600 Garsington Road, Oxford, OX4 2DQ, UK
The Atrium, Southern Gate, Chichester, West Sussex, PO19 8SQ, UK

For details of our global editorial offices, for customer services, and for information about how to apply for permission to reuse the copyright material in this book please see our website at www.wiley.com/wiley-blackwell.

Library of Congress Cataloging-in-Publication Data
Coady, David, 1965–
What to believe now : applying epistemology to contemporary issues / David Coady.
    p.   cm.
  Includes bibliographical references and index.
  ISBN 978-1-4051-9993-3 (hardcover : alk. paper) – ISBN 978-1-4051-9994-0
(pbk. : alk. paper)
  1. Knowledge, Theory of.   2. Ethics.   I. Title.
    BD176.C63 2012
    121–dc23

                                                    2011038289
A catalogue record for this book is available from the British Library.

This book is published in the following electronic formats: ePDFs 9781444362091; ePub 9781444362107; mobi 9781444362114

Set in 10/12pt Palatino by SPi Publisher Services, Pondicherry, India

1   2012

He who says "Better to go without belief forever than believe a lie!" merely shows his own preponderant private horror of becoming a dupe. ... It is like a general informing his soldiers that it is better to keep out of battle forever than to risk a single wound. Not so are victories either over enemies or over nature gained. Our errors are surely not such awfully solemn things. In a world where we are so certain to incur them in spite of all our caution, a certain lightness of heart seems healthier than this excessive nervousness on their behalf.

William James, "The Will to Believe"

they were afraid to be with him,
or to think much about him for fear they might believe him

John Dos Passos, *The 42nd Parallel*

Contents

Preface

In this book, I attempt to show how epistemology, the study of knowledge and justified belief, can be relevant to issues of contemporary concern. I address questions about what we can know and what we are justified in believing, not in the abstract ahistorical way of most traditional epistemology, but through an explicit consideration of the practicalities of working these things out at the beginning of the twenty-first century. I argue that epistemology would benefit from an applied turn, analogous to the applied turn which ethics has undergone in recent decades.

To some extent, this applied turn has already begun, under the banner of "social epistemology." Although the concerns of this book partly overlap with the concerns of social epistemology, not all social epistemology is particularly applied and not all applied epistemology is particularly social. This book is centrally concerned with practical questions about what we should believe, and how we should pursue knowledge, wisdom, and other epistemic values. Although many of these questions are (in some sense) social questions, not all of them are, any more than all questions in applied ethics are social questions.

Each chapter of this book (after the first) picks up from where the preceding chapter left off. Nonetheless each chapter can be read on its own if the reader is so inclined. The earlier parts of the book tend to be more discursive and expository than the later parts. Readers who are not particularly interested in current philosophical debates about expertise or democracy may choose to skip ahead to Chapters 4 through 6, which are more directly engaged with debates going on outside philosophy departments (and even outside universities). These three chapters are unified by two closely related themes, the importance of free public channels of communication and the dangers of overcredulous deference to formal authority.

There is very little technical language in this book. The main exception is Chapter 2, which includes some discussion of Bayesianism and probability. Again, readers should feel free to skip this if they like.

In preparing the present work, I have made use of previously published materials as follows: Chapter 1 includes some brief passages from Coady (2010); Chapter 2 includes some brief passages from Coady (2006d); Chapter 4 includes some passages from Coady (2006c); Chapter 5 includes some passages from Coady (2007b); and Chapter 6 includes passages from Coady (2011).

I am indebted to many more people than I can think to acknowledge here. I owe a very special intellectual and personal debt to my father, Tony Coady. I am also greatly indebted to Charles Pigden who first got me interested in applied epistemology through his work on conspiracy theories. Both men have taught me that that passion and good humor are compatible with good reasoning, and that good philosophy can promote good causes. I would like to thank Alvin Goldman for his uncanny ability to ask the right questions. Nothing remotely like this book could exist without him. I would also like to thank my wife Diana Barnes, my mother Margaret Coady, my brother Ben Coady, and my colleagues at the University of Tasmania – James Chase, Lucy Tatman, and especially Richard Corry for his invaluable feedback and support over the last few years. I would also like to thank Andrew Alexandra, Wayne Christensen, Steve Clarke, Brian Keeley, Neil Levy, and Julie Barnes. Thanks also to Tiffany Mok, Jeff Dean, and the people of Wiley-Blackwell for their patient assistance. And thanks also to Jenny Roberts for all her help.

1

Introduction

Epistemology has always been, at least in part, a normative discipline. It is in the business of prescription, not mere description. It characterizes certain states and practices as good, bad, or indifferent. Not content to say how the world is, it aims to say how it should be. The normative dimensions of epistemology are a consequence of the two concepts which are standardly used to define the subject, *knowledge* and *justified belief*.

Aristotle famously said that "all men by nature desire to know" (*Metaphysics*, 1.980a). He recognized that knowledge seeking is a pervasive feature of human life. Knowledge is desirable for instrumental reasons (i.e., as a means to other goods), but it also seems to be, at least sometimes, an intrinsic good as well (i.e., something that is good whether or not it leads to further goods). Accordingly, one of the central tasks of epistemology has been to investigate how we should go about acquiring this good.

The normative implications of the concept of *justified belief* are equally clear. To call a belief justified is, *at the very least*, to give a consideration in favor of that belief. I will be adopting and defending a stronger position in this book, sometimes called "the guidance conception of justification" (Pollock, 1986, p. 10), according to which to

What To Believe Now: Applying Epistemology to Contemporary Issues,
First Edition. David Coady.
© 2012 David Coady. Published 2012 by Blackwell Publishing Ltd.

call a belief justified is simply to say that we ought to believe it, and to say that a person is justified in believing something is simply to say that he or she ought to believe it.

Whether epistemology is understood as an investigation into how to acquire knowledge or as an investigation into what we ought to believe, it is natural to compare it to ethics, which has long been the paradigm of a normative discipline within philosophy. It is particularly natural to compare the problem of working out what we ought to believe, to the problem which Plato thought of as the central problem of ethics, that of working out how we ought to live (*Republic*, Book 1, 352).[1]

Analogies of this kind have recently led several philosophers to develop epistemological theories that are explicitly inspired by ethical theories. But although epistemology has been willing to turn to ethics for theoretical guidance, it has been much more reluctant to follow the lead of ethics in another way. Whereas the work of philosophers like Peter Singer and Jonathan Glover has transformed the study of ethics in recent decades, by addressing contemporary social and technological issues, the study of epistemology remains quite abstract and ahistorical. It is true that some epistemologists have applied their theorizing to contemporary issues (and a handful have even called that work "applied epistemology"), but applied epistemology, unlike applied ethics, remains an obscure and underdeveloped subject. For many people, including many professional philosophers, "applied philosophy" is virtually synonymous with "applied ethics."

This view of the scope of applied philosophy is not inevitable, and one of the chief tasks of this book will be to argue that it is too limited. The information revolution and the knowledge economy have radically changed the way that we acquire knowledge and justify our beliefs. These changes have altered our epistemic landscape as surely as the sexual revolution and breakthroughs in reproductive technology have changed our moral landscape. The latter changes provided a good deal of the impetus for the applied turn in ethics, but the former changes have so far failed to result in a comparable turn in epistemology. Such a turn is surely inevitable, and this book aims to contribute to it. Hence this book will not only do some applied epistemology, it will also constitute an argument for the importance of applied epistemology as an emerging field of research.

It has often been observed that the applied turn in ethics of the last few decades is not a radical departure from tradition, but a rediscovery of an earlier approach to the subject.[2] This would be equally true of an applied turn in epistemology. Although the expression "applied epistemology" seems to be quite new, the practice of applying epistemology to issues of topical concern is not. One classic example of applied epistemology is David Hume's argument against belief in miracles (1966/1748, Section 10). The question of whether one could be justified in believing stories of miracles from the Bible and other religious or historical texts was of great interest to Europeans in the middle of the eighteenth century.[3] Epistemological considerations have also played a significant role in the history of political philosophy. For example, John Locke (1999/1689) argued for religious toleration, partly on the grounds that no government can be sure that the official religion is correct, which means that no government can be sure that it is not persecuting the true religion. Likewise, John Stuart Mill (2008/1859) argued that since no one person has infallible access to the truth, we are most likely to converge on the truth in the course of debate sustained by laws protecting free speech.

In recent decades, however, epistemology has been somewhat sidelined in political philosophy, which has increasingly come to be thought of as a branch of ethics. This is an overly narrow view. Politics *does* raise ethical issues, which political philosophy has rightly taken on. But it also raises epistemological issues, which, in recent years, political philosophy has been less willing to address.[4] For example, although some of the public debates about the 2003 invasion of Iraq concerned ethical issues (e.g., the principles of just war theory), most of them concerned epistemic issues (e.g., the nature of the evidence for weapons of mass destruction, or what we could know of the real intentions of the governments prosecuting the war). For the most part, philosophers, including those who emphasize the relevance of philosophy to contemporary political issues, denied that philosophy had anything to contribute to the latter debates. I hope this book will encourage them to rethink this attitude.

Before doing applied epistemology, we need a bit of theory to apply. In what follows, I will survey some of the theoretical positions to be found in contemporary normative epistemology. I will not end up endorsing any of these positions or offering any unified theoretical position of my own. There are two reasons for this. First, I am not particularly interested in making a case for any purely theoretical position. This is a work of applied philosophy. As such, I want my arguments to be persuasive to a wide range of readers with a wide range of theoretical commitments.[5] Second, I genuinely think that an eclectic approach is best. Each of the theoretical positions I consider will offer some genuine insight, despite their limitations, and will serve as valuable instruments if used with care.

Veritism

Alvin Goldman has recently proposed a normative epistemological theory called "veritism," which is inspired by consequentialist ethical theory in general, and utilitarianism in particular. Knowledge occupies the role in veritism that happiness or utility occupy in utilitarianism; just as happiness or utility is the one intrinsic value in traditional utilitarian ethics, knowledge is the one intrinsic value in veritistic epistemology. In both cases, other valuable items, "such as actions, rules, or institutions, are taken to have instrumental value insofar as they tend to produce states with fundamental value" (Goldman, 1999b, p. 87).

Before evaluating veritism we need to briefly consider the nature of the value on which it focuses. What is knowledge, that is, what does the word "knowledge" mean? Attempts to define knowledge go back at least as far as Plato.[6] Since Plato, knowledge has standardly been characterized as a species of belief; knowledge is belief with certain (desirable) characteristics. Although there has been great controversy over precisely what those characteristics are, there has been no real controversy about one of them, truth. If someone knows p, then p must be true. But although truth is clearly a necessary condition for knowledge, most philosophers have followed Plato in denying that it is sufficient. Indeed Plato's way of framing the problem of defining knowledge, as the problem of specifying what distinguishes *mere* true belief from knowledge, has dominated the literature.[7]

Despite having made some very influential contributions to this literature, Goldman has recently challenged the principal assumption on which it is based, the Platonic view that truth is not sufficient for knowledge. He argues that very often talk of knowledge is just talk of true belief:

> The sentence "You don't want to know what happened while you were gone" seems to mean: You don't want to have the truth about what happened in your belief corpus. It does not seem to require the translation: You don't want to have a justified belief in the truth about what

happened. So I believe there is an ordinary sense of "know" in which it means "truly believe." (Goldman, 1999b, p. 25)

Although Goldman recognizes that this is not the only way in which the word "know" is used, he stipulates that it is knowledge in this "thin" sense that is accorded fundamental or intrinsic value in veritism.

Goldman does an excellent job countering a variety of arguments that truth is unachievable, or not a fundamental or intrinsic value. Throughout this book I will assume what I take to be the commonsense view, that he is right about this: truth (or at least a reasonable approximation to it) is quite often achievable, and truth (or approximate truth) is often valued, and valuable, for its own sake.

Veritism is, however, susceptible to criticisms which closely resemble certain common criticisms of the utilitarianism on which it is modeled. These criticisms come in two broad categories: first, those which insist that there is more than one intrinsic value that normative epistemology should be concerned to maximize or promote, and second, those which insist that there are "value side-constraints"[8] on *how* the value or values in question should be pursued. I will consider criticisms of both kinds.

Error Avoidance

We have seen that veritism characterizes acquiring true belief (i.e., knowledge in the thin sense) as the only intrinsic epistemic good. Where does that leave the value of avoiding false belief (i.e., avoiding error)? Goldman considers the possibility that the acquisition of true belief and the avoidance of false belief might be two distinguishable values, but rejects the idea, claiming that there is a way to unify them by blending them "into a single *magnitude* or *quantity*" (Goldman, 2002, p. 58).

This requires him to translate the "categorical" approach to epistemology in which we talk only of belief, disbelief, and suspension of judgment (or having no opinion) into the "degrees of belief" (or subjective probability) approach in which beliefs are given values between 0 and 1, where 1 represents complete subjective certainty that the proposition in question is true and 0 represents complete certainty that it is false. Goldman says that we should identify belief *simpliciter* with having a degree of belief close to 1, while disbelief *simpliciter* is identified with having a degree of belief close to 0, and suspension of judgment (or having no opinion) is identified with having a degree of belief close to

0.5. Now, consider a particular true proposition, *p*. Having a high degree of belief in this truth is equivalent to having a low degree of belief in the falsehood *not-p*. So the value of true belief (i.e., of having a high degree of confidence in a particular truth) is equivalent to the value of error avoidance (i.e., of having a low degree of confidence in its negation). Thus seeking truth and shunning falsehood are, Goldman argues, simply two ways of looking at the same thing.

Goldman's argument identifies having no opinion with suspending judgment (and with having a roughly 0.5 degree of belief).[9] But this is clearly wrong. Someone who has never heard of Caracas will have no opinion about whether Caracas is the capital of Venezuela. But that person has not suspended judgment, nor does she have a (roughly) 0.5 degree of belief. You can neither suspend judgment about, nor have any degree of belief in, a proposition you have never considered. Goldman presupposes that everyone has some degree of confidence – high, low, or in between – in every proposition. But this is not true. For each of us, there are many propositions which we neither believe nor disbelieve, and which we do not assign any subjective probability either. And it is precisely because some strategies lead us to form more beliefs than others that there can be a conflict between the goals of truth seeking and error avoidance.

Strategies which exclusively emphasize error avoidance will inevitably lead to fewer beliefs than strategies which exclusively emphasize truth acquisition. William James recognizes this often overlooked point in the following passage:

> There are two ways of looking at our duty in the matter of opinion, – ways entirely different, and yet ways about whose difference the theory of knowledge seems hitherto to have shown very little concern. *We must know the truth*; and *we must avoid error*, – these are our first and great commandments as would-be knowers; but they are not two ways of stating an identical commandment, they are two separable laws ... Believe truth! Shun error! – these we see are two materially different laws; and by choosing between them we may end by coloring differently our whole intellectual life. We may regard the chase for truth as paramount, and the avoidance of error as secondary; or we may, on the other hand, treat the avoidance of error as more imperative, and let truth take its chance. (James, 2007/1897, Part VII, pp. 17–18)

Of course Goldman recognizes that the absence of true belief (being ignorant) is different from the presence of false belief (being misinformed). But his unified approach to epistemic value leads him to the position that these "vices," though distinguishable, can be "ordered" in a way which implies that the former is less epistemically or intellectually vicious than the latter:

> Does this scheme of veritistic value accord with commonsense notions about intellectual attainments? I think it does. If a person regularly has a high level of belief in the true propositions she considers or takes an interest in, then she qualifies as "well-informed." Someone with intermediate levels of belief on many such questions, amounting to "no opinion," qualifies as uninformed, or ignorant. And someone who has very low levels of belief for true proposition – or equivalently, high levels of belief for false propositions – is seriously misinformed. Since the terms "well-informed," "ignorant," and "misinformed" seem to reflect a natural ordering of intellectual attainment, our scheme of veritistic value seems to be on the right track. (Goldman, 2002, p. 59)

But it is not at all clear that commonsense is on Goldman's side here. Although being well-informed[10] is certainly, at least *prima facie*, a higher level of intellectual attainment than being either ignorant or misinformed, it is not so clear that we should rank being ignorant ahead of being misinformed. Should we say that someone who has no opinion about whether Caracas is the capital of Venezuela has achieved more intellectually than someone who believes that Caracas is not the capital of Venezuela?[11] I submit that, without some contextual guidance, our intuitions simply get no traction on the question. I conclude that Goldman is wrong to suppose that ignorance and error can be put on a single scale on which ignorance is ranked higher than error. In Chapter 6 I will argue that Goldman's view that error is inherently worse than ignorance leads him to express unjustifiable concerns about the epistemic dangers of the blogosphere.

Proceduralism

One could accept the argument up to this point while retaining the spirit, if not the letter, of veritism. Truth acquisition and error avoidance, though distinguishable, are closely related; furthermore, they are both characteristics of the outcome of inquiry (or its absence), rather than of the way in which inquiry is (or is not) conducted. In other words, the argument so far is compatible with epistemic consequentialism, though not of the unified kind preferred by Goldman. In what follows, I will argue that epistemic consequentialism fails to do justice to the *intrinsic* value of acquiring, holding, or avoiding beliefs in some ways rather than others. In particular, it fails to do justice to the intrinsic value of doing these things in rational or justified ways, rather than irrational or unjustified ways. This *proceduralist* critique of consequentialist epistemology is reminiscent of critiques of consequentialist ethics, which insist that there is a moral value to certain kinds of actions, which is (at least partially) independent of their consequences or anticipated consequences.[12]

Epistemic consequentialists will not of course deny that the way in which we acquire, hold, and/or avoid belief matters. Like most people, they will insist that the process by which we do these things should (at least usually) be justified, by means of evidence, argument, and so on. Nonetheless, they will insist that the value of justification (or at least the value of "epistemic justification"[13]) is purely instrumental. Laurence Bonjour expresses this view in the following passage:

> The basic role of justification is that of a *means* to truth ... if epistemic justification were not conducive to truth ... if finding epistemically justified beliefs did not substantially increase the likelihood of finding true ones, then epistemic justification would be irrelevant to our main cognitive goal and of dubious worth. It is only if we have some reason for thinking that epistemic justification constitutes a path to truth that we as cognitive beings have any motive for preferring epistemically justified beliefs to epistemically unjustified ones. (Bonjour, 1985, pp. 7–8)

It is not obvious that Bonjour and Goldman are right about this. In particular, it is not obvious that we should think of justification as valuable only insofar as it helps us to believe what is true or avoid believing what is false. Consider an example to test your intuitions about this issue.

David Lewis (2000) has discussed what he takes to be a puzzling feature of the way academics are appointed to philosophy departments. From the premise that universities "exist for the sake of the advancement of knowledge" (p. 187) he draws the following conclusion:

> By and large and *ceteris paribus*, we would expect the materialists in the philosophy department to vote for the materialist candidate, the dualists to vote for the dualist, and so forth ... I say this not out of cynicism. Rather, it seems to be how they *ought* to vote, and unabashedly, if they are sincere

in their opinions and serious about doing the best they can, each by his own lights, to serve the advancement of knowledge. (Lewis, 2000, p. 189)

But, of course, this is not how they typically behave. Rather than openly promoting the views which they consider right by appointing those who agree with them, "an appointing department will typically behave as if the truth or falsehood of the candidate's doctrines are weightless, not a legitimate consideration at all" (p. 190). Lewis explains this attitude by postulating a tacit treaty between academics with opposing views. According to the terms of this treaty, those with truth on their side should "ignore the advantage of being right" and not promote their own views in return for those who do not have this "advantage" agreeing not to promote their views. We ignore the truth of a particular candidate's doctrines:

> Because if we, in the service of truth, decided to stop ignoring it, we know that others, in the service of error, also would stop ignoring it. We have exchanged our forbearance for theirs. If you think that a bad bargain, think well who might come out on top if we gave it up. Are you so sure that knowledge would be a winner? (Lewis, 2000, p. 200)

Despite the ingenuity of this argument, I doubt many people will be convinced by it. They are likely to object to the premise that the promotion of true belief is the fundamental value for which universities and philosophy departments exist. The natural thing to say is that it is *the process* by which beliefs are acquired and justified that is of fundamental or intrinsic value rather than, or at least as well as, the outcome of that process.

If this were not the case, it seems we should assess students' essays on the basis of the truth of the positions they argue for. But, of course, this is precisely what we struggle to avoid. Instead we try to assess them on the basis of how well they justify (or rationally defend) the positions they argue for, whether or not those positions are true. Again, it seems that when we do this, we are committed to the view that it is the process by which students arrive at and defend their conclusions which is of fundamental importance, rather than the truth of those conclusions.

There are, of course, responses that Lewis, Goldman, Bonjour, et al. could make to these objections. But I won't pursue the issue further here. It is enough to note that a purely consequentialist approach to epistemology seems counterintuitive for reasons which closely resemble the reasons many have found purely consequentialist approaches to ethics counterintuitive.[14] What is more, even if epistemic consequentialism is correct, not everyone is liable to be persuaded of its correctness in the foreseeable future and I don't want nonconsequentialists to stop reading now. Hence I will not adopt a purely consequentialist approach in this book.

Nor will I adopt a purely proceduralist approach. Such an approach would, to use Goldman's words, treat justification as "sharply disconnected from truth" (Goldman, 2002, p. 55). Throughout this book I will assume that any form of inquiry which consistently fails to arrive at the truth, or which consistently leads to falsehood, cannot be justified. Like truth, justification seems to be both intrinsically and instrumentally valuable.

Other Values?

I have argued that a plurality of fundamental or intrinsic values have a role to play in normative epistemology. Are there any values that I have not considered? The value of happiness (one's own or that of other people) certainly seems to be a consideration people sometimes take into account when considering what to believe. What is more, it is a value that can notoriously come into conflict with the value of truth as well as the value of justification (or at least the value of epistemic justification). This is the basis of Pascal's argument for belief in God. According to Pascal, we should have this belief, not because it's likely to be true (he claims that it is just as likely to be true as not), and not because it is justified by the evidence (he denies that it is), but because (roughly speaking) it is in our interests to believe.[15]

To avoid theological controversies, I will use a slightly different example, adapted from William James's "The Will to Believe." Jones is being pursued by a wild animal, when his path is blocked by a deep canyon. The only way he can hope to survive is by jumping across it, but all the available evidence suggests the canyon is too wide and he is unlikely to make it. However, he is enough of a psychologist to know that if he believes he will succeed, he is more likely to succeed. It seems to me clear that in these circumstances, Jones ought to believe the following proposition:

I will succeed in jumping over the canyon.

Objections to this claim are likely to come from two directions. Some philosophers will object on the grounds that it would be impossible for him to believe (a). Since (it is often said), ought implies can, it cannot be the case that he ought to believe something which he cannot believe. I will take up this position, as part of a broader discussion of the degree to which our beliefs are under our control, in the next section. For now, I will assume what I take to be the commonsense view, that Jones might be able to get himself to believe (a). The question is "Should he believe it?"

A position called *evidentialism*, often associated with W. K. Clifford, holds that we are always obliged to form our beliefs in accordance with the available evidence. In this case, the available evidence does not support (a), so an evidentialist will say that Jones should not believe (a), no matter what advantages belief may bring. Clifford's argument for evidentialism appeals to broadly veritistic considerations, pointing out the many advantages that truth can bring to both individuals and societies. He claims that anyone who holds a belief that is contrary to the available evidence is setting a bad example, and thereby committing a "sin against mankind" (Clifford, 1947/1877, p. 77).

I am confident that this is usually true, but the current example seems to be a clear exception to the rule. While there may be a sense in which anyone who takes the principled stance of refusing to even try to believe (a), on the grounds that it's not supported by the evidence, is being rational, it should also be clear that there is another broader, and in this case decisive, sense in which they are being irrational. A procedure that leads Jones to believe (a) would be justified in the sense that concerns us in this book. Jones would be justified in believing (a) because, all things taken into account, Jones should believe (a).

Many epistemologists would concede this, but brush aside such "pragmatic" considerations as beyond the proper scope of epistemology. On their view, what Jones should, all things considered, believe is a question for decision theorists or ethicists, not epistemologists. I see no reason to narrow the concerns of epistemology in this way. Epistemology, and especially applied epistemology, should be broad enough in its concerns to engage with any factors that may be relevant to the issue of what we should believe. Again the analogy with ethics is useful. Some people think of normative ethics as offering a specific kind of advice, which can be weighed against other potentially action-guiding considerations, for example, prudential or aesthetic considerations. The problem with this approach to ethics is that it leaves the point of the subject obscure and open to endless contention. It is better to think of ethics, in the broad and traditional way, as a subject concerned with how we should live, all things considered. Likewise epistemology (or at least normative epistemology) should be concerned with what we should believe, all things considered.

Controlling Our Beliefs?

The above discussion assumed that Jones could believe (a) if he wanted. But many philosophers would challenge this assumption. They claim that we have little or no control over our beliefs. If they are right, this is a problem, not merely for that example, but also for the analogy between ethics and normative epistemology with which we began. In fact, it seems to me that much of the resistance to the development of applied epistemology as a subject on a par with applied ethics[16] comes from a view, found among many working epistemologists, that whereas we can control our actions (the domain of ethics), we have little or no control over our beliefs (the domain of epistemology). I say this is wrong. I say that we often exercise voluntary control over our beliefs, just as we often exercise voluntary control over our actions. This makes me a proponent of what Alvin Goldman has called "the dubious thesis of doxastic voluntarism" (Goldman, 1999a, p. 275).[17] The first thing to say in defense of doxastic voluntarism is that it seems to be supported by common sense. We often talk, for example, of deciding what to believe about this or that matter or of struggling to decide what to believe about some other matter.[18] I say that such talk should be taken at face value. The burden of proof is on the other side.

Arguments against doxastic voluntarism go back at least as far as Hume, who claimed that belief "depends not on the will, but must arise from certain determinate causes and principles, of which we are not masters" (Hume, 1967/1740, p. 624). Hume's position is intimately connected with the theory of ideas, which he inherited from the empiricist tradition. This tradition has a notoriously passive conception of human psychology, which few contemporary philosophers are likely to fully endorse.[19] Nonetheless, many contemporary philosophers do adopt a passive conception of the psychology of evidence evaluation, according to which the available evidence either leads us to form a certain belief or it does not. Choice does not come into it. As Richard Feldman puts it, "we are at the mercy of our evidence" (Feldman, 2001, p. 83).[20]

This claim is sometimes generalized to cover the full range of doxastic attitudes, that is, not only our beliefs, but also the degree of confidence with which we hold those beliefs. According to Neil Levy, for example, propositions have "an immediate subjective probability for us. In the light of the evidence available to us, we are simply struck by the likelihood that a given proposition is true or false" (Levy, 2007a, p. 136). I shall argue shortly that this completely passive conception of belief formation is wrong. Even if it were right, however, and we have no control over what we believe *given our evidence*, it would not follow that we have no control over what we believe. Levy himself effectively acknowledges this when he says that "though we may not be able to control what beliefs we form on the basis of our evidence we can certainly control our evidence gathering activities (if we can control anything)" (Levy, 2007a, p. 144). Although Levy characterizes himself as an opponent of doxastic voluntarism, he concedes that we do in this way exercise some "indirect" control over what we believe. We exercise some control over our evidence-gathering activities, and hence over our eventual beliefs, when we choose to investigate one subject rather than another, as well as when we choose to conduct our investigation in one way rather than another. Opponents of doxastic voluntarism tend to be dismissive of this kind of indirect control, claiming that it is of marginal significance and perhaps not really a form of control at all.[21] But this is a mistake. Many (indeed arguably almost all) of the things we control we control indirectly. I am certainly in control of the words that appear in this book (if I am in control of anything) but my control is indirect. I control them by controlling other things, such as the movement of my fingers over my keyboard. Even the movement of my fingers is (at least arguably) indirect, since I control it by sending signals via my nervous system to the muscles in my fingers.[22] So even if it were true that we only have indirect control over our beliefs, that would not imply that this control is less extensive than, or fundamentally different in kind from, the control we ordinarily take ourselves to have over most of our actions.

So far I have assumed, for the sake of argument, the correctness of the view that *given our evidence* we have no control over what we believe. Now I want to challenge it. On the face of it, our beliefs are determined, not only by our evidence, but also by the attitude we adopt towards that evidence. Hence, on the face of it, we can exercise control over our beliefs, not only by controlling our evidence-gathering activities, but also by choosing to adopt one rather than another attitude to the strength of the evidence we end up with. We often talk, for example, of *deciding* that some evidence is compelling, or that that some evidence should be ignored. Of course, this way of speaking might be misleading. Perhaps when we talk of someone deciding that a piece of evidence is compelling, we really mean that he or she forms the belief (nonvoluntarily of course) that the evidence in question is compelling. Similarly, perhaps when we say that someone chooses to ignore a piece of evidence, we really mean that he or she forms the belief (again nonvoluntarily) that it isn't really evidence at all. Such moves are always possible, but they should be motivated by something more than a dogmatic commitment to the view that given our evidence we cannot help believing what we believe.

Although Bernard Williams (1973) has argued that it is logically impossible to directly control our beliefs, most opponents of "believing at will" accept that it is logically possible; they just think that as a matter of fact no one can do it. In the following passage William Alston presents an influential "argument" to that effect:

> My argument for this, if it can be called that, simply consists in asking you whether you have any such powers. Can you, at this moment, start to believe that the United States is still a colony of Great Britain, just by deciding to do so? If you find it too incredible that you should be sufficiently motivated to try to believe this, suppose that someone offers you $500,000,000 to believe it, and you are much more interested in the money than in believing the truth. Could you do what it takes to get that reward? (Alston, 1989, p. 122)

Many philosophers have found this persuasive. Nikolaj Nottelmann, for example, endorses Alston's view, observing that no matter how hard he might try he cannot bring himself to believe that there is a blue cat in front of him (2006, p. 560).

Speaking for myself, I cannot bring myself to believe either that the United States is still a colony of Great Britain or that there is a blue cat in front of me. But it does not follow from the fact that there are limits to what we can choose to believe that we cannot choose to believe at all, or even that we have little choice about what to believe. There is no disanalogy between beliefs and actions here. It does not follow from the fact that I cannot lick my elbow (try it) or fly to Mars that I have little or no control over my actions.[23]

I expect many people will be unconvinced, and continue to insist that neither they nor anyone else can ever choose what to believe.

Such people can believe whatever they like.[24] In this book it will be presupposed that we have significant control, not only over our evidence-gathering activities, but also over what we end up believing, and hence that when I offer advice about what to believe (or how to go about believing), readers will be able to decide for themselves whether or not to take that advice.

Duties to Believe and Responsibility for Belief

William Alston's argument against doxastic voluntarism is one step in an argument against what he calls "the deontological conception of justification," according to which, to say that a belief is justified is to say that it is one's duty or obligation to believe it. Since, he claims, having a duty to believe something implies having control over whether or not to believe it, and (according to him) we do not "in general" have such control, it follows that we do not in general have duties or obligations to believe, and that justified belief should not be understood in these terms (Alston, 1989, p. 196). Needless to say, I do not accept this argument, because I do not accept the premise that we do not in general have control over what we believe. I say we have duties to believe certain things. Some of these duties may be peculiar to the circumstances in which we find ourselves, others are (almost) universal. It seems clear, for example, that we all have a duty to believe that the Holocaust occurred, because this belief is well-evidenced, true, and an important reminder to us all of what people can do.

Nonetheless, I don't accept the deontological conception of justification. On my view, to say that a person's belief is justified is simply to say that he or she ought to believe it. In other words, as I said earlier, I endorse the guidance conception of justification. But although the guidance conception of justification tends to be closely associated with the deontological conception of justification, they really should be distinguished.[25] Intuitively, it seems clear that we are not duty-bound to believe everything that we ought to believe, any more than we are duty-bound to do everything we ought to do.[26] To start with, if one has a duty to believe (or, for that matter, do) something, that implies that it is important that one believe (or do) it, and not everything that one ought to believe (or do) is particularly important. Furthermore, duties are, at least typically, duties to other people, and many of the things we ought to believe do not in any significant way concern other people.[27] We ought to believe everything we have a duty to believe, but the converse is not true. We do not have a duty to believe everything we ought to believe.

Arguments against doxastic voluntarism have not only been used to challenge commonsense views about our duties to believe, they have also been used to challenge commonsense views about our responsibility for our beliefs. Although Neil Levy concedes that we may *sometimes* be responsible for our beliefs, he claims that such responsibility is rare, much rarer than we usually think (2007a, p. 149). He uses the example of Dr Fritz Klein, a concentration camp doctor who tried to reconcile his role in the Holocaust with his Hippocratic oath by claiming (and, we will assume, believing) that "The Jew is a gangrenous appendix in the body of mankind"[28] to illustrate his position. Levy is aware that most people would view Klein as blameworthy, not merely for his actions, but also for the beliefs that motivated his actions (indeed it is hard to see how he could be responsible for his actions unless he was responsible for the beliefs that led to them). Nonetheless, Levy thinks it is unlikely that Klein was responsible for this belief.

As we have seen, Levy thinks the only control we have over our beliefs is indirect, through our control of our evidence-gathering activities. Hence, according to him, any responsibility we have for our beliefs is also indirect. But, he goes on to argue, such indirect responsibility is rare, because it is inconsistent with certain common attitudes, one of which is moral certainty:

> When I am morally certain that *p*, I cannot be expected to gather further evidence for or against *p*. There must be some doubt to set me on the path to checking or altering my beliefs by evidence-gathering. Certainty precludes the need (in my eyes) for me to engage in evidence-gathering, and thereby excuses me of indirect responsibility for my beliefs. (Levy, 2007a, p. 145)

Since, according to Levy, indirect responsibility is the only kind of responsibility we can have for our beliefs, it follows that holding a belief with certainty excuses us of any responsibility for it at all. This is, as Levy recognizes, extremely counterintuitive. Intuitively, it seems clear that moral certainty would not excuse Klein of responsibility for his belief. If anything, it would make him more culpable.[29]

I have already argued against the view that we only have indirect control over our beliefs; hence I don't accept Levy's view that we can only ever be indirectly responsible for our beliefs. But I would also insist that even if Klein did only have indirect control over his belief, moral certainty would not excuse him of responsibility for it. Levy assumes that, although Klein may have some control over his belief (through his control of his evidence-gathering actions or omissions), he has no control over the degree of confidence with which he holds that belief. But the very evidence-gathering activities or omissions that lead him to hold the belief also lead him to whatever degree of confidence he has in it. Hence, if Klein were morally certain of his belief, he may well have been responsible, not only for having the belief, but also for being so certain of it.

I am not saying that Klein definitely was responsible for his belief, or for his certainty (if he was certain). Perhaps he was subject to brainwashing from an early age, which left him literally incapable of considering the possibility that his belief might be false. In such circumstances (arguably) he would not be responsible. But in such circumstances, it would be *the reasons for* his moral certainty that (arguably) would excuse him, not *the mere fact* that he was morally certain.[30]

I conclude that the commonsense view that we are typically, though not always, responsible for our beliefs, just as we are typically, though not always, responsible for our actions, is correct. Indeed the reason we are typically responsible for our actions is that they are to a large extent the result of beliefs for which we are responsible. Because people are typically responsible for their beliefs, we may be justified in praising or blaming others for their beliefs or being proud or ashamed of our own beliefs. Other responses associated with responsibility may not be justified. It is (at least usually) wrong to punish people for what they believe, though it may well be appropriate to punish them for acting on their beliefs. There are good pragmatic and moral reasons for not converting thought-sins into thought-crimes.[31]

Virtue Epistemology

The discussion so far has assumed that normative epistemology is exclusively concerned with evaluating belief (or degrees of belief).[32] In recent decades, several philosophers have challenged this belief-based approach to epistemology. They advocate instead an approach known as *virtue epistemology*. Like veritism, virtue epistemology is a theoretical approach to normative epistemology which is explicitly modeled on a theoretical approach to ethics. Whereas veritism is modeled on consequentialism, virtue epistemology is modeled on *virtue ethics*.

Since the late 1950s, virtue ethics has challenged act-based approaches to ethics. Virtue ethicists argue that the locus of ethical evaluation should not be the difference between right and wrong action, but the difference between good (i.e., virtuous) and bad (i.e., vicious) people. Appealing to ancient Greek, and particularly Aristotelian, traditions, they construe the principal task of ethics as the identification of moral virtues, where these are understood as dispositions to act in good ways. In an analogous way, virtue epistemologists claim that the central task of normative epistemology is not the evaluation of beliefs, but the evaluation of people and their epistemic virtues (or, to use the Aristotelian language, "intellectual virtues").

Of course, one can evaluate people and their intellectual virtues as well as their beliefs. Alvin Goldman (2002), for example, has offered an account of intellectual virtue which is derived from his veritism. But this certainly does not make him a virtue epistemologist. What distinguishes virtue epistemology from other approaches to normative epistemology is the belief that intellectual virtue is conceptually prior to knowledge and justified belief. According to virtue epistemologists, we can't understand what it is for a belief to be justified or to qualify as a piece of knowledge, until we understand what an intellectually virtuous person would be like. Hence, one prominent virtue episte-mologist has defined knowledge as being (roughly) true belief grounded in intellectual virtue (Sosa, 1991, p. 277), and another has defined a justified belief as being (roughly) a belief that an intellectually virtuous person would have (Zagzebski, 1996, p. 236). Whatever one thinks of these issues of conceptual priority, it should be clear that an adequate applied epistemology should have something to say about the nature of intellectual virtue and how to go about cultivating it.

The Greek poet Archilochos famously said "The fox knows many things, but the hedgehog knows one big thing" (Gerber, 1991, Fragment 201). Linda Zagzebski (1996, p. 45) has accused contemporary belief-based epistemology of idealizing the fox at the expense of the hedgehog.[33] There is a great deal of truth in this. The only intellectual virtue recognized in much contemporary epistemology is the virtue of *being well-informed* (i.e., knowing a lot of things). But it should be clear that this virtue is distinct from, and can come at the expense of, a much more important intellectual virtue, *wisdom*, which involves, in part, knowing what is worth knowing. Goldman's veritism seems a particularly clear example of an approach to epistemology which idealizes the fox at the expense of the hedgehog, since it treats maximizing truth-possession (i.e., being extremely well-informed) as the fundamental epistemic value. Although Goldman acknowledges that not all truths are equally valuable, because not all are equally interesting, he thinks this problem is easily dealt with:

> We can no longer suggest that higher degrees of truth-possession are all that count in matters of inquiry. But can't we incorporate the element of interest by a slight revision in our theory? Let us just say that the core epistemic value is a high degree of truth-possession *on topics of interest*. (Goldman, 2002, p. 61)

But this is not the minor modification Goldman seems to think. Whether a topic is of interest or not is often a matter of degree. Hence we are often faced with the problem of simultaneously maximizing two values, interest and truth. How do we compare the intellectual attainments of a fox who knows many moderately interesting things, with the attainments of a hedgehog who knows just one extremely interesting thing? Much of the appeal of veritism was that it offered us the hope of treating normative epistemology as a simple matter of promoting one quantifiable value. This hope appears to be unfounded.

There is another way in which the fact that some topics are more deserving of investigation than others makes epistemology a much messier business than purely belief-based approaches to epistemology suggest. It is not as if there is a fixed set of topics in which we take (or should take) an interest, and our task is just to work out what we should believe about those topics. Preliminary investigation of a topic may reveal that it is, or is not, worth further investigation, or it may reveal some other topic that is more deserving of investigation. Hence questions about what we should believe are inseparable from questions about what we should investigate. Neither kind of question has any absolute priority. Applied epistemology cannot afford to ignore questions about what topics are interesting (or important) if it hopes to provide useful advice to people wondering what to believe. Nor can it ignore the fact that different topics are interesting or important at different times. In this book, I am concerned with what we should believe and how we should pursue knowledge now, at the beginning of the twenty-first century. Like most philosophers, I am fond of the eternal verities, but in this book I will confine my attention to issues of current interest. There is no guarantee that they will retain that status, but that does not in any way diminish their significance.

For the most part, I will be concerned, even more specifically, with issues of interest in Western societies (particularly English-speaking ones). This is not because I think these societies are more important than others; rather it is because I know them best, and I assume that most of my readers will be similarly placed. As we shall see, some of the issues (e.g., the reliability of the blogosphere versus the conventional media) cannot be addressed without considering the social/political context in which they are raised, and some of the concepts (e.g., that of a *conspiracy theory*) may not be found in other societies. It is the nature of applied philosophy to be heavily dependent on time and place. It is not just that what one says may be interesting in one society, but not another; what one says may actually be true in one society, but not another. In several places, I will argue that certain contemporary epistemologists have an excessively *a priori* approach to some of these issues. Applied epistemology, like applied ethics, needs to engage closely with contemporary social and political realities.

Applied Epistemology and Social Policy

Let's take the analogy between applied ethics and applied epistemology a step further. Applied ethics consists of two parts, the part concerned with questions about individuals and their behavior (e.g., How much of our income, if any, should we donate to the poor?), and the part concerned with questions of social policy (e.g., Should the tax system be used to redistribute wealth?). We can make a similar division within applied epistemology. This book is principally concerned with questions about individuals, what they should believe and how they should pursue knowledge and/or wisdom. But epistemology, like ethics, can also be applied to questions of social policy.[34] Such applications are an important part of the branch of epistemology known as "social epistemology."

Alvin Goldman has applied his veritism to social epistemology, calling the result "veritistic social epistemology" (from now on VSE). VSE aims to evaluate social policies in terms of their "knowledge impact" (Goldman, 1999b, p. 6). VSE, like veritism more generally, is modeled on consequentialist, and more particularly utilitarian, moral theory (Goldman, 1999b, p. 87), with knowledge in the thin sense (i.e., true belief)

Table 1.1

	t1	*t2*
S1	DB(p) = 0.4	DB(p) = 0.7
S2	DB(p) = 0.7	DB(p) = 0.9
S3	DB(p) = 0.9	DB(p) = 0.6
S4	DB(p) = 0.2	DB(p) = 0.8

playing the role in the former that happiness or utility plays in the latter. Some people reject utilitarianism as a general guide to life, but consider it to be defensible as a guide to social policy (e.g., Goodin, 1995). For similar reasons, one may reject veritism as a general theory of normative epistemology (perhaps for some of the reasons I discussed earlier), but accept it as a guide to social policy (i.e., accept VSE).

Before considering the plausibility of this position, we should get a clearer picture of the way VSE is suppose to work. Goldman (1999b, p. 93) invites us to imagine that there is a community of four agents S1–S4, and a certain true proposition, p, which is of interest to them. At time t1 the agents have degrees of belief (DB) in p (identified with subjective probabilities) as shown in Table 1.1. A certain social policy π is enacted, with the result that at a later time t2 the agents have new degrees of belief in p, shown in the next column of the table. In this situation, social policy π has positive veritistic value (V-value), because it increases the mean degree of belief in the correct answer to the question of interest (from 0.55 to 0.75).

Not surprisingly, VSE is vulnerable to criticisms which are analogous to common criticisms of utilitarian approaches to social policy. Just as utilitarian approaches to social policy have been criticized, on the grounds that they ignore justice (or more specifically justice in the distribution of happiness or utility), VSE may be criticized for ignoring a distinctively epistemic form of justice (i.e., justice in the distribution of knowledge, understood as true belief, or interesting or important true belief).[35]

What would a just distribution of knowledge be like? When answering this question, it is natural to consider well-known principles of distributive justice for other kinds of goods. Someone inspired by John Rawls's Difference Principle (Rawls, 1971, pp. 75–83), for example, might say that the most epistemically just social policy would be one which maximized the knowledge of the least knowledgeable members

Table 1.2

	π	ψ
S1	DB(p) = 0.5	DB(p) = 0.7
S2	DB(p) = 0.7	DB(p) = 0.9
S3	DB(p) = 0.4	DB(p) = 0.2
S4	DB(p) = 0.6	DB(p) = 0.8

of the community. So, for example, when comparing the veritistic merits of two practices, π and ψ, in a community of four people, we might decide that their outcomes, measured in degree of confidence in some true proposition of interest p, will be as indicated in Table 1.2. In this situation, although ψ is to be preferred to π by the standards of VSE, because it has greater V-value (the mean degree of true belief being 0.65, whereas the mean degree of true belief under p is 0.55), π is to be preferred to ψ by the standards of what we might call the Epistemic Difference Principle, because the least knowledgeable member of this community would be better informed as a result of π than as a result of ψ. Hence π, according to that principle, is more epistemically just than ψ.

Now, I am not advocating the Epistemic Difference Principle. It is open to some of the same objections that have been leveled against the original Difference Principle on which it is modeled (and perhaps others). For example, someone with libertarian sympathies, like Robert Nozick, might object to both the Epistemic Difference Principle and VSE, on the grounds that they seek to impose a pattern (Nozick, 1974, pp. 208–10) in the distribution of knowledge, and so ignore historical questions about where the knowledge in question came from and how it came to be distributed in the way it is. In other words, they both ignore questions about who had intellectual property in the knowledge in the first place, and hence they have the potential to violate the rights of holders of intellectual property who should be able to transfer their knowledge (or not to transfer it) to whomever they choose.

I will not attempt to adjudicate these disputes here. My intention has just been to argue that VSE neglects questions about justice in the distribution of knowledge, and that this constitutes an objection to VSE. Goldman could try defending VSE against this objection by pointing out that VSE was not meant to provide us with an all-things-considered evaluation of social policies. Goldman acknowledges that veritistic considerations may be outweighed by other considerations, including considerations of justice. At one point, for example, he explicitly states that concerns for procedural justice might legitimately lead a court of law to exclude evidence which would be admissible on purely veritistic grounds (Goldman, 1999b, p. 284).

This response would be right, as far as it goes, but it would miss the point of the current objection. For the kind of justice under consideration is distinctively epistemic (indeed it is specifically veritistic). To be clear, my objection is not that general considerations of justice can rightly trump considerations of maximizing true interesting belief (though this is of course true); rather my objection is that considerations about the just allocation of such belief can rightly trump considerations about maximizing it.

Am I doing epistemology or ethics here? Although I have been talking up to this point as though epistemology and ethics are distinct, though analogous, enterprises, strictly speaking epistemology (or at least normative epistemology) is not *merely* analogous to ethics, it is a part of ethics. Belief-based epistemology is a part of ethics, because believing, as one of the things we do (albeit not always voluntarily), is a kind of acting (and not merely comparable to acting as I earlier supposed). Likewise virtue epistemology is a branch of ethics, because intellectual virtues, such as wisdom, are among the virtues required of a good life. Epistemology is the branch of ethics specifically concerned with intellectual goods, one of which is knowledge.[36] Hence Goldman's VSE should be understood as an ethical theory, and it is perfectly appropriate to criticize it on ethical grounds.

Suppose, by way of comparison, that an economist examined various public policies for their impact on wealth, and provisionally endorsed policies which would maximize overall (or average) wealth. We may suppose that the economist's endorsement is only provisional because he or she accepts that noneconomic values may sometimes trump the maximizing project. Nonetheless, the economist's position would certainly (and I think rightly) be criticized if it fails to address questions about the justice or injustice of wealth distributions that would result from the social policies he or she has provisionally endorsed. This criticism would not be external to the economist's project, nor should it be dismissed on the grounds that it concerns ethics *rather than* economics. Applied economics, like applied epistemology, is a branch of applied ethics.

Although epistemology is a branch of ethics, the distinction between epistemology and ethics is so well entrenched in philosophical debate, and often so useful, that it will sometimes be convenient to talk as if they are distinct (i.e., nonoverlapping) subjects. This practice is harmless, so long as we bear in mind that when we do so we are construing ethics narrowly as a subject concerned with "outward" actions *rather than* beliefs, or with moral virtues *rather than* intellectual virtues.

Notes

1 Toward the end of this chapter, I will argue for a stronger position, namely that the problem of working out what we ought to believe can be treated as part of the problem of working out how we ought to live, and that epistemology (or at least normative epistemology) can not only be compared to ethics, it can be treated as a branch of ethics. Nonetheless, it will usually be convenient to treat ethics and epistemology as separate disciplines.

2 See, for example, Edel, Flower, and O'Connor (1994, pp. 1–8) who point out that Aristotle, Aquinas, Hobbes, Bentham, and Kant all did what would now be called "applied ethics."

3 Of course it's still an interesting question, at least for many people. However, the secularization of society since Hume's time means that it is not interesting for as many people as it would once have been.

4 There are some exceptions. As we shall see in Chapter 3, there is a substantial contemporary literature on the epistemology of democracy, and, as we shall see in Chapter 5, some of the current literature on the epistemology of conspiracy theories is explicitly presented as political philosophy.

5 In this way, my approach is comparable to Peter Singer's approach to the ethics of our treatment of nonhuman animals. Although Singer himself is a utilitarian, he tries to construct arguments which will persuade a wide range of people, including people who don't share his theoretical commitment to utilitarianism.

6 The topic is discussed in both the *Theaetetus* and the *Meno*.

7 It has usually been assumed that justification is another necessary condition for knowledge. Before Edmund Gettier (1963) it was usually assumed that truth and justification were both individually necessary and jointly sufficient.

8 The term comes from Nozick (1974, p. 29).

9 The identification of suspension of judgment with having a (roughly) 0.5 degree of belief is questionable (see Coady, 2010, p. 107). But, whatever you think about this, the real flaw with Goldman's argument is its identification of this state (or these states) with having no opinion.

10 I shall shortly challenge the idea that it is the preeminent intellectual attainment.

11 Caracas *is* the capital of Venezuela.

12 Such critiques of consequentialist ethics are usually called "deontological." I will avoid that word here, however, since it is often used in episte- mology to refer to a view about the nature of justification (i.e., that it is to be understood in terms of a duty or obligation), rather than a view about the value of justification (i.e., that it is intrinsically valuable). I take the term "proceduralism" from Goldman (1999b, pp. 75–9).

13 Epistemic justification is often contrasted with pragmatic (ethical or prudential) justification. You might be epistemically justified in believing something (i.e., the available evidence and arguments indicate that it is true); nonetheless you might (at least arguably) not be all-things-considered justified in believing it, because it is in not in your interests to believe it or because you have a moral obligation not to believe it. I will discuss this issue further in the next section.

14 This includes many who think that their intuitions are wrong and consequentialist ethics is right.

15 Strictly speaking he doesn't claim that belief is definitely in our interests, just that it has greater expected utility than disbelief.

16 This is certainly not the only reason. The word "epistemology" is unfamiliar and unattractive to many people, and, as a result, few people outside of professional epistemology have taken much interest in the subject.

17 Doxastic voluntarism is not popular. I don't know anyone else who has explicitly embraced it.

18 Indeed, one prominent contemporary philosopher has declared "the fundamental problem of epistemology to be that of *deciding* what to believe" (Pollock, 1986, p. 10, my emphasis).

19 It tends to adopt a passive view of perception and desire, as well as belief.

20 Similar views have been expressed by Robert Audi, who says that "belief is more like a response to external grounds than a result of internal volitive thrust" (Audi, 2001, p. 98), and John Heil, according to whom "believers are largely at the mercy of their belief-forming equipment" (Heil, 1983, p. 357).

21 Alston (1989) describes this kind of control as "weak" (p. 118). Adler just stipulates that when he speaks of controlling beliefs he is "speaking of *direct* control" (Adler, 2002, p. 57).

22 Of course one needn't *consciously* send signals to one's muscles in order to raise one's hand, but then one doesn't necessarily consciously control one's evidence-gathering activities either.

23 Not only are there things that most of us could not bring ourselves to believe, there are things that most of us cannot help believing. Again, there is no disanalogy between beliefs and actions here. Some actions are voluntary; some are not.

24 This is more than a facetious joke. It is a reminder of my earlier point that ordinary forms of thought and language presuppose that we have extensive control over what we believe.

25 Alvin Goldman, for example, critically discusses the "guidance-deontological conception of justification" (1999a, pp. 271–4).

26 Likewise to say that someone should do something is not necessarily to say that they are duty-bound to do it.

27 I do not deny that one may have duties to oneself, as Kant, for example, thought. Nonetheless, the paradigm cases of duty do seem to involve other people.

28 The original source for this quote is Lifton (1986, p. 16).

29 Intuitively it seems the more certain one is of something one shouldn't believe, the more blameworthy one is.

30 Moral certainty is not the only doxastic attitude Levy thinks is incompatible with responsibility for belief. He claims that Klein would be responsible for his belief that Jews are a gangrenous appendix in the body of mankind "only if he is less than morally certain that this is the case, if he thinks it matters greatly whether he is right, if he believes that further evidence is available for the proposition and that gathering the evidence is worth the trouble" (2007a, p. 147). Unless all these conditions are met, Klein cannot be expected to investigate further, and so is not responsible. We have seen that Levy just assumes that Klein has no control over the degree of confidence with which he holds his belief. He also seems to just assume that Klein's attitude to the importance of what he believes is not under his control, and that his beliefs about the availability of further evidence and the desirability of acquiring it are not under his control. But once we have accepted (as Levy has) that we have at least some control over our beliefs and over our attitudes towards our beliefs, none of this can be assumed.

31 I thank an anonymous reviewer for suggesting this way of putting the point.

32 Our concern with knowledge has also been a concern with belief, since we have treated knowledge as a kind of belief, that is, true belief, or justified true belief, or justified true belief with some further condition or conditions.

33 Zagzebski is discussing Isaiah Berlin's (1978) interpretation of the Archilochos fragment, rather than the fragment itself. Berlin's discussion of the fragment is largely responsible for its current fame.

34 Questions of social policy are not central to this book, but they do come up in several places. The Postscript is entirely devoted to a social policy issue.

35 Goldman does discuss the distribution of veritistic value, and acknowledges that maximizing this value may not always be desirable (see 1999b, p. 96). His discussion in this passage is not, however, about the justice or otherwise of various distributions, but about their efficiency, given a certain goal, that of promoting "the community's interest." For example, considerations of efficiency may mean that some information should only be distributed on a "need to know" basis.

36 As we have seen, justified belief and wisdom are also epistemic goods.

2

Experts and the Laity

Nullius in Verba

(Motto of the Royal Society)

"Should I believe you or my rock-hard nipples?"

(Jon Stewart asks Al Gore a question about
global warming on The Daily Show)

I have characterized "What should we believe?" as one of the central questions of normative epistemology. Often, however, there is a prior question that needs to be addressed, namely "Whom should we believe?" Often we can't work out what to believe (or how confident we should be of our beliefs) on our own. In these circumstances, we may seek the guidance of experts.[1] A lot of recent work in epistemology has emphasized the extent to which we are all (albeit in different ways and to different degrees) epistemically dependent on experts. There are at least two reasons for the current interest in this topic.

First, it has become increasingly clear that much of the epistemology we inherited from both the empiricist and rationalist traditions was overly individualistic. The paradigm of knowledge and justification

What To Believe Now: Applying Epistemology to Contemporary Issues,
First Edition. David Coady.
© 2012 David Coady. Published 2012 by Blackwell Publishing Ltd.

in the empiricist tradition is an individual's perceptual encounter with an object of enquiry; in the rationalist tradition it is an individual's own powers of reasoning. Both traditions downplay the extent to which we are dependent on others, especially experts or those we judge to be experts, for many of the things we believe and many of the things we claim to know.

The second reason for the current interest in this topic is that our reliance on experts seems to be increasing. Human knowledge is expanding rapidly and becoming increasingly specialized. It is no longer the case, if indeed it ever was, that we can justify many of our beliefs by direct observation or by working them out from first principles. Instead we find ourselves regularly deferring to people we judge to be experts.

So we were always more epistemically reliant on those we judge to be experts than many philosophers recognized, and we are becoming more and more reliant on them as our body of knowledge (or at any rate our body of belief) expands, and many parts of it become increasingly specialized.

What is an Expert?

Although I rejected Goldman's purely veritistic approach to epistemology in the last chapter, a purely veritistic approach to defining expertise seems more promising.[2] Being well-informed may not be the most important intellectual virtue, but it does seem to be the most important virtue of the expert *qua* expert. We do not go to experts seeking wisdom; we go to them seeking correct answers to our questions.

So I say that being an expert is simply a matter of being well-informed about a subject, that is, having a significantly greater store of accurate information about it than most people (or most people in one's community). Goldman thinks this is too simple. He complicates the concept in three ways, none of which, in my opinion, are justified.

First, whereas I have characterized expertise in purely comparative terms, Goldman thinks there is a noncomparative component to the concept as well: "Being an expert is not simply a matter of veritistic superiority to most of the community. Some non-comparative threshold of veritistic attainment must be reached, though there is great vagueness in setting this threshold" (Goldman, 2001, p. 91). I simply don't share the intuitions Goldman appeals to in this passage and see no need to complicate matters in this way. If some individuals are significantly better informed than most people about a subject, or most people in their community, then I think they should be considered experts on it, whether or not they are well-informed from a God's-eye point of view.

Second, Goldman suggests that one can be an expert, not only by having significantly more true beliefs about a subject than most people, but also by having significantly fewer false beliefs about it than most people (2001, p. 91). This seems wrong. If one could be an expert on a subject just by having significantly fewer false beliefs about it than most people, one could acquire expertise in a subject by the simple expedient of taking little or no interest in it. Someone who takes little interest in a subject will acquire few beliefs about it and will *eo ipso* acquire few false beliefs about it. But the idea that one could acquire expertise about a subject by being largely or entirely ignorant of it is obviously counterintuitive. Experts are typically much more interested in the subjects on which they have expertise than laypeople are. Hence they inevitably acquire more beliefs about those subjects and so run a greater risk of believing falsehoods about them than laypeople do.[3] So it is quite possible (indeed it is probably common) for experts to have more false beliefs (and perhaps even a greater ratio of false beliefs to true beliefs) in their domains of expertise than most people. In the previous chapter, I argued that the virtue of acquiring true beliefs should be distinguished from the virtue of avoiding false beliefs. The former virtue seems central to our concept of expertise in a way that the latter virtue does not.

Third, Goldman claims that there is also a dispositional element to the concept of expertise. An expert must have a capacity (or disposition) to form beliefs in true answers to new questions which may be posed within his or her domain of expertise. I'm inclined to think that this is an unnecessary complication. We would *ceteris paribus* expect people who are well-informed about a subject to be more able to accurately answer new questions that arise within it than people who are ignorant of it. The very capacities and dispositions, for example, inferential skills and interests, that led them to answer the old questions more accurately can be expected to lead them to answer new questions more accurately as well. My own view is that we should treat such capacities and dispositions as evidence that someone is an expert, rather than as "part of what it is to be an expert" (Goldman, 2001, p. 91).[4] Suppose Jones has acquired significantly more accurate information about a subject than most people, but that, as a result of some cognitive impairment, Jones is no longer able to accurately answer new questions that arise about the subject. Is Jones an expert? It seems to me that Jones is an expert, at least until such a time that the subject in question has changed (or lay knowledge of it has expanded) to the point that Jones's store of accurate information on the subject is no longer significantly greater than most people's. Certainly Jones will be able to fulfill the practical role of the expert, that is, being someone laypeople can go to in order to receive accurate answers to their questions. This is not to deny that there is a concept of expertise in which capacities (or skills) are central. Some people are experts at playing the piano or sexing chickens. But, like Goldman, I say that this kind of expertise should be distinguished from the "cognitive expertise" which is our concern here.

Given this account of expertise, and given the value we place on truth, the case in favor of being epistemically dependent on experts, when we can identify them, should be clear. Believing a proposition, or increasing our confidence in it, on the grounds that an expert believes it, or has a high degree of confidence in it, is justifiable insofar as we want to increase our chances of believing, or having a high degree of confidence in, the truth. Although I have argued, in the previous chapter, that truth is not the only fundamental value to consider when deciding what to believe, it clearly is *a* fundamental value.

Some Reasons for Lay Skepticism of Experts

It is quite common to hear people offer warnings against making ourselves epistemically dependent (or at least overly epistemically dependent) on experts. These people accept, of course, that we do rely heavily on experts for much of what we believe, but they think of this as an undesirable state of affairs. This skepticism comes in a variety of forms, some more legitimate than others.

Sometimes the skeptic is simply not using the word "expert" in the way I have recommended. They are using a *reputational* rather than an *objective* concept of expertise. By "experts" they mean "those who have the reputation for being experts," and their skepticism about expertise is just skepticism about whether the people who are widely believed to be experts deserve their reputation, either because there are no objective experts on the subject in question or because some other group of people are the real objective experts.

This form of skepticism is undoubtedly appropriate for some domains, but in others it is quite clear both that there are objective experts and that reputation is a good indicator of who those experts are. We don't usually have much difficulty identifying experts in (say) microbiology, number theory, or eighteenth-century Russian history. They are, to a large extent, the people who have a reputation for being experts in those fields. Other cases are less clear. Are there objective experts in morality, and if so, who are they? I will address this question at the end of this chapter. For now, it is enough to recognize that, on some subjects, skepticism about reputational expertise may well be justified. When it is justified, however, it only promotes confusion to say that we should not trust experts in the domain in question. Rather, we should say that those who have the reputation for being experts in that domain are not really experts.

A second, more general, reason for being skeptical of experts is that the practice of relying on experts can seem elitist, since it implies that some people's opinions are more valuable than others. Two things should be said about this. The first is that some people's opinions *are* more valuable than others, because some people *are* better informed than others. The second is that it is not as if there are two groups of people, the experts and the novices. We are all novices with respect to some subjects, and (I would suggest) experts with respect to others.

Indeed, if I am right that an expert is simply someone who is significantly better informed about a subject than most people, it should be pretty clear that almost everyone is an expert on many subjects. I am significantly better informed than most people about what I had for breakfast this morning; hence I am an expert on the subject. This sounds like a strange thing to say, of course, but that does not mean it is false. Some assertions sound strange because they are obviously false; other assertions sound strange for pragmatic reasons, even though they are true. I think this falls into the latter category. I am reluctant to describe myself as an expert on what I had for breakfast this morning, not because it isn't true, but because it sounds as if I am boasting about something which is nothing to boast of.

Expertise and Testimony

A third reason for concern about our epistemic reliance on experts stems from concern about our epistemic reliance on testimony. If we are to believe something on the grounds that an expert believes it, we must first know what the expert believes, and the normal way to find out what people believe is through their testimony, that is, through their written or spoken assertions. This is not the only way of finding out what other people, including experts, believe; sometimes, for example, we find out what others believe through their nonverbal behavior, and sometimes we find it out through the testimony or non-verbal behavior of third parties. Nonetheless, in most cases, we can rely on expert opinion only to the extent that we can rely on the testimony of the expert in question.

Skepticism about the testimony of others has ancient precedents,[5] but it came into its own in the early-modern period. The idea that we should rely on our own sensory experiences and our own inferences from them *as opposed to* the word of others was central to the zeitgeist of the time and closely associated with both British Empiricism and the scientific revolution (the motto of the Royal Society was "Nullius in Verba," which may be translated as "Nothing on Testimony"). John Locke gave voice to this skepticism in the following passage:

> I hope it will not be thought arrogance to say, that perhaps we should make greater progress in the discovery of rational and contemplative knowledge if we sought it in the fountain, in the consideration of things themselves, and made use rather of our own thoughts than other men's to find it: for I think we may as rationally hope to see with other men's eyes as to know by other men's understanding. ... The floating of other men's opinions in our brains makes us not one jot the more knowing, though they happen to be true. What in them was science is in us but opiniatrety. (Locke, 1961/1690, p. 58)

Locke's position here is extremely counterintuitive, perhaps more so today than in his own time. Many of the things we take ourselves to know with a very high degree of certainty have not come from drinking "the fountain" of "things themselves," but rather from our attending to the thoughts and understandings of other men and women, transmitted to us (directly or indirectly) through their testimony. For example, I know that there is a brain inside my skull, though I have never seen it or indeed any other brain. I know that there is a country called "Iraq" though I have never been there. And I know that Fermat's Last Theorem is true, even though I have never seen the proof, and doubt that I would understand it if I did. These are not *merely* my opinions (though of course they are my opinions); they are things I know, and I can only know them because I can trust the testimony of experts.

If beliefs that we derive from others are in some way inferior to beliefs that we acquire "on our own," that is not because we are less entitled to them or less entitled to be sure of them. Quite often we are entitled to be more confident of the testimony of others than of the "testimony" of our own senses. What is more, we sometimes should dismiss beliefs derived from our own observations and inferences in the face of expert testimony that those beliefs are not true. Surely a mediocre mathematician should prefer the consensus of the mathematical community to his or her own reasoning about whether Fermat's Last Theorem is true. Surely most of us would (and should) prefer the predictions of meteorologists to inductions from our own experiences, when trying to work out what tomorrow's weather will be like. At any rate, it should be clear that nonexperts in these cases should defer to experts insofar as their goal is to believe the truth.

Reductionism

Nonetheless, the Lockean ideal of working out what to believe for ourselves, rather than relying on experts, is undeniably appealing. A position, sometimes called *reductionism*, retains something of the spirit of this ideal, while conceding that we should sometimes (perhaps often) trust what experts say. Reductionists are not skeptical about expert testimony; they accept that it can be a source of knowledge and justified belief. But they insist that its status as a source of these things is derivative from some other, supposedly more fundamental, source. Since reductionism is closely associated with the empiricist tradition, that more fundamental source is usually understood to be the individual's own observations.

For the sake of clarity, we should note two things that the debate between reductionism and antireductionism is *not* about. First, it is not about whether our reliance on expert testimony is based on evidence, or whether, on the other hand, it is "blind" or "partially blind."[6] The fact that the debate has sometimes been presented in these terms is a product of an unfortunate tendency to contrast knowledge based on trust with knowledge based on evidence.[7] This is a false dichotomy. Knowledge based on trust can be (and often is) also based on evidence, evidence that the person we are trusting is in fact trustworthy. Reductionists have sometimes presented their position as the only alternative to gullibility or naivety about the word of others,[8] and it must be admitted that some antireductionists have sometimes said things which make them sound gullible. Nonetheless the real debate is not about *whether* novices should require evidence of the trustworthiness of putative experts before believing what they are told (all sides should agree that they should,[9] at least when the topic is sufficiently important); rather it is about the form that evidence should take. The reductionist asserts, and the antireductionist denies, that the evidence must be reducible to the individual's own observations (or whatever the preferred reductive base is). Hence the reductionist allows that novices should sometimes trust expert testimony, but insists that this trust should be subordinate to the novice's trust in his or her own powers of observation (as well, perhaps, as his or her own powers of inductive reasoning[10] from those observations).

Second, the debate between reductionism and its opponents should not be conflated with a certain debate about childhood learning. Reductionism has sometimes been associated with an idea, popular in the empiricist tradition, that children find out *entirely* from their own observations that some (indeed most) of the things they are told are true. Opponents of this view claim that children could never, on their own, acquire sufficient evidence to work this out.[11] The eighteenth-century Scottish philosopher Thomas Reid was an early proponent of the latter view, claiming that children begin with an attitude of unqualified trust in authority, and that only later does their "mature reason" learn "to suspect testimony in some cases, and disbelieve it in others; and set bounds to that authority to which she was at first entirely subject" (Reid, 1970/1764, p. 197). Alvin Goldman has defended reductionism by arguing that children may after all be in "a position to get good inductive evidence that people usually make claims about things they are in a good position to know about" (Goldman, 2001, p. 87). Whatever you may think about this debate, it should be distinguished from the debate about reductionism, understood as a normative thesis about what we should believe and how we should pursue knowledge now. So understood, reductionism offers us advice. The question is whether it is good advice.

To get a clearer picture of the kind of advice reductionism has to offer, consider the following example. Suppose a putative expert makes an assertion p concerning which I am a novice, and I am wondering whether I should believe p as a result of the putative expert's testimony (or whether I should increase my confidence in p and if so by how much). Some of the evidence available to me is likely to consist in the testimony of other putative experts, whose expertise may be confirmable by still further putative experts, and so on. Reductionists will insist that this process of confirming the expertise of one person by consulting further putative experts must come to an end with a justification expressed entirely in terms of my own observations; as J. L. Mackie put it: "if an infinite regress is to be avoided, we must come back at some stage to what the knower observes for himself" (Mackie, 1970, p. 254).[12]

On the face of it, the desirability of pursuing this ideal depends on who we are, and on the circumstances in which we are placed. If I have reason to believe that my own observations and the inferences I make from them are highly reliable, that is, they almost invariably cause me to form true beliefs, *and* I have reason to believe that the testimony of putative experts I encounter tends to be unreliable, that is, it is often not true, then the reductionist ideal would be plausible, because it would describe a reasonably reliable way of forming beliefs. In following the reductionist ideal I would be making a less reliable source of information (what putative experts say) subordinate to more reliable sources (my own powers of observation and inductive reasoning), and this would surely be at least presumptively rational. But although reductionism seems to offer good advice for people in this position, most of us are not in this position. Our own powers of observation and reasoning are not more reliable than the testimony of putative experts. And it is simply egotism to think otherwise. Of course people *sometimes* mislead us (intentionally or otherwise), but our own epistemic resources sometimes mislead us as well. If our own epistemic resources are in some sense *more fundamental* sources of knowledge and justification than what we are told by others, that is not because they are always, or even typically, more reliable.

Intellectual Autonomy and Information Cascades

If you were only interested in your chances of believing truths and steering clear of falsehoods, then you would be right to treat expert testimony as just another source of information, no different from your own powers of perception or reasoning. All these sources of knowledge and justification are usually, but not always, reliable.

Nonetheless, reliability is not the only value at stake, and the analogy between expert testimony and these other sources of information can be taken too far. My reliance on expert testimony, unlike my reliance on my own sensory organs or powers of reasoning, involves some sacrifice of my *intellectual autonomy*. When I believe something because a putative expert testifies to it, I am believing it because (I judge) someone else believes it, rather than because I worked it out for myself. Why is intellectual autonomy valuable? A partial answer is that intellectual autonomy is valuable for some of the same reasons that autonomy in general is valuable. For one thing, my self-respect is intimately connected with my ability to do things for myself, and one of the most important of these things is working out what to believe. Another reason to think intellectual autonomy is valuable is that we cannot be sure that experts will always be available (in fact we can often be sure they won't). Hence we need practice at working things out for ourselves, so that we will have the skills we need when there is no other way of getting the information we want.

But there is more to the value of intellectual autonomy than this. Intellectual autonomy serves an important social function. This can be seen by considering the phenomena economists call *information cascades*. Information cascades can occur when people express their beliefs (through testimony or by some other means) about a certain matter in a sequence.[13] If the early beliefs show a clear pattern, the information inferred from this pattern may outweigh any information that individuals later in the sequence have which conflicts with it. Hence, they follow "the crowd," rather than their own "private evidence." Information cascades are ubiquitous. On a reasonably fine day I am wondering whether to take an umbrella to work. I look out the window to see if others are carrying umbrellas. If enough of them are, I do too, even though many of them may only be carrying umbrellas because they have seen that others are doing the same, and even though whatever private evidence I have indicates that rain is unlikely. Now there may be nothing wrong with ignoring my private evidence and following the crowd from a purely self-interested epistemic point of view. Copying other people's beliefs can be a more reliable belief-forming practice than trying to work out what to believe on one's own, but it can also be antisocial (or selfish, to put it bluntly).

This can be seen clearly from some of the experimental work on information cascades. The following experiment (Anderson and Holt, 1997) provides a useful context for discussion. At the beginning of the experiment, there are two outwardly indistinguishable urns. One of them, which we will call "the predominantly white urn," contains twice as many white marbles as dark marbles. The other, which we will call "the predominantly dark urn," contains twice as many dark marbles as white marbles. One of these urns is chosen at random, and volunteers are asked to draw one marble from it, in sequence, and guess which urn they are drawing from. Those who guess correctly are rewarded with two dollars. The volunteers do not have any direct information about the color of marbles drawn earlier in the sequence. They only have two pieces of evidence to base their guess on, the color of the marble that they themselves have drawn, and the guesses of those earlier than them in the sequence.

Now, what should you do when these two forms of evidence conflict? Suppose, for example, that you have drawn a white marble, but everyone before you has guessed that it is the predominantly dark urn. If there is only one person ahead of you, and you can assume that he or she is rational, then you can infer that he or she has drawn a dark marble. Hence one dark marble and one white marble have been drawn and it is equally likely to be either urn. Almost everyone in this situation chooses to rely on their private evidence, that is, they will guess that it is the predominantly white urn.[14] However, suppose that there are two people ahead of you and they have both guessed that it is the predominantly dark urn. Now, it seems clear, you should agree with the people ahead of you, even if your private evidence points in the opposite direction. You have good reason to believe that the first two marbles are dark, and that outweighs any evidence you can get from the one marble you have drawn. In general, whenever the first two guesses match, the third person should follow, regardless of the color of the marble he or she draws. Not only should the third person follow, so should the fourth, the fifth, and so on, even if their private evidence points in the other direction.

Notice that everyone in such an information cascade is being individually rational. If they are only interested in promoting their own chances of guessing correctly, they really should follow the crowd. Nonetheless, in following the crowd, they are doing those who follow them a disservice, by concealing their private evidence from them, and so increasing the likelihood that their guesses will be wrong.

The danger of information cascades provides some reason to be wary of making ourselves epistemically dependent on others in certain circumstances. But it does not provide a general reason for being skeptical of expert testimony. Part of the reason experiments like the one described above often lead to information cascades is that there are no real experts involved. Everyone in the group has precisely the same amount of private information, so no one is significantly better placed than anyone else when answering the question at issue.[15]

In what follows, I will assume that we should sometimes (indeed quite often) be epistemically dependent on experts, and that our principle concern in doing so is to increase our own chances of believing the truth about the question at issue. In other words, I will put aside any concerns we might have about failing to "do our bit" for the epistemic well-being of our society.

Disagreement Among Experts

It is one thing to note that we should trust experts on certain questions, but what should laypeople believe when the experts disagree? This is a problem which regularly confronts jurors. Scott Brewer explains their dilemma in the following passage:

> When experts disagree about the truth of some evidentiary proposition *e*, the nonexpert must decide whom to believe on the scientific issue. But, *ex hypothesi*, the nonexpert does not have sufficient competence in the expert discipline to be able to make the choice on substantive grounds, so how can the nonexpert make that choice? If we assume honesty on the part of each expert, this can seem especially puzzling in that it may look like we are expecting greater ability to discern the scientific truth from the nonexpert than we are from the expert. (Brewer, 1998, p. 1595)

This is a problem for everyone, not just jurors. In recent years a number of philosophers have discussed this problem.[16] It seems to be a particularly pressing issue at the beginning of the twenty-first century, when experts disagree over a wide variety of issues about which laypeople should (and arguably must) adopt some doxastic attitude. A prime example of such an issue is climate change. How can laypeople decide whether or not to believe that human activity is causing the earth to get warmer when (it seems) the experts themselves are divided on the matter?

Going by the numbers

One intuitively plausible response to this problem is to appeal to the numbers on either side of the issue. All else being equal, it would seem, if there are more experts on one side than on the other, it is rational for a layperson to take the side of the larger group of experts. I'm sure I speak for many people when I admit that when asked to defend my belief in anthropogenic climate change, I can do little more than point to the fact that the overwhelming majority of climatologists (presumably the experts on the topic) believe in it. By pointing to this fact, I seem to be appealing to the following idea:

> … numbers would seem to be very weighty, at least in the absence of other evidence. Each new testifier or opinion-holder on one side of the issue should add weight to that side. So a novice who is otherwise in the dark about the reliability of the various opinion-holders would seem driven to agree with the more numerous body of experts. (Goldman, 2001, p. 98)

Despite the intuitive plausibility of this idea, Goldman and several other contemporary philosophers reject it. They claim that there is only evidential significance in the fact that the numbers are on one side of an issue if, and to the extent that, those on that side formed their opinions independently of one another. Goldman himself expresses this idea by saying that "if two or more opinion-holders are totally *non-independent* of one another, and if the subject knows or is justified in believing this, then the subject's opinion should not be swayed – even a little – by more than one of these opinion-holders" (Goldman, 2001, p. 99). In a similar vein, Thomas Kelly claims that "numbers mean little in the absence of independence" (Kelly, 2010, p. 148). Likewise, Adam Elga argues that the accumulation of testimony on one side of an issue "should move one only to the extent that one counts it as independent from opinions one has already taken into account" (Elga, 2010, p. 177). He claims that this is "completely uncontroversial" and that "every sensible view on disagreement should accommodate it" (p. 178).

Nonetheless, I think it is wrong, and in what follows I will defend the practice of "going by the numbers" against this objection.[17] In particular, I will offer a (qualified) defense of my own appeal to the authority of numbers in forming an opinion about global warming.[18] Ben Almassi applies the Goldman/Kelly/Elga thesis to the topic of global warming when he says that "were one to discover that all climatologists believe in global warming entirely on the basis of a single scientist's research, while global warming skeptics believe on mutually independent grounds, the novice bystander ought not to be swayed by the numbers favoring global warming" (Almassi, 2007, p. 378).[19] This seems to me to be wrong. I will argue that *if I were* to discover that the climatologists who believe in global warming do so entirely on the basis of a single scientist's research, while those on the other side of the debate reach their conclusions on mutually independent grounds, I *may* still be rationally be swayed by the numbers favoring global warming. Whether, and in what way, such a discovery should affect my confidence in global warming cannot be decided in the abstract. Such a discovery *could* rationally reduce my confidence in global warming, but equally it could rationally increase my confidence, or leave it unaffected. It would all depend on the details.

So what does *dependence* mean in this context, and why should its presence undermine the rationality of "going by the numbers"? Goldman explains dependence in terms of conditional probability. Suppose there are two opinion-holders X and Y and a hypothesis H, let X(H) be X's believing H and Y(H) be Y's believing H. To say that Y's belief is totally dependent[20] on X's belief is to say:

$$P(Y(H)/X(H) \& H) = P(Y(H)/X(H) \& \sim H)$$

In other words, Y would be just as likely to share X's opinion that H when it is false as when it is true. In this situation, Goldman calls Y a *nondiscriminating reflector* of X with respect to H. According to Goldman, in order for Y's opinion to have any evidential worth above and beyond X's opinion, it is necessary for Y to be more likely to share X's opinion that H is true when it is true than when it is false. In other words:

$$P(Y(H)/X(H) \& H) > P(Y(H)/X(H) \& \sim H)$$

In this situation Y's belief is at least partially *conditionally independent* of X's belief.

This may seem plausible. Consider an extreme case, which Goldman discusses (2001, pp. 98–9). Suppose X is a "guru" and Y is a "follower" who believes whatever X believes. If X believes H, Y is certain to believe H. Hence Y is just as likely (that is, with probability 1) to share X's opinion if it is true as he or she is if it is false:

> … a follower's opinion does not provide any additional grounds for accepting the guru's view (and a second follower does not provide any additional grounds for accepting a first follower's view) even if all the followers are precisely as reliable as the guru himself (or as one another) – which followers must be, of course, if they believe exactly the same things as the guru (and one another) on the topics in question. (Goldman, 2001, p. 99)

Goldman concludes that Y's agreement with X about H will only provide evidence of H for a third person if that person has evidence that Y has a "more-or-less autonomous causal route to belief, rather than a causal route that guarantees agreement with X" (2001, p. 102). He mentions three forms that such autonomy could take – access to independent eyewitnesses, access to independent experiments, and a process of reasoning with X about the truth of H.[21] The presence of some autonomy in any of these forms would make Y "poised to avoid belief in H even though X believes it" (p. 102).

People who value epistemic autonomy (as I hope we all do) are likely to associate the language of "gurus" and "followers" with connotations of irrationality, which may prejudice clear discussion of the issue. It is important to remember that one is only a nondiscriminating reflector with respect to *a particular belief* of another. You could be a nondiscriminating reflector of another person with respect to one of that person's beliefs and still be as discriminating as you like about any or all of his or her other beliefs.

It is also important to note that Goldman quite rightly does not think that there is anything wrong, as such, with being a nondiscriminating reflector. In fact, the problem he is addressing, about which experts a novice should believe, is a problem about which experts a novice should nondiscriminately reflect. Goldman stipulates (2001, p. 90) that novices have no prior opinions (or at least none to which they feel they can legitimately appeal) about the topic. Hence a novice can have no autonomous causal route (in Goldman's sense) to the belief he or she ends up with.

An illustration may be helpful here. Suppose that I have just traveled to a new community and am told by X, who purports to be a meteorologist, that it will be hot tomorrow (proposition H). Suppose, as a result, I attach some credibility to H. Next I encounter Y who also believes that it will be hot tomorrow. Goldman's position implies that I would be irrational to allow Y's belief to increase my confidence that it will be hot tomorrow if Y is a nondiscriminating reflector of X with respect to H. That is, according to Goldman, I should only take Y's belief as confirming evidence that H if Y's belief that H is at least partly conditionally independent of X's belief that H. Furthermore, the same would be true no matter how many people I find in this community who believe that tomorrow will be hot. As Goldman says, it makes no difference how many people "share an initial expert's opinion": "If they are all non-discriminating reflectors of someone whose opinion has already been taken into account, they add no further weight to the novice's evidence" (2001, p. 102).

Goldman presents his formal argument for this position in Bayesian terms. The novice should update his or her belief in H in light of the evidence that X believes H in accordance with the following "likelihood quotient":

$$\frac{P(X(H)/H)}{P(X(H)/\sim H)}$$

And the novice should update his or her belief in H in light of the evidence that X and Y believe it in accordance with this likelihood quotient:

$$\frac{P(X(H)\,\&\,Y(H)/H)}{P(X(H)\,\&\,Y(H)/\sim H)}$$

Now, normally you would expect (2) to be larger than (1), but, as Goldman spills some ink demonstrating, when Y is a nondiscriminating reflector of X with respect to H, that will not be so: (1) and (2) will be equivalent.

Although mathematically impeccable, this argument involves an illegitimate assumption, namely that the probabilities in question, and hence the ratios between them, will remain constant throughout the enquiry. Perhaps the clearest way to see why this cannot be assumed is to concentrate, not on the updating process itself, but on its end result, the degree to which the novice should believe H (that is, the probability the novice should assign H).

After learning that X believes H, the novice updates his or her degree of belief in H by assigning it the "new" probability $P(H/X(H))$. After learning that Y believes H as well, the novice again updates his or her degree of belief in H; this time assigning it the probability $P(H/X(H)\,\&\,Y(H))$. In general, the latter value will be greater than the former; however, if Y is a nondiscriminating reflector of X with respect to H, these values will be the same. Hence, in this case, updating the novice's degree of belief from the former to the latter involves no increase in his or her confidence in H.

The presupposition of this argument that $P(H/X(H))$ will remain constant for the novice throughout the enquiry is not justified, because Bayesian probabilities are subjective. They are measurements of the degree to which it is rational to believe something, given certain evidence. Hence probabilities can change as the available evidence changes. It is therefore wrong to think of a Bayesian probability as something which has, in Goldman's words, "already been taken into account" (2001, p. 102). Goldman's argument assumes, in effect, that knowing or justifiably believing that $P(H/X(H))$ and $P(H/X(H)\&Y(H))$ are equivalent is a reason for the novice to assign a lower value than he or she otherwise would (or previously had) to the latter. But this ignores the possibility that it might instead be a reason to assign a higher value than he or she would (or previously had) to the former.[22]

Why should we consider the latter possibility? Because the existence of a nondiscriminating reflector of a person with respect to a proposition can itself be evidence in favor of that proposition. Suppose, that Y is a nondiscriminating reflector of X with respect to H, *because Y knows or is justified in believing that H is within a domain in which X is an expert.* Y believes H because X does, and would do so even if H were false, but Y's concurrence with X still provides the novice with evidence for H, because the novice rationally believes Y to be a reliable judge about whether X is a reliable judge about whether H is true. The novice's confidence in X's expertise concerning H is rationally increased by his or her confidence in Y's meta-expertise.[23] Y's meta-expertise consists in Y's knowledge of (or justified belief about) the scope and extent of X's expertise.[24]

Suppose, to return to my earlier example, that X is, as he claims, a meteorologist. Suppose further that everyone else in the community believes what he says about tomorrow's weather because they know him to be well-qualified and invariably accurate in his weather predictions up until now. My confidence that it will be hot tomorrow may be rationally increased by the fact that many apparently sensible people believe it. In making this assessment I may quite rationally be indifferent to the issue of whether all but one of them are nondiscriminating reflectors of the other. In fact, the degree by which my confidence is increased by the concurrence of the many may be greater if I discover that all but one of them are completely (conditionally) dependent in this way, than it would have been if I had discovered instead that they all had a partially autonomous causal route to their belief. Suppose, for example, that the only even partially autonomous causal routes to belief available to the nondiscriminating reflectors are intuitive inductions from their own personal experiences. They may be poor meteorologists, but good judges of meteorologists, and I, as a novice, may rationally judge that this is so. Hence, Goldman's claim that "a follower's opinion does not provide any additional grounds for accepting the guru's view" is not generally true. It would only be true if we could presuppose that followers are invariably unreliable judges of gurus. And we can't.

Of course, "followers" (i.e., nondiscriminating reflectors) exhibit a particularly extreme form of dependence. Dependence is often, perhaps usually, a matter of degree. The Goldman/Elga/Kelly view is that the greater the dependence is, the less the evidential significance of numbers will be:

> Whatever evidence is afforded for a given claim by the fact that several billion people confidently believe that that claim is true, that evidence is less impressive to the extent that the individuals in question have not arrived at that belief independently. That is, the evidence provided by the fact that a large number of individuals hold a belief in common is weaker to the extent that the individuals who share that belief do so because they have influenced one another, or because they have been influenced by common sources. (Kelly, 2010, p.147)

Goldman draws the following conclusion about how novices should respond to disagreement among experts:

> The appropriate change in the novice's belief in H should be based on two sets of concurring opinions (one in favor of H and one against it), and it should depend on *how reliable* the members of each set are and on *how (conditionally) independent* of one another they are. (Goldman, 2001, p. 103)

He claims that this conclusion seems to get the right result in the following case:

> If scientific creationists are more numerous than evolutionary scientists, that would not incline me to say that a novice is warranted in putting more credence in the views of the former than in the views of the latter (on the core issues on which they disagree). At least I am not so inclined on the assumption that the novice has roughly comparable information as most philosophers currently have about the methods of belief formation by evolutionists and creationists respectively. (2001, pp. 103–4)

In a footnote attached to this passage, Goldman makes it explicit that he is "assuming that believers in creation science have greater (conditional) dependence on the opinion leaders of their general viewpoint than do believers in evolutionary theory."

But it's not at all clear that this assumption is correct. I, for example, am a believer in evolutionary theory on the core issues on which it contradicts creationism, but my beliefs in this area are all highly dependent on the opinion leaders of that general viewpoint. I suspect this is true of many other believers in evolutionary theory. But even if Goldman's assumption is correct, our previous discussion makes it clear that this is not *on its own* a reason for a novice to prefer evolutionary theory to creationism. It is only a reason when combined with the further assumption (which is surely correct) that creationist followers lack relevant meta-expertise. In other words, they are not particularly good at identifying objective experts in this area.

In fact this doesn't seem to be a very good case study. Hardly any reasonably educated person can be a complete novice in this dispute, and even people who are relatively uninformed don't have to look far to see internal inconsistencies in the creationist position. A better example is global warming. Most climatologists believe the earth is warming and that it is to a large extent caused by human activity; a small minority disagree. As things stand, many people, including myself, have little but this bare fact to go on when deciding what to believe. Nonetheless I think we are justified in agreeing with the larger group of experts, just because it is larger. Goldman's position implies that if we were to discover that the beliefs of some members of the larger group of experts were highly dependent on others, our confidence in the proposition about which they agree should be reduced. But, as I hope I've made clear, this need not be the case. We may quite rationally be indifferent to the discovery of these dependence relations. We may even quite rationally see them as evidence justifying an increase in our confidence in the proposition in question.

In fact, I assume that the scientists who believe in anthropogenic climate change have not reached their conclusions entirely independently of one another. The Goldman/Elga/Kelly view implies that recognition of this (probable) fact should reduce the collective authority of these scientists in the eyes of laypeople, and that we should be less confident of expert consensus (or near consensus) in a proposition to the extent that it is the product of teamwork. But this seems to be clearly wrong. The fact that a scientific consensus (or near consensus) is not the result of scientists independently arriving at the same conclusion should not undermine its significance from a novice's perspective. If anything, it should strengthen it.

45

Although expertise and meta-expertise are logically distinguishable, they overlap to a large extent. Because experts typically work closely with other experts on the same subject, we can usually assume that experts will be able to recognize other experts, and be able to recognize those who have greater expertise than themselves. Consider the far-fetched scenario, envisioned by Almassi, in which we (novices) discover that the scientific consensus (or near consensus) on global warming is based entirely on a single scientist's research. A novice *might* construe this discovery as evidence that the scientist responsible for all the research has exceptional expertise (after all, a lot of people who we have reason to think are meta-experts appear to regard this scientist as having exceptional expertise). In fact, I don't think that would be the appropriate response to this situation, but that has nothing to do with abstract considerations about the nature of dependence. Rather, it concerns a feature of this particular topic, which is apparent even to novices such as myself. Research on global warming and its causes clearly requires people to take measurements in a wide range of places over long periods of time, and it is obvious that these measurements could not be performed adequately by a single scientist. If we were to discover that the majority of climatologists were irrational enough to think otherwise, our opinion of their intellectual capabilities and hence our faith in their conclusions, would rationally be reduced. But no general considerations about the rationality of "going by the numbers" can be deduced from this. No one has suggested that the number of experts on either side of a question is the *only* consideration laypeople can take into account when deciding whom to believe.

The arguments of contending experts

To what extent can the arguments that experts put forward in support of their views help laypeople work out what to believe? It is tempting to be skeptical. If the novice cannot work out the truth-value of the expert's claim to start with, why should he or she be any better at working out the strength of the expert's argument for that claim? Sometimes, novices cannot even understand the arguments of experts, still less work out whether their premises are true, or whether, if they were true, they would support the expert's position.

Following Goldman, I will distinguish between the *esoteric* and the *exoteric* statements within an expert's argument. Esoteric statements belong to the expert's domain of expertise and as such their truth-values are inaccessible to the novice. Exoteric statements are outside the expert's domain of expertise, and their truth-values may be accessible to the novice:

> Not only are novices commonly unable to assess the truth-values of the esoteric propositions, but they also are ill-placed to assess the support relations between the cited evidence and the proffered conclusion. Of course, the proponent expert will claim that the support relation is strong between her evidence and the conclusion she defends; but her opponent will commonly dispute this. The novice will be ill-placed to assess which expert is in the right. (Goldman, 2001, p. 94)

Such a novice is in a difficult position, but not, according to Goldman, an entirely hopeless one. Even if the arguments of contending experts are largely or entirely esoteric, one expert can exhibit *dialectical superiority* over another, and this may be a plausible indicator that he or she has greater expertise than the other expert. The novice may be rationally convinced by *the way* the expert has argued, rather than by *what* the expert has argued, by the nature of the expert's "performance," rather than by the plausibility of the expert's premises or the strength of his or her inferences.

How is a novice to judge whether one performance is superior to another? Goldman's answer focuses on the way the experts respond to ostensive counterevidence. The greater *the number* of ostensive rebuttals an expert makes to ostensive counterevidence, the greater the *speed* with which he or she does this, and the greater the *smoothness* with which he or she does this, then, all else being equal, the greater the confidence the novice should have in the expert's expertise (Goldman, 2001, pp. 95–6).

Why should these things be thought of as indicators of superior expertise? Goldman has little to say about this issue, but David Matheson has offered an interpretation and defense of Goldman's position, which draws on Goldman's distinction between *primary* and *secondary* questions in a domain of expertise. Primary questions are "the principal questions that are of interest to researchers or students" investigating the domain, whereas secondary questions "concern the existing evidence or arguments that bear on the primary questions, and the assessments of the evidence made by prominent researchers" (Goldman, 2001, p. 92). Suppose that "Whether *p*?" is a primary question of domain *E*. Matheson makes the following claim about Goldman's "marks" of superior expertise:

> These marks constitute in general, good evidence for thinking that the expert knows enough answers to secondary questions in *E* to put her in a better position to know the answer to primary questions in *E* than almost anyone else, and hence in a better position to know the answer to the question of whether *p* … (Matheson, 2005, p. 150)

It is important to emphasize that this kind of *indirect* evidence for the superiority of one argument to another can be quite unreliable.[25] The readiness of an expert to give a lot of quick, smooth responses to ostensive counterevidence *may* be evidence that he or she has superior expertise on the topic. On the other hand, it may merely be evidence that he or she is an expert in the dark art of rhetoric, an art which consists, to a large extent, in knowing how to appear to be an expert. As Brewer has noted, there is "a lucrative market" in this appearance, which has been "traded at high prices since the days of the sophists and finds exceptionally robust business in adversarial legal systems" (Brewer, 1998, p. 1622).

In fact, it is quite easy to imagine circumstances in which the marks Goldman associates with superior expertise should lower, rather than increase, an expert's credibility in the eyes of laypeople. The quickness and smoothness of an expert's responses to ostensive counterevidence *may* be, as Matheson suggests, a sign that the expert knows the debate inside out; but it may instead be a sign that the expert is not giving the ostensive counterevidence the consideration it deserves. Matheson himself argues that, all else being equal, the greater an expert's "receptivity to new ostensive evidence" relevant to a question, the greater the credence a novice should give the expert's testimony on that question (Matheson, 2005, pp. 151–2). This seems right. But surely one sign that someone is receptive to new ostensive evidence is that they are willing to take time to respond (perhaps hesitatingly) to it.

A similar point can be made about Goldman's other mark of superior expertise, the *number* of ostensive rebuttals made to ostensive counterevidence. The fact that one expert offers more ostensive rebuttals to ostensive counterevidence than another expert *may* be a sign that the former expert has superior expertise. On the other hand, it *may* be a sign that the latter has superior expertise. Given the imperfect nature of our understanding of the world, we should expect that even the greatest experts will often be unable to offer effective rebuttals to all apparent counterevidence to their views, and we may reasonably be suspicious of experts who think they can. We *may* reasonably construe their attitude as evidence that they are fixated on a view to the point that they are unwilling to admit the existence of any evidence against it.

Goldman is right that there are marks of dialectical superiority, which novices can use to make reasonable judgments about which experts have greater expertise. But I doubt whether any of these marks are universal. It seems much more likely that marks of dialectical superiority are dependent on subject matter and the context in which the arguments are presented. If there were universal marks of dialectical superiority, it is reasonable to suppose that practitioners of rhetoric would be familiar with them by now, and would have learnt how to acquire them or successfully imitate them. This would have the effect of undermining their status as marks of superior expertise. Attempts to identify marks of expert argumentative performance are reminiscent of attempts by psychologists to identify marks of honesty. Sometimes it is possible to know whether someone is being honest. Sometimes it may even be easy. But we have reason to be suspicious of the usefulness of rules for identifying honest speech, which purport to apply independently of the subject matter of the speech or the context in which it is delivered.

A novice who is ill-placed to evaluate the plausibility of the premises of an expert's argument or the strength of its inferences may still sometimes make a reasonable judgment about whether to accept it on the basis of the expert's performance. All else being equal, an expert's responses to ostensive counterevidence should be *reasonably* quick and smooth, but not *excessively* quick or smooth. How quick and how smooth should they be, if they are to be rationally persuasive? This cannot be answered *a priori*. The same goes for Goldman's other mark of expert argumentative performance. Experts should, all else being equal, be able to offer ostensive rebuttals to some of the ostensive counterevidence presented by rival experts, and we have *prima facie* reason to be suspicious of the claims of those who have little or nothing to say in response to those who disagree with them. On the other hand, we may also have *prima facie* reason to be suspicious of experts who attempt to rebut all ostensive counterevidence. Sometimes a novice may reasonably conclude that the very fact that experts disagree about something shows that not all the evidence points the same way. If so, then a novice may reasonably be suspicious of an expert who claims that *all* the evidence against his or her view can be rebutted.

Evidence of dishonesty

Working out which experts to believe is not just a matter of working out which of them have greater expertise, that is, which are more likely to know the truth; it is also a matter of working out which are more likely to report the truth. Sometimes novices should choose to believe one expert rather than another, because the former, but not the latter, has interests and/or biases which give him or her a reason to lie.

Although the presence of such interests and/or biases *may* give a novice reason to suspect that the expert with a reason to lie is lying, it need not. Goldman goes too far when he says, "if two people give contradictory reports, and exactly one of them has a reason to lie, the relative credibility of the latter is seriously compromised" (Goldman, 2001, p. 104). Although he characterizes this proposal as coming directly from "common sense and experience," it is clearly not, in general, true. One can recognize that someone has a reason to lie, but still be justified in being morally certain that they are not lying (if one can be justified in being morally certain of anything). Motive is one consideration to be taken into account when trying to determine whether someone is lying, but it is clearly not the only consideration.

Interests and/or biases *can* constitute evidence that an expert is lying, but that is not the only way they can undermine the reliability of an expert's testimony. As Goldman notes, they "can exert more subtle distorting influences on an expert's opinions, so that their opinions are less likely to be accurate even if sincere" (2001, p. 104). Nonetheless, these subtle distorting influences should still, I think, be understood in terms of dishonesty, so long as we construe dishonesty in a suitably broad manner, one which recognizes that it can occur *prior* to the testimony in question and involve self-deception.

I argued, in the previous chapter, that people sometimes believe things, because it is in their interests to believe them.[26] People may have an interest in believing a proposition, because they have an interest in testifying convincingly that it is true and cannot do so unless they believe it themselves. Hence an interest may cause an expert (or indeed any speaker) to testify falsely, by first causing him or her to believe falsely. Those who suggest that the testimony of climate skeptics should be given less weight if they are employed by fossil fuel interests, need not be suggesting that these people are lying. At least they need not be suggesting that they are lying *at the time of their testimony*. But they are, in my view, still suggesting the *possibility* of some form of dishonesty. At least, the suggestion is, this interest makes self-deception *prima facie* more likely.[27]

Moral Expertise

Rather than attempting a complete list of the factors laypeople may take into account when assessing the testimony of rival experts, a task which I suspect could never be completed, I will finish this chapter by considering a case study in which the attribution of expertise has been highly controversial. This will lead directly into the themes of the next chapter.

I earlier raised the issue of whether there are any experts in morality. There are of course reputational experts in morality; at least, there are people who have a reputation for moral expertise in some communities. For example, many religious leaders are treated as moral experts by their followers, who think of them as being significantly more likely than most people to have accurate answers to moral questions.[28] Professional philosophers, especially moral philosophers, also have something of a reputation for moral expertise in certain quarters. Their moral expertise seems to be assumed by those who appoint them to ethics committees, for example, as well as by those in the media who seek out their opinions on moral issues of topical interest.

Nonetheless, most professional philosophers modestly reject any claim to objective moral expertise, or at least deny that they have such expertise in virtue of their status as professional philosophers (or professional moral philosophers).[29] C. D. Broad expresses this view in the following passage:

> Moral philosophers, as such, have no special information not available to the general public, about what is right and what is wrong; nor have they any call to undertake those hortatory functions which are so adequately performed by clergymen, politicians, leader-writers … . (Broad, 1952, p. 244)

Broad does not deny that there are moral experts. He merely denies that moral philosophers *qua* moral philosophers are moral experts.

Indeed, Broad seems to imply that certain other people, politicians, clergymen, and so forth, may have a better claim to expertise in this area.[30] Most professional philosophers who deny that they are experts on morality, however, pretty clearly do so on the grounds that no such people exist. It is usually assumed by both sides of this debate that if there are moral experts, they are to be found among the ranks of professional philosophers.

To suppose that any person or group of people are (objective) experts on morality is to suppose controversially both that there is such a thing as moral truth[31] and that some people have access to significantly more of it than others. In what follows, I will put aside the former reason for being skeptical of moral expertise, and assume, what I take to be the commonsense view, that some moral beliefs (i.e., beliefs about what is good or bad, right or wrong, etc.) are true,[32] and hence that it is possible to have moral knowledge, at least in the "thin" sense discussed in the previous chapter, according to which knowledge is simply true belief.

Renford Bambrough has argued that moral experts "disagree so much and so radically that we hesitate to say they really are experts" (Bambrough, 1967, p. 164). But, as David Archard has noted in response, extensive and radical disagreement is to be found among acknowledged experts in a wide variety of fields, including statistics, physics, and biology (Archard, 2011, p. 121). I would add that Bambrough may be exaggerating the degree of disagreement about morality to be found among so-called experts on the subject. It all depends, of course, on who we suppose the so-called experts are. Let's assume for the moment, as Archard does, that the only serious candidates for moral expertise are professional moral philosophers. Disagreement about morality among them, though real, is not particularly extensive or radical. Utilitarians and Kantians, for example, agree about a wide range of moral judgments. They agree that murder is usually wrong and that telling the truth is usually right. Indeed, it could be argued that they only disagree when it comes to some quite far-fetched thought experiments. Their disagreements seem quite minor and superficial compared with the extensive and profound disagreements to be found among physicists over the merits of string theory, to take just one example.

Archard's own reason for thinking that professional moral philosophers are not moral experts is different. It is based on the fact that "moral philosophers see themselves as required to construct moral theory on the foundations of common-sense morality" (Archard, 2011, p. 123). Although he concedes that there are moral philosophers who are highly critical of *some* aspects of common-sense morality, he insists that their arguments nonetheless are founded in common-sense morality, where that is understood as "a set of core moral precepts" such as "Don't kill innocents, Don't lie, Don't break promises, and so on" (2011, p. 124). Even the most radical moral philosophy cannot reject all the precepts of commonsense morality. This means that moral philosophers cannot have *significantly* more true beliefs about morality than most people, who presumably accept commonsense morality more or less uncritically. Hence, Archard concludes, moral philosophers are not moral experts, though he does concede that his argument leaves open the possibility that they might have a "selective and limited" expertise in morality (p. 125).

I think Archard is right that moral philosophy is, or at least should be, built on foundations of common sense, but it's not clear that this distinguishes moral philosophy from any other area of thought, including those in which there clearly are experts. This was certainly the view of Thomas Reid, who said that "All knowledge and all science must be built upon principles that are self-evident; and of such principles every man who has common sense is a competent judge" (Reid, 2006/1785, p. 331). This does not mean that science cannot go beyond common sense, nor does it mean that it cannot contradict common sense. It just means that in science, as in morality, or any other enquiry, common sense is the starting point, and that if our conclusions involve a *total* rejection of common sense, we should construe that as a *reductio* of our premises.

I agree with Archard's conclusion that there are no experts in morality, or at any rate that any expertise in morality is likely to be selective and limited, but my reasons for thinking this are quite different from his. They can be brought out through a critique of Peter Singer's argument that moral philosophers have a good claim to being moral experts. Singer's conclusion is based on the following three facts about (most) moral philosophers. First, they have a general training in philosophy which should make them "more than ordinarily competent in argument and in the detection of invalid inferences." Second, they have "specific experience in moral philosophy" which gives them "an understanding of moral concepts and the logic of moral argument." Third, they have the time to "think full-time about moral issues" (Singer, 1972, p. 117). The problem with Singer's position is that it implicitly presupposes that acquiring moral knowledge is largely an *a priori* matter, that extensive knowledge of morality can be acquired just by sitting around thinking and/or arguing with others. One does not have to be either an irrationalist or an emotivist about morality to see the limits of such an approach.

In fact, Singer himself does not endorse a purely *a priori* approach to moral knowledge, conceding that "to be moral experts, it would be necessary for moral philosophers to do some fact-finding on whatever issue they were considering" (1972, p. 117). But this concession significantly undermines his argument. After doing some fact-finding on a moral issue, moral philosophers can *at most* claim to have expertise on one moral issue, not on morality itself. I suggest that no one is an expert on morality, because morality is too vast and amorphous a subject for anyone to be *significantly* better informed than *most* people about it, and this is true even of people who devote their entire lives to investigating the subject.

I anticipate the following objection. The fact that a subject is vast and amorphous can't be a good reason for thinking there are no experts on it. Science is a vast and amorphous subject, but there are clearly experts on science. That's what scientists are! I reply that although scientists were once experts on science, they no longer are. This is not, of course, their fault. Rather, science has become the kind of loose baggy monster morality was all along.[33] Of course, some people are better informed about science than others. But I submit that no one is so well-informed about it that they should be treated as an expert on it. What is more, being a scientist is neither necessary nor sufficient for being scientifically well-informed. Although it is probably the case that most scientists are scientifically better informed than most people, there are clearly some scientists who are quite ignorant of what scientists working in other branches of science do, or who wrongly think that the methods of their branch of science characterize science as a whole. What is more, I submit that there are plenty of nonscientists who are scientifically better informed than some practicing scientists.[34]

The relation between science and scientists is similar to the relation between morality and moral philosophers.[35] There are experts on a range of moral issues and some people are morally better informed than others, but no one stands out from the crowd to such an extent, on the subject of morality as a whole, that they should be thought of as experts (to any significant degree) on the subject. There may well be people who are morally better informed than most, but being a moral philosopher is neither necessary nor sufficient for being morally well-informed. A person may be morally well-informed for a variety of reasons. These *could* include those mentioned by Singer, such as training in moral philosophy or time devoted to thinking about morality, but they could include many other things, involving the agent's experiences and character.

Now I don't want to exaggerate the significance of my denial that there are moral experts. Like science, morality may not admit of an expert/novice relation, but it does admit of a well-informed/ill-informed relation. What is more, it may be the case, for all I have said so far, that the ill-informed should defer to the moral views of the well-informed, just as novices should usually defer to the views of experts. Again, we may appeal to the analogy with science. Shouldn't the morally ill-informed defer to the opinions of the morally well-informed, just as (surely) the scientifically ill-informed should defer to the opinions of the scientifically well-informed?

I think the answer is "no," for two reasons, one factual and one moral. The factual reason is that information relevant to moral judgments tends to be more widely distributed within a community than information relevant to scientific judgments. Hence the difference between morally well-informed people and everyone else will not be as great as the difference between scientifically well-informed people and everyone else. The moral reason is that it is important for people to work out the answers to moral questions for themselves. Intellectual autonomy is important, as we saw earlier, but it is particularly important when it comes to working out the answers to moral questions. As we shall see in the next chapter, democracy not only requires citizens to engage in moral thinking, it requires them to draw conclusions about morality in a reasonably autonomous way.

Notes

1   Another option is to suspend judgment about the matter. But, for obvious reasons, this is not always a wise or responsible option.
2   As we shall see, I don't think Goldman's own account of expertise is sufficiently veritistic.
3   Oliver Scholz claims that a nonexpert in a domain "may have more true and fewer false beliefs" in it than an expert (2009, p. 193). I agree with the second part of this claim, but not with the first.
4   Of course it may be difficult for nonexperts to assess this evidence, since, as nonexperts, it may be difficult for them to assess whether answers to new questions in the domain are true.
5   See for example Plato, *Theaetetus*, 201.

6 John Hardwig (1991) presents the debate in these terms. On page 693 he describes knowledge based on trust as "partially blind"; on page 699 he describes it simply as blind.

7 See, for example, Goldman (2001). Goldman describes some critics of reductionism, in particular Tyler Burge and Richard Foley, as giving license to "blind" trust.

8 See for example, Fricker (1994, 1995).

9 There may be exceptions, that is, circumstances in which we should trust people without considering evidence of their reliability. I may, for example, trust a complete stranger to tell me the approximate time, because I know that most people are reliable enough for my purposes about that subject.

10 For this reason, reductionism is sometimes called "inductivism."

11 This argument is very similar to Noam Chomsky's (1980) well-known "poverty of stimulus" argument against purely empiricist approaches to language learning.

12 Mackie describes the reductionist ideal as the "ideal of the autonomous knower" (1970, p. 254).

13 People often express their beliefs in the form of testimony, that is, they explicitly assert their beliefs, but, as noted earlier, they may also express their beliefs through their nonverbal behavior.

14 It is an interesting question whether following one's private evidence in this situation is rational. However, we need not answer this question here. The point is that most people do follow their private evidence, and that most people are aware that most people behave that way.

15 Although everyone has the same amount of private information, those later in the sequence have more public information than those earlier. This public information is of little use to them, however, because of the likelihood of information cascades.

16 See, for example, Goldman (2001), Matheson (2005), Coady (2006d), and Scholz (2009).

17 It's necessary for me to discuss this topic at length, because it is important, not only for this chapter, but also for the next two chapters, and because the opposite view is so widespread. If you don't need any convincing of my view, you should skip ahead to the next section.

18 My defense is qualified, because I realize I could and should do more to inform myself about this important subject.

19 Almassi (2007) is a review of Crease and Selinger (2006).

20 In fact, as we've seen, Goldman says "totally non-independent" rather than "totally dependent," but I find the double negative awkward and potentially confusing.

21 Notice that the third of these routes to belief does not appear to be genuinely autonomous. Certainly it doesn't seem to be autonomous in the same way the other two routes to belief are.

22 In this argument I've been assuming that the novice discovers that X believes H before discovering that Y believes H. What if the novice simultaneously discovers that X and Y believe H? Just as Bayesian probabilities can change over time, they can vary across possible worlds. So, we cannot assume that knowing or justifiably believing that $P(H/X(H))$ and $P(H/X(H)\&Y(H))$ are equivalent is a reason to assign a lower value than would otherwise have been assigned to the latter, rather than a reason to assign a higher value than would otherwise have been assigned to the former.

23 I borrow the term "meta-expert" from Goldman (2001, p. 97). He doesn't define the term, but I believe my usage is consistent with his.

24 Y knows the scope of X's expertise if he or she knows which questions X can answer with a high probability of accuracy. Y knows the extent of X's expertise if he or she knows how high that probability is.

25 Goldman himself (2001, p. 96) acknowledges this point.

26 I also argued that this could be rational.

27 There are paradoxes associated with the concept of *self-deception*, which have led some philosophers to doubt that people really can deceive themselves (e.g., Paluch, 1967; Haight 1980). Nonetheless commonsense and scientific research (Sahdra and Thagard, 2003) suggest that self-deception is not only real, it is widespread. I assume therefore that these paradoxes can be resolved, but it would be inappropriate for me to try to resolve them here.

28 They are also often thought of as exceptionally moral people, which is a different thing. The relation between being a moral person and being a moral expert is an interesting topic, but beyond the scope of the current work.

29 Peter Singer (1972) is a notable exception.

30 Broad may not be entirely serious about the adequacy with which these people perform their "hortatory functions." As Peter Singer points out, these so-called experts "have done so badly that 'morality', in the public mind, has come to mean a system of prohibitions against certain forms of sexual enjoyment" (Singer, 1972, p. 115).

31 Noncognitivists claim that "moral beliefs" are neither true nor false. Error theorists claim that they are all false (or at least that we have no reason to believe any of them are true).

32 Readers who are uncomfortable with this assumption should feel free to substitute "assertable," or "acceptable," or some other term of commendation in place of "true" in what follows.

33 This should not be surprising since moral reasoning has been going on a lot longer than scientific reasoning and it is something that almost everyone does.

34 The widespread assumption that scientists are experts on science is responsible for a great deal of confusion in the public debate about climate

change. Even those who are aware that a geologist (say) may not be an expert on climate, often assume that he or she will be better-informed than most people about the subject. But this need not be the case.

35   The relation between history and historians is another useful analogy.

3

Epistemic Democracy

"Democracy is the worst form of government, except for all those other forms that have been tried from time to time."

(Winston Churchill, House of Commons, November 11, 1947)

I suspect that some contemporary philosophers are reluctant to endorse the idea that there are moral experts, and are especially reluctant to endorse the idea that *they* are moral experts, for historical reasons. These ideas are closely associated with antidemocratic traditions in philosophy which date back to Plato's notorious argument that philosophers are uniquely qualified to rule because of their moral expertise. For obvious reasons, most contemporary philosophers would not want to be associated with this idea. In what follows, I will distinguish Plato's claim that politics should be left to experts from his claim that the relevant experts are experts on morality. We have already seen that there is some reason to be skeptical about whether there are moral experts. But even if there are no moral experts, there may still be political experts.[1]

What To Believe Now: Applying Epistemology to Contemporary Issues,
First Edition. David Coady.
© 2012 David Coady. Published 2012 by Blackwell Publishing Ltd.

Plato's argument that politics should be left to experts is based on a series of analogies between politics and other fields, such as navigation and medicine, in which there are acknowledged experts. He claims, for example, that ordinary people are no more qualified to guide "the ship of state" than they are to navigate a real ship (*Republic*, VI, 488a–9a). Plato has left would-be defenders of democracy with the problem of explaining what is wrong with this kind of analogy.

Of course, the political systems Plato thought of as democratic were quite different from contemporary democracies (or at least the political systems that we[2] are likely to think of as democratic). For one thing, contemporary democracies are representative rather than participatory. If we think of the politicians elected to make decisions on our behalf as political experts, it might seem that we can reconcile democracy with expertise and so avoid Plato's problem. Unfortunately the problem just reappears at another level. Suppose you are persuaded of Plato's view that political decisions should be left to experts. How are these experts to be identified? Presumably those best qualified to identify them would be meta-experts in politics, that is, people who are significantly better than most at identifying people with first-order expertise in politics. Who are they? Whatever answer one gives to this question,[3] it should be clear that ordinary people are no more meta-experts about politics than they are experts about it. Presumably Plato would have found representative democracy just as objectionable as participatory democracy. Extending his medical analogy, we could compare representative democracy to an institutional arrangement in which the population as a whole is given the power to determine who is qualified to be a doctor. This is surely a job best left to the appropriate medical associations.

One way of responding to Plato's problem, which I will clarify and defend in this chapter, comes from epistemic democrats, who defend democracy on the grounds that it "exceeds other systems in its ability to 'track the truth'" (Goldman, 2008, p. 111). The Condorcet Jury Theorems (Condorcet, 1994/1785) have been central to the work of many epistemic democrats.[4] These theorems show that, in certain circumstances,[5] the probability of the majority of a group identifying the truth will be greater than the probability of any one of the group's members identifying the truth, and that the larger the group is, the more likely it is that the verdict of the majority will be accurate. Condorcet draws our attention to the fact that not all cases of rational epistemic dependence on others involve expertise. Sometimes a crowd, especially a large crowd, is more reliable as a source of truth than even the most expert member of the crowd.[6]

Arguably, the Condorcet Jury Theorems are applicable to jury voting, but not to voting in democratic elections. It is pretty clear that a juror's vote is (or can reasonably be thought of as) a statement, and hence as something with a truth-value. In the case of a criminal trial, for example, a juror's vote seems to be a statement about whether or not the defendant is guilty (or whether or not the defendant is guilty beyond all reasonable doubt). It is not so clear what votes in democratic elections are saying. In fact, as we shall see, there is a controversy about whether they are saying anything at all.

The view that votes in democratic elections are, or should be thought of as, statements or opinions (i.e., things with a truth-value) is sometimes called the *statemental* or *cognitive* theory of voting. Rousseau provides an influential version of the theory in the following passage:

> When a law is proposed in the People's assembly, what they are being asked is not exactly whether they approve the proposal or reject it, but whether it does or does not conform to the general will, which is theirs; everyone states his opinion about this by casting his ballot, and the tally of the votes yields the declaration of the general will. Therefore when the opinion contrary to my own prevails, it proves nothing more than I made a mistake and that what I held to be the general will was not. (Rousseau, 1967/1762, p. 124)

There are four controversial claims here, which we would do well to separate: first, voters in a democratic election are offering an opinion (the statemental theory of voting); second, they are all offering an opinion about the same topic; third, the topic about which they are offering their opinion is something called "the general will"; fourth, the outcome of their vote carries great epistemic authority, so great that it proves that the opinion of those who voted for a different outcome was wrong. We will consider these claims in order.

Are Votes Statements?

The statemental theory of voting is standardly presented as though it were in competition with certain other theories of voting, in particular the *preferential theory* (Estlund, 1990, p. 398; Christiano, 1995, pp. 401–4;

Goldman, 1999b, p. 316), according to which votes are expressions of preference, and the *resource theory* (Christiano, 1995, pp. 410–13; Goldman, 1999b, p. 317), according to which votes are resources or powers which allow voters to play a role in collective decisions. I will argue that we don't need to choose between these theories. Being a statement is compatible with being an expression of preference. Hence the statemental and preferential theories could both be true. Furthermore, both theories are compatible with the resource theory, and so all three theories could be true. In fact, I think they are all true.

Some critics of the statemental theory seem to assume that if votes are statements, they are *merely* statements; that is, they don't do anything other than state that something is the case. Alvin Goldman, for example, seems to make this assumption in the following criticism of the statemental theory:

> Voting cannot simply consist in making a statement that something is (say) in the common interest, because not every such statement counts as a vote. People who have no vote on a given subject – because they live in a different district, or do not belong to the relevant organization – can make statements about the common interest to their heart's desire without thereby voting. (Goldman, 1999b, p. 317)

Advocates of the statemental theory of voting should willingly concede that voting doesn't "simply" consist in making a statement[7]; it consists in making a statement in a particular institutional context.

In one sense, a statement is a particular kind of (assertoric) speech act; in another sense it is an abstract entity, the meaning (or propositional content) of such a speech act. Advocates of the statemental theory of voting clearly are (or at least should be) thinking of votes as statements in the former sense, as speech acts, things located at particular places and times, rather than as any sort of abstract entity.

This should make it clear that the statemental theory is compatible with the preferential theory, because some statements (i.e., some assertoric speech acts) are expressions of preference (this is particularly obvious of statements that take the form "I prefer such-and-such"). It should be equally clear that the statemental theory is compatible with the resource theory. A statement, understood as a kind of speech act, can be a resource or power (think, for example, of the statements put into a contract). Hence accepting the preferential theory or the resource theory is no reason for rejecting the statemental theory.

In fact, the statemental theory embodies an important aspect of the way in which we think about voting in democratic elections. Your vote is "your voice," and to cast it is to "send a message." Indeed it is a sign of how difficult it is not to think of voting this way that even Goldman, who rejects the statemental theory, has no qualms about invoking the distinction between sincere and strategic voting, characterizing the latter as "casting a ballot in a way that misrepresents one's genuine preferences" (Goldman, 1999b, p. 344). Surely one cannot misrepresent one's preferences unless one is, at least implicitly, saying something about them.

I submit that a minimal account of voting, which all parties should accept, is that votes in democratic elections are statements. Many of the substantive issues that divide democratic theorists are (or can be reasonably construed as) disagreements about what those statements are about.

What Do Votes Say?

If votes are statements, what is the subject matter of those statements? One view is as follows:

(1) Each vote is a statement about the voter who casts it.

Advocates of (1) can be further subdivided as follows:

(1a) Votes are statements of voter preference.
(1b) Votes are statements of voter self-interest (i.e., what is good for the voter).

These views are often conflated, because of a more or less implicit assumption that all preferences are ultimately self-interested. But although (1a) and (1b) should be distinguished, they do have something important in common, namely that by identifying votes with a kind of self-description, they are committed to the view that each vote (in a given election) is a statement about a different subject. This means they are incompatible with the epistemic approach to democracy. Voting can't be a good way of tracking the truth about a certain subject if each vote is a statement about a different subject (Estlund, 1990). As we saw, the Condorcet Jury Theorems presuppose that each voter is answering the same question. Consequently, epistemic democrats will reject (1a) and (1b) and embrace the following position instead:

(2) Each vote (in a given election) is a statement about the same subject.

Advocates of (2) can be further divided as follows:

(2a) Votes are statements about the general will.
(2b) Votes are statements about the common interest (i.e., the common good).

As we saw, Rousseau advocated (2a), but (2b) has been a more popular view.[8] Hence most of the debate between (1) and (2) has effectively been a debate between (1b) and (2b), the view that votes are statements of self-interest and the view that they are statements of the common interest.

Critics of (2b) have rightly pointed out that there are situations in which voters do (and should) vote in accordance with their self-interest, rather than the common interest. Thomas Christiano (1995, pp. 406–7) and Alvin Goldman (1999b, p. 316) both use an example in which a group of sightseers are deciding where to go, to make this point:

> There seem to be many cases where it is most unnatural to interpret a vote as a statement about the common interest. Suppose a group of people wish to take a sightseeing trip together, but they must first agree on where to go. A good way to decide where to go is to take a vote and see which destination is most popular. Here it is natural to encourage everyone to vote on the basis of his or her own interest. Must each vote nonetheless be interpreted as a statement that the voted-for destination is the *group's* preferred destination? That is highly implausible. Sally may know antecedently that most members of the group prefer, say, Yosemite to Yellowstone, even though she prefers Yellowstone. When she votes for Yellowstone, must we interpret her vote as a statement that the group's interest is to go to Yellowstone? That would be absurd. (Goldman, 1999b, p. 316)

Goldman is right that it would be absurd to view votes in this context as statements about the group's interest (still less as statements about the "group's preference"), but we shouldn't automatically assume that this kind of voting provides a satisfactory model for voting in democratic elections (any more than we should automatically assume that jury voting provides such a model). In fact, I will argue that, although the sightseers in this example may think of their approach to collective decision making as "democratic," this is extremely misleading. It results from an unfortunate tendency to see balloting as the be-all and end-all of democracy.

Why do Goldman and Christiano's sightseers provide a bad model for democratic politics? First, there is the size of the group. Since there would presumably be relatively few sightseers, each of them would have a significant chance of affecting the outcome. This is decidedly not the case in modern representative democracies, where elections are never decided by a single vote. Goldman and Christiano claim that their sightseers should be urged to consider only their self-interest. Whether or not that is true,[9] the consequences of this kind of counsel in "real" elections would be disastrous. If voters in modern democracies were guided purely by self-interest, they wouldn't vote at all.

Goldman and Christiano implicitly assume that an individual's behavior *qua* citizen is, and should be, motivated by the same considerations that motivate his or her behavior *qua* consumer. Because consumer behavior is (and presumably should be) largely (though not necessarily entirely) motivated by self-interest, so must voting behavior. This is quite a common assumption, explicit in the work of social choice theorists such as James Buchanan and Gordon Tullock, according to whom "the average individual acts on the basis of the same over-all value scale when he participates in market activity and in political activity" (Buchanan and Tullock, 1962, p. 20). But if this were true, only irrational people would vote, and that, I think, is a sufficient *reductio* of the view.[10]

The fact that voting does not appear to be usually motivated by self-interest[11] does not, of course, mean that it is motivated by altruism. Since you can be confident your vote will not affect the outcome of an election, you cannot use it to promote the interests of others any more than you can use it to promote your own interests. As Mancur Olson observed, the futility of "imperceptible" contributions holds regardless of "whether behavior is selfish or unselfish" (1965, p. 64). My point is that just as no voter can rationally hope to influence the outcomes of a "real" election at all, *eo ipso* no voter can rationally hope to bring about an electoral outcome which is in his or her interests.

It would be possible to hold that votes are statements of self-interest, even though most voters don't appear to be motivated by self-interest. The meaning of a vote might be quite different from the motivation behind it. Perhaps a vote is a statement of self-interest, which voters make, even though they know (or easily could know) that there is no realistic possibility that their votes will promote those interests.

If this is understood as an empirical claim about voter intentions, the evidence seems to be against it. Kinder and Kiewiet (1981), for example, found that, in the United States, voters' views of the economy as a whole was a much better predictor of their voting behavior than their views about their own economic circumstances. James Surowiecki, after reviewing empirical literature of this kind, concludes that most voters seem "interested in picking the best man for the job, not just the best man for themselves" (Surowiecki, 2004, p. 265). That does not mean, of course, that considerations of self-interest have no influence on the way people vote. They obviously have a significant influence. But that is no reason to suppose that votes are statements of self-interest, rather than statements about the common good. There is a widespread tendency for people to think that their own interests coincide with their community's interests, whether or not they do.[12] Hence the fact that many, perhaps all, voters, are biased by considerations of self-interest does not mean that votes are not statements about the common good. Many, and perhaps all, statements about the common good, whether or not they take the form of votes, are biased by considerations of self-interest.

This brings us to a second reason for thinking that Goldman and Christiano's sightseers are a bad model for democratic politics. A group of sightseers, bearing no particular relation to each other beyond a shared desire to see certain sights, have no special duties toward one another. By contrast, a group of citizens voting in a democratic election, do have such duties, and empirical studies indicate that a "sense of duty" is the best predictor of whether people will vote (Surowiecki, 2004, p. 264).

Those who insist that votes are statements of self-interest need not be deterred. They could say that they are making a normative, rather than an empirical, claim. Perhaps votes should be understood as statements of self-interest, even though most voters don't seem to think of their votes that way. We can make a distinction between voter meaning and vote meaning, which is analogous to Paul Grice's (1989) distinction between speaker meaning and linguistic meaning. A speaker can mean something by a statement which is quite different from what the statement itself (a linguistic entity) means. The speaker's meaning is determined by his or her intentions, whereas the statement's meaning is determined by normative considerations (i.e., standards of correct usage). Likewise, a voter might mean something by his or her vote which is quite different from what the vote itself means. The voter's meaning is determined by the voter's intentions, whereas the vote's meaning is determined by normative considerations (i.e., how the vote should be interpreted). So voters might mean to make a statement about one thing (such as the common good), but their vote could nonetheless be a statement about something else (such as their self-interest).

The view under consideration attributes widespread error to voters. According to it, voters should be guided solely by considerations of self-interest, even though they often aren't. Why might one think that? It is sometimes suggested that the alternative, voting for the common good, is too unclear a goal. Joseph Schumpeter, for example, has argued against the view that democracy is an attempt to identify the common good on the grounds that the common good is "bound to mean different things to different individuals and groups" (Schumpeter, 1992, p. 250). In support of this claim he gives several examples of people disagreeing with one another about what is in the common good and asserts (without argument) that these disagreements cannot be settled through rational argument. But even if Schumpeter were right about this, his conclusion does not follow from his premise. There is a difference between disagreeing about what is in the common good and disagreeing about what the "common good" means, just as there is a difference between disagreeing about whether a certain object is a cat and disagreeing about what the word "cat" means.

Even if Schumpeter is right that people do mean somewhat different things by "the common good," that would not show that votes should not be thought of as statements about the common good. Arguably, people also mean somewhat different things by "self-interest."[13] Both of these concepts may be somewhat ambiguous, but there are plenty of circumstances in which it is perfectly clear whether or not they apply. There is enough shared meaning for us to talk to each other and (usually) understand each other.

Richard Posner (2003) argues that voting should be driven by self-interest on epistemic, rather than conceptual, grounds. He claims that it "is far more difficult to form an informed opinion about what is good for society as a whole than it is to determine where one's self-interest lies" (Posner, 2003, p. 131). There are two problems with this as an argument for self-interested voting. First, the fact that doing something is relatively easy need not be a conclusive argument in favor of it. There may be a good reason for taking the more difficult option. I will return to this point later. The second problem is that Posner's claim that it's easier to work out what is in one's own interests than it is to work out what's in the interests of one's society is extremely dubious. Posner claims that "reasoning about the most effective means to a given end – instrumental reasoning, the type involved in self-interested action – is a good deal more straightforward than reasoning about ends, the type of reasoning required for determining what is best for society as a whole" (Posner 2003, 131–2). But this presupposes a contrast between self-interest and collective interest that close examination will not support. Is reasoning about self-interested action always purely instrumental? It doesn't seem to be. People often reason, not only about which means will promote their interests, but also about which ends – knowledge, power, wealth, and so on – are in their interests. It may be objected that although these things are ends with respect to some means, they are not *ultimate ends*, because they are themselves means to some further end (presumably happiness); so self-interested reasoning is still all *ultimately* instrumental. But this conception of self-interested reasoning, as a matter of promoting some single goal over the course of one's life, is highly controversial (and, in my opinion, morally and psychologically facile).[14] There is, of course, a trivial sense in which all reasoning about self-interested action is instrumental; all such reasoning is about the means to a certain end, namely the promotion of one's own well-being. But that doesn't establish Posner's asymmetry between self-interested reasoning and reasoning about the interests of society as a whole. There is also a trivial sense in which the latter kind of reasoning is instrumental; it is reasoning about the means to promote a certain end, namely the well-being of society as a whole.

Even though Posner's argument that people are better at self-interested reasoning than they are at reasoning about the common good is poor, it's tempting to think that experience shows his conclusion is true. Posner and Schumpeter both cite numerous examples of people who can reason soundly when trying to advance their own interests, but who reason poorly when it comes to politics:

> The typical citizen drops to a lower level of mental performance as soon as he enters the political field. He argues and analyzes in a way which he would readily recognize as infantile within the sphere of his real interests. He becomes a primitive again. His thinking becomes associative and affective. … The picture of the prettiest girl that ever lived will in the long run prove powerless to maintain sales of a bad cigarette. There is no equally effective safeguard in the case of political decisions. (Schumpeter, 1992, pp. 262–3)

There clearly is something to this rather depressing line of thought.[15] Nonetheless, it is not a good reason for thinking that votes should be understood as statements of voter self-interest rather than statements about the common good. If people are usually better at working out what is in their own interests than they are at working out what is in the common good, that is because they have had more practice at doing it. Whereas people are often in a position to promote their own interests to a significant degree, they are rarely as well placed when it comes to promoting the common good. But, as we have seen, voters are not faced with a choice between trying to advance their own interests and trying to advance the common good, because voters know (or at least are in a position to know) that they can do neither (hence the problem of why people vote). If people reason poorly about politics or are badly informed about politics, then they are less likely to vote the way they should, and this will be true whether you think they should vote for political outcomes that would promote their own interests, or for those that would promote the common good. Both challenges require significant political knowledge[16] and sound reasoning, and we have seen no reason to think that one challenge is inherently more difficult than the other.[17]

What about the other version of the theory that votes are self-descriptions, that is, (1a), the view that each vote is just a statement about the voter's preference? Voters may be mistaken about their self-interest as well as about the common good, but how could they be mistaken about their own preferences? Well in fact they can. It is important to recognize that the issue is not what policies or candidates voters *think* they would prefer at the time of voting, but what policies or candidates they would in fact prefer, were they to be implemented or elected. Again, I see no reason for supposing that voters are better at identifying which political outcomes they would prefer than they are at identifying which political outcomes are in the common good (assuming they would prefer something other than the common good).

Suppose, for the sake of argument, that I am wrong, and voters are usually better at identifying political outcomes that they would prefer than they are at identifying political outcomes that would promote the common good, it does not follow that they should try to vote for the former rather than the latter. There might be a good reason for thinking that voters should try to vote for the latter rather than the former, even though they are less likely to be successful. In fact, we have already seen such a reason. We saw earlier that treating votes as statements about the common good, unlike treating them as statements of self-interest or as mere statements of preference, is consistent with the guiding idea of epistemic approaches to democracy, namely that democracy can (at least partially) be justified by its truth-tracking properties. If democracy is, as epistemic democrats claim, better than rival political systems, because it is a more reliable way of coming up with correct answers to certain questions, then each vote in a given election must be a statement about the same subject. If we treat each vote merely as a statement about the voter who cast it, then we give up on this kind of justification of democracy.

That wouldn't necessarily mean that we would give up on democracy itself. As Surowiecki has noted, there are fundamental differences about what democracy is for at stake here:

> Do we have it because it gives people a sense of involvement and control over their lives, and therefore contributes to political stability? Do we have it because individuals have the right to rule themselves, even if they use that right in ridiculous ways? Or do we have it because democracy is actually an excellent vehicle for making intelligent decisions and uncovering the truth? (Surowiecki, 2004, p. 261)

Is the idea that democracy is a good way of uncovering the truth too ambitious? I hope not, because the other justifications mentioned above are clearly unsatisfactory for anyone with a genuine commitment to democracy. The first treats democracy as a mere means to the end of political stability. But there are plenty of nondemocratic ways of achieving political stability. We don't want the argument for democracy to be contingent on the claim that it is the best way to achieve political stability, for it often isn't. What is more, even if democracy is the best way of achieving political stability, political stability is not always desirable. Plenty of objectionable regimes are stable and it is at least arguable that it would be better if they were less stable. The reasons democracy allegedly contributes to political stability, the "sense of involvement and control" it gives people over their lives, are also problematic. They suggest that it doesn't really matter if people really have such involvement and control, as long as they feel they do. This is obviously unsatisfactory, since similar feelings could be achieved by mass hypnosis or drugs.[18]

Justifying democracy on the grounds that "individuals have the right to rule themselves" is equally problematic. Individuals may well have the right to rule themselves (at least up to a point), but it is not at all clear how that right relates to democracy. As J. S. Mill pointed out, democracy doesn't involve individuals ruling themselves; it involves a group of individuals (or the majority thereof) ruling itself. This was the basis of his concerns about the "tyranny of the majority" (Mill, 2008/1859, Ch. 1 para. 4). There has always been a tension within liberal democratic theory between those who emphasize the liberal aspect of it (understood as an outlook which emphasizes the value of individual rights), and those who emphasize the democratic aspect of it. Hence civil libertarians like Mill see guarantees of individual rights as an important check on unconstrained democracy, while philosophers like Charles Taylor have the opposite concern, namely that "the stress on rights as dominant over collective decisions" could "undermine the very legitimacy of the democratic order" (Taylor, 1993, p. 112).

I have argued that the theory that votes in democratic elections are statements about the common good is descriptively and normatively better than the theory that they are statements of self-interest and the theory that they are mere statements of preference. Not only is it more accurate, if it is understood as an account of what voters think they are doing, it is also better, if it is understood as an account of what they should be doing. The view that votes are statements about the common good is perfectly consistent with the fact that some voters don't think of their votes that way. Christiano and Goldman both seem to assume that if some voters regard their votes as statements about self-interest, then they cannot be statements about the common good (Christiano, 1995, pp. 406–7; Goldman, 1999b, pp. 316–17). But this assumes that the meaning of a vote is determined by the intentions of the voter. We have already seen what is wrong with this assumption. The meaning of a statement is not in general determined by the intentions of the speaker, but by public rules of meaning, and votes, as a kind of statement, have a publicly determined meaning, even if some voters mean something else by them. The issue we have been addressing is not what voters mean, but what their votes mean. Fortunately, as we have seen, most voters seem to understand the meaning of their votes better than some democratic theorists.

We are led to the inescapable conclusion that voters who regard their votes as statements of self-interest or as mere statements of preference are not properly participating in the democratic process (like those who do not know how to fill in a ballot paper). It does not of course follow that they should be prevented from voting; there would be obvious practical and moral objections to any attempt to do that. But it does follow that they should be educated about the nature and value of democracy.[19]

Although the view that votes are statements about the common good is preferable to the view that they are statements of self-interest and the view that they are mere statements of preference, it does not seem to be quite right. If we conceive of votes as statements about the common good, we are ruling out *a priori* the rationality of voters taking into account any other consideration whatsoever. We should at least leave open the possibility that voters could rationally vote for certain policies (e.g., not to attack a foreign country, or to give animals legal rights, or give refugees asylum), not because these policies promote the common good of the voters (though they may do that), but just because, in their opinion, they are right.

Someone defending the view that votes are statements about the common good could try to accommodate this objection by arguing that it is based on too narrow an understanding of the group, whose interests are at stake in democratic elections. Perhaps votes should be understood as statements about a good which is common, not only to the community of voters, but to a broader community that includes foreigners, animals, and so on. Unfortunately I don't think this will work. In the first place, it is not clear who or what should be included in the broader community whose good voters should be considering. In the second place, there is a danger that the broader we make the community, the weaker we make the special obligations that members of a political community should have to one another.

I conclude that votes in a representative democracy are statements about who, all things considered, are the best candidates for certain jobs, where these jobs are defined as being principally (though not exclusively) concerned with the goal of promoting the common good.[20]

The Epistemic Authority of Electoral Outcomes

One concern we might have about epistemic democracy concerns its implications for intellectual autonomy (a topic we discussed in the previous chapter). If, as epistemic democrats suppose, democratic elections track the truth with a not insignificant degree of reliability, it seems that their outcomes should carry a certain epistemic authority, and that as a result there should at least be a presumption in favor of conforming our beliefs to electoral results, just as there is a presumption in favor of novices conforming their beliefs to the beliefs of experts.

The problem can be brought out through a discussion of Richard Wollheim's well-known "paradox of democracy" (Wollheim, 1969). Wollheim asks us to suppose that in an election between two alternatives, A and B, a democratically minded person votes for A, but B wins. It seems, according to Wollheim, that such a voter is committed to the following contradictory beliefs:

(a) I think A should be enacted; after all, I voted for it.
(b) I think B should be enacted, because it's the democratic choice.

One way of resolving the paradox, which Wollheim considers, is that the voter should simply reject (a). On this view, the electoral result should lead a true democrat to change his or her mind and withdraw support from A and give it to B.

This was the position of Rousseau, who, as we saw, claimed that the epistemic authority of democratic elections is so great that if the opinion contrary to your own prevails, that proves you were mistaken. Rousseau implies that democracy is not merely a relatively good way of tracking the truth, but an infallible guide to the truth. Consider the implications of this view for how voters should approach their task. If we assume that voters are sincere, that is, they are trying to make an accurate statement with their vote, then their task is equivalent to making a prediction about the outcome of the election. Given this, we can see why Rousseau might have thought of votes as statements about "the general will" rather than (say) the common good. The logical consequence of his view is that each voter should try to work out how the other voters (or a majority or plurality of them) will vote, and conform his or her vote to their infallible collective judgment.

Of course, epistemic democrats need not be committed to the view that the general will is infallible. Nonetheless it does appear that they are committed to the view that the outcome of a democratic process is more reliable than the judgment of any single voter. After all, if there were a voter whose judgment was more reliable than the democratic process, it seems there would be no need for the democratic process. So it seems that epistemic democrats should, insofar as their goal is to believe the truth, change their minds if an opinion contrary to their own prevails in an election. Furthermore, it seems that if they have a reasonable belief that an opinion contrary to their own will prevail in an upcoming election, they should change their minds, and insofar as they want to make an accurate vote (remember votes are statements), they should vote for the outcome they believe will prevail even if all the other available evidence indicates that it is wrong.

This position is clearly paradoxical, since a vigorous and rational opposition seems to be an essential feature of democracy. Hence it is important to work out how epistemic democrats can resist making their beliefs subordinate to actual or anticipated electoral outcomes, and avoid what Robert Goodin has dubbed "the paradox of persisting opposition" (Goodin, 2002).[21] There are at least two responses an epistemic democrat can make to this problem. Together they reduce the worry, without altogether eliminating it.

First, it is important to note that epistemic democrats are not committed to the view that democracy tracks the truth with much reliability, just that it tracks the truth more reliably than any feasible alternative system of government. It is possible to be misled here by the role the Condorcet Jury Theorems have played in many epistemic justifications of democracy. These theorems show that the majority of a group *can be* more reliable (i.e., likely to be right) than any single member of the group. But the epistemic case for democracy isn't dependent on this possibility. Epistemic democrats only need to defend the weaker, and hence more plausible, view that a majority is more likely to be right than any individual or group with a realistic chance of assuming nondemocratic power.[22] Most people are not in any position to assume nondemocratic power. Hence, contrary to the above argument, an epistemic democrat need not view the judgment of the majority as more reliable than his or her own judgment. This brings out a flaw in Plato's argument against democracy. Even if we were to grant him that there are political experts (whether or not they are philosophers), there is no reason to think that rule by these experts is a realistic alternative to democracy. The version of epistemic democracy I have been defending isn't committed to the view that democracy tracks the truth about (roughly) the common good better than any other *possible* system, it is only committed to the view that it tracks it better than any realistic alternative. What are the realistic alternatives to democracy, that is, the rule of the people? A quick glance at history and current affairs shows that the systems of government that have challenged democracy in the past, and continue to challenge it to one degree or another all over the world, include the rule of kings, of aristocrats, of priests, of the rich, of the military, and of the secret police. It should be obvious that, even if there are experts at tracking the truth about (roughly) which policies are in the common good, none of these individuals or groups have any great claim to such expertise.

Second, even if we were to accept that the results of completely democratic elections should be rationally compelling, it is very far from clear what the practical implications would be, because we cannot just assume that the elections we are familiar with are completely democratic. There are two problems. One is to specify the kind of voting system that would be genuinely democratic.[23] The other is to specify the knowledge conditions that must be met by a community in order for its decisions to be genuinely democratic. Clearly a community that is entirely ignorant of, or mistaken about, "the choices" it is presented with is not making a genuinely democratic choice at all.

Knowledgeable Voters

The epistemic conception of democracy I have been defending implies that elections, even if they are conducted freely and fairly,[24] are not sufficient for democracy. Democracy also requires voters to be reasonably well-informed about the nature of the available options. Alvin Goldman gives some reasons for pessimism about this, at least in the United States, when he notes that "One principal and consistent finding by American political scientists is that ordinary American citizens have a minimal, even abysmal, knowledge of textbook facts about the structure of American government, the identity of their elected officials, and fundamental facts about contemporaneous foreign policy" (Goldman 1999b, p. 317).

There is no denying that some of these examples of voter ignorance or error are significant. It is particularly regrettable when citizens are ignorant of, or misinformed about, the structure of their own government.[25] Nonetheless, we should be careful not to read too much into findings of this kind. Goldman supposes that identifying the information that voters need (what he calls "core voter knowledge") is a task for political scientists (1999b, p. 320). But to suppose that this is a task for any group of experts or putative experts, whether they be political scientists, political philosophers, or political journalists,[26] is clearly inconsistent with the spirit of epistemic democracy. If the people as a whole are wise enough to be allowed to answer primary political questions (e.g., "Who are the best candidates?" or "What are the best policies?"), as epistemic democrats suppose, then they should be wise enough to be able to identify the kinds of information they need in order to answer them as well. If we could trust political scientists, or any other group smaller than the people as a whole, to identify the information we need in order to vote the way we should, then we could also presumably trust them to identify whom we should vote for as well, and we cannot.

Goldman's discussion of democracy is part of a broader project called "veritistic social epistemology," which I discussed in Chapter 1. This project consists in identifying social policies that promote certain kinds knowledge, where knowledge is understood simply as true belief. Goldman says that "we" need to address the question "What kinds of knowledge (or information) is it essential that voters should have?" (1999b, p. 320) before "we" evaluate our social policies with a view to remedying any epistemic shortcomings we find in the voting population. But this is a fundamentally undemocratic idea. It presupposes that "we" are in a better position than voters to know what they need to know, that if only we could get them to believe certain things that we have antecedently identified as both true and relevant, we would improve our democratic practices. This is the ideal, known in Indonesia as "guided democracy," according to which voting can be left to the people as a whole, so long as the information on which they base their vote is controlled by an elite. It should be obvious that guided democracy is not really democracy at all.

I have argued that epistemic democrats don't have to be committed to the view that there are no political experts. But the epistemic case for democracy would certainly be stronger if it could be shown that there are none. If there are political experts, the epistemic argument for democracy is precarious, because it is contingent on the available alternatives. Fortunately, I think we can make a good case that there are no political experts, or at least that there are no political experts in the required sense. There are, of course, people who have expertise on a wide range of matters relevant to political life.[27] But to be political experts, in the relevant sense, a person would have to be significantly better (i.e., more reliable) than most at answering questions about which political outcomes would promote (roughly speaking) the common good of the voting community. My argument in the previous chapter that there are no experts in morality, or at least that any expertise in this vast area is very limited, seems to apply *mutatis mutandis* to politics, understood in this way. Information relevant to questions about the common good will inevitably be widely distributed, and no one can plausibly claim to have significantly more of it than most people. There are of course people who have a legitimate claim to forms of expertise that might be labeled "political," including politicians, public servants, political scientists, political philosophers, and political journalists. But none of these people are experts on politics as such, because none of them are experts on which candidates or policies will promote the common good. Contrary to political realists like Morgenthau (1967, p. 16), the political is not autonomous. If it were, it could be mastered, and there might be experts on it. But there aren't, because politics is implicated in almost every area of human thought and activity. Hence, information relevant to questions about the common good of a community might come from any member of the community, from someone who is well-versed on the causes of World War I to someone with detailed knowledge of the impact of fuel prices on truck drivers. We cannot hope to come up with reliable answers to questions about the common good if we don't ask enough people.

The epistemic account of democracy I have defended requires voters who are reasonably well-informed. How well informed, and about what topics? Answers to these questions will vary considerably from society to society. The best way to answer them is through an aspect of the democratic process itself, that is, through public discussion. The issue of how little knowledge and how much error is compatible with democratic institutions is closely related to another difficult and subtle issue, namely the extent of an individual's obligation to be well-informed about politics. It has often been remarked that an obligation on the part of citizens to seek out accurate information about politics is a precondition of democratic life. But what is the extent of this obligation? Conversely, to what extent are we entitled to put politics aside for the sake of pursuing our private goals? Is the obligation to be politically well-informed greater for some people (e.g., political journalists, political scientists, etc.) than for others? Again it seems that the correct answer to these questions will vary from society to society, and again it seems that they are best answered through the democratic process itself.

Deliberative Democracy

The position I have been defending is closely related to a conception of democracy that has come to be called "deliberative democracy." According to deliberative democrats, debate and argument are defining features of democracy. No decision can be considered truly democratic unless it has been preceded by public deliberation. Although deliberative democracy is sometimes presented as an alternative to epistemic democracy (Miller, 1992, p. 56), this is a mistake. Properly understood, deliberative democracy is a form of epistemic democracy. In fact, it is precisely the epistemic "pretensions" of deliberative democracy that at least one of its critics objects to:

> Deliberative democracy is political democracy conceived of not as a clash of will and interests, or as an aggregating of preferences … None of these conceptions would be epistemically robust. None of them even has epistemic pretensions – they are about power and interests rather than truth. Deliberative democracy, in contrast, is political democracy conceived of as the pooling of different ideas and approaches and the selection of the best through debate and discussion. (Posner, 2003, pp. 106–7)

Posner goes on to dismiss deliberative democracy as absurdly utopian, and certainly his description of it does make it sound rather unrealistic. But as we've seen, an epistemic democrat doesn't have to be committed to the view that democracy inevitably leads to the "best" (i.e., most accurate) answers, only that it tends in the long run to lead to more accurate answers than feasible alternatives. Likewise, a deliberative democrat, as a kind of epistemic democrat, doesn't have to be committed to the infallibility of the deliberations he or she advocates.

Another feature of deliberative democracy that can be seen as objectionable is its tendency to downplay the significance of elections and voting. Some deliberative democrats have expressed themselves in ways which make it appear that they are committed to a conception of democracy in which the deliberative process is all that is required, and that elections and voting procedures can either be ignored or else be understood as a part of that process. Jon Elster, for example, calls deliberative democracy "decision making by discussion among free and equal citizens" (Elster, 1998, p. 1), which seems to imply that democracy requires nothing more than discussion. But it does require something more. It requires a procedure (i.e., a ballot), which allows the opinions voters have at the end of their discussion to be transformed into a decision that everyone can accept, though not necessarily agree with. Similarly, Amartya Sen, after rejecting conceptions of democracy focused exclusively on ballots and elections, advocates a "broader" conception of democracy, in which it is identified with "public reason."

He goes on to say that balloting "can be seen as just one part" of the process of public reasoning (Sen, 2009, p. 327). But this is counterintuitive. It is natural to distinguish between "public deliberation (or reasoning)" and "public choice," and see votes and elections as examples, though not necessarily the only examples,[28] of the latter. Decision making, whether it is individual or collective, should be distinguished from the reasoning which precedes it, not treated as an aspect of it.

This is a semantic point, but it is not a trivial one. To characterize democracy entirely in terms of deliberation, reasoning, or discussion, is to neglect something that should be central to any account of democracy – political power. After all, public deliberation, reasoning, and discussion have gone on in some highly authoritarian and nondemocratic regimes. Sen characterizes the Emperor Ashoka as a democrat (Sen, 2009, p. 331), on the grounds that he allowed, indeed encouraged, his subjects to engage in free and open public debate. But Ashoka's subjects lacked something which citizens of democracies must have, namely the collective power to enforce the results of their deliberations. I earlier argued that the statemental theory of voting is true, but I also suggested that it is not the whole truth. Although votes are statements, they are not *merely* statements. Votes are also resources, which voters can use to exercise political power. Democracy, and hence democratic theory, therefore, consists in two parts, the deliberative part and the electoral part, and we should recognize the importance of each and not conflate them.

I have said that deliberative democracy, properly understood, is a kind of epistemic democracy. It is epistemic democracy accompanied by a particular view of how voters come to have the opinions which they can then go on to state with their vote.[29] Deliberative democracy, correctly understood, is the view that voters should form their opinions in the light of public argument and debate, and that a system of government is less than fully democratic if and to the extent that voters don't form their opinions in this way.

One reason epistemic democracy has sometimes been thought of as distinct from, and even in conflict with, deliberative democracy is the close association between epistemic democracy and the Condorcet Jury Theorems. These theorems assume that voters' opinions are probabilistically independent of one another. But, as several critics of epistemic democracy have noted (Bartels, 1996; Goldman, 1999b, p. 319), this is an unrealistic assumption. Voters interact with one another and so influence one another's opinions. Deliberative democrats claim that at least some voter interaction, the kind that takes the form of debate and argument, is a good thing, indeed that it is an essential ingredient of democracy. But for epistemic democrats who base their case on the Condorcet Jury Theorems, any such interaction appears to be a problem.

Some epistemic democrats have responded to this apparent problem by claiming that debate and argument do not really undermine probabilistic independence. Robert Goodin, for example, approvingly cites the following passage by James Hawthorne:

> The kind of independence that is relevant to Jury theorems … is not at all the kind of restriction on voter communication that some have taken it to be. Rather, in this context *probabilistic independence* means that after the public debate each voter assesses the merits and votes his or her own judgment. Thus, *probabilistically independent voting* means *independent voting* as the term is commonly understood – *voting one's conscience* rather than as part of a block or faction. (Goodin, 2002, p. 120)

But this is false. Probabilistically independent voting does not mean voting one's conscience. It means that the likelihood that one will vote for the correct option is independent of how others vote, and public debate will very likely undermine that. After all, if one voter persuades another to vote the same way he or she is voting, the latter's vote will not be probabilistically independent of the former. There would be little point in having a public debate if we knew in advance that no one would persuade anyone to vote their way.

Condorcet's assumption that votes are probabilistically independent of one another made his calculations easier, but epistemic democrats don't need this assumption. As we saw in the previous chapter, the widespread view that independence is a precondition for the rationality of "going by the numbers" is false, and Thomas Kelly, to take just one example, is mistaken when he claims that "the evidence provided by the fact that a large number of individuals hold a belief in common is weaker to the extent that the individuals who share that belief do so because they have influenced one another, or because they have been influenced by common sources" (Kelly, 2010, p. 147). So the fact that voters do not form their opinions independently of one another need not undermine the core claim of epistemic democracy that aggregating votes in a democratic election is the best way of tracking the truth.

Although we saw in the previous chapter that lack of independence among opinion holders *need not* undermine the rationality of going by the numbers, we also saw that it *can* in certain circumstances, because of the possibility of information cascades. It might seem that this possibility is irrelevant to democratic decision making, since information cascades can only occur when people offer their opinion in a sequence, whereas in democratic elections citizens offer their opinion at (effectively) the same time at the ballot box. Nonetheless, two relatively recent phenomena in Western societies can lead to information cascades, which can undermine the reliability of democratic decisions. One is the emergence of reasonably accurate and widely publicized opinion polls. The other is the tendency of mainstream media to present political news in strategic rather than policy terms (Patterson, 1993). Increasingly, public debate within the mainstream media is not about identifying the best policies or the candidates who are most likely to implement them, but about which candidates are winning and which candidates have momentum. The more or less explicit implication is that the candidates most likely to win are the best candidates.

It is not important that citizens vote independently of one another. Requiring them to do so would be both impractical and inconsistent with the central insight of deliberative democracy. But it is important that citizens vote independently of their views about who will win the election. Since, according to epistemic democrats, the outcome of a reasonably democratic election constitutes evidence relevant to the statements voters are making with their vote, there is a danger of voters voting for candidates on the grounds that they expect them to win. If enough voters ignore their private evidence and follow the crowd in this way, then elections will be less reliable guides to the truth.

Conclusion

Critics of epistemic democracy often pride themselves on their hard-headed "realism." They treat the task of giving a theory of democracy as a matter of describing what the governments we tend to think of as democratic have in common. This approach seems to me to be a mistake, and one with dangerous implications, as it effectively assumes that our naming practices are infallible. Rather than starting with the question "What do the so-called democracies have in common?" we should start with the question "What account of democracy offers the best response to those, like Plato, who advocate the rule of a political elite?"

81

Nonepistemic democrats tend to characterize democracy, not as an alternative to the rule of political elites, but as a method by which political elites gain power. Hence Posner, for example, endorses a definition of the democratic process according to which it is "a competitive power struggle among members of a political elite ... for the electoral support of the masses" (Posner, 2003, p. 130).[30] If you took the word "electoral" out of this definition, it would obviously be too broad. Almost every system of government is characterized by competition for power among members of a political elite who seek the support of the masses, as well as the support of other political elites. Putting the word "electoral" back into the definition narrows its extension somewhat, but not nearly enough. We have already seen that identifying democracy with voting and elections is a mistake. As Sen points out, "A great many dictators in the world have achieved gigantic electoral victories even without any overt coercion in the process of voting, mainly through suppressing public discussion and freedom of information, and through generating a climate of apprehension and anxiety" (Sen, 2009, p. 327). Any attempt to characterize democracy in terms of *how* an elite group acquires political power misses the central defining feature of democracy. Democracy consists in political power being in the hands of the people as a whole, rather than in the hands of an elite.

It will be objected that this is an unachievable ideal, because some people will always have a greater share of political power than others. It is true that democracy is an unachievable ideal. In this respect, it is like other unachievable political ideals, such as justice or freedom. There will never be a perfectly just or free society any more than there will ever be a perfectly democratic one, but that does not mean that these ideals should be dismissed as impractical. Democracy, like justice and freedom, is a political ideal, with enormous practical significance as a tool for evaluating and improving existing political arrangements.

Notes

1 As Renford Bambrough has noted, Plato and Aristotle thought "the relationship between ethics and politics was so close as to make them virtually one inquiry" (1967, p. 153). This attitude is quite alien to a lot of modern thought about politics, especially the school of thought known as "political realism." I shall have more to say about the relation between ethics and politics later in this chapter.

2 By "we" I mean myself and anyone likely to read this book. The term "democracy" has come to have such positive connotations, especially since the end of World War II, that most governments describe themselves as "democratic," even those *we* tend to think of as the antithesis of democracy (e.g., the Democratic Republic of North Korea).

3 We saw in the previous chapter that although experts on a subject are not necessarily meta-experts, they very often will be.

4 See, for example, Grofman and Feld (1988), and List and Goodin (2001).

5 I will discuss those circumstances in some detail later in this chapter.

6 This idea is discussed in some depth in Surowiecki (2004).

7 We can put aside for now Goldman's suggestion about what the statement might be about.

8 In fact, even some followers of Rousseau seem to find his concept of "the general will" obscure and metaphysically dubious, and have quietly replaced talk of it with talk of the "common good" or the "common interest" (e.g., Estlund, 1990).

9 It is certainly not obviously true. If, for example, one sightseer thinks the group should go to Yosemite rather than Yellowstone (for whatever reason), then he or she might very well vote for Yosemite even though going there is not in his or her own interests. The only reason I can think of for dismissing this as irrational would be a dogmatic insistence that all rational actions must be entirely motivated by self-interest.

10 Of course there are philosophers who think that voting is irrational on precisely these grounds. I think they have an excessively narrow (i.e., purely instrumental) conception of rationality. In my view, to describe something as irrational necessarily involves an element of condemnation. Voting is clearly not a practice that should be condemned; at least it should not be condemned by proponents of democracy. A good discussion of the alleged irrationality of negligible contributions can be found in Richard Tuck (2008).

11 At least, voting is not motivated by self-interest, in the sense that individuals do not vote in order to bring about electoral outcomes that are in their self-interest. Someone might insist that voters are nonetheless motivated by self-interest, because they are motivated by the desire to feel good about themselves or look good in the eyes of others. While I find such views highly implausible, I will not argue against them here, since they are irrelevant to my argument.

12 As General Bullmoose, a character in *Li'l Abner*, says, "What's good for General Bullmoose is good for the USA."

13 Those who think the concept of *self-interest* is clearer than the concept of *common interest* (or common good) seem to be reasoning in something like the following way. My self-interest (what is good for me) consists in maximizing my happiness and minimizing my unhappiness over the course of my life. There is no similarly uncontroversial understanding

of the common interest (or the common good). We could try saying that it consists in maximizing the happiness and minimizing the unhappiness of the greatest possible number of people. But that would commit us to classical utilitarianism, which is a highly controversial doctrine. The problem with this line of argument is that the above account of self-interest is also highly controversial (in fact I think it is just as controversial as the utilitarian account of the common good), because it presupposes the contestable claim that my interests are to be understood in purely hedonistic terms, as well as the contestable claim that happiness in the distant future is as important as immediate happiness. Of course, one could try to give a different account of self-interest, but I submit that (unless it were a trivial truth) it would also be highly controversial.

14 It seems to be a relic of classical utilitarianism, which has been largely abandoned by consequentialists of the twentieth and twenty-first century, who tend to have much more nuanced and realistic views of human motivation.

15 There is, however, some irony in Schumpeter's example, since buying cigarettes is hardly a good example of rational self-interested action. It gives us some reason to be wary of Schumpeter's confidence in people's ability to work out what is in their own interests.

16 I will have more to say about what that consists in shortly.

17 Though of course some people may find one challenge more difficult than the other. For example, someone who has been educated to think that there is no such thing as society, and therefore no such thing as the common good, will find it difficult to identify policies that promote the common good.

18 In fact, it seems pretty clear that if voting does give people a sense of control over their own lives, that feeling is an illusion, since, as we have seen, one cannot reasonably hope to influence the outcome of an election with one's vote.

19 I am heavily indebted to John Dewey (1997/1916) for my views about the importance of democratic education and the centrality of the concept of *the common good* to that education.

20 It would be nice if this community were always well-defined. Unfortunately it is not. For example, what is the job of a politician elected to a national legislature from a local district? Should he or she be principally concerned with promoting the nation's interests or the district's interests? I have no satisfactory answer to this question.

21 According to Goodin (2002, p. 109) the problem is that it appears that "even relatively small electoral majorities should prove rationally compelling and opposition ought rationally to vanish."

22 This is one way of interpreting Winston Churchill's famous statement on democracy quoted in the epigraph to this chapter.

23   That is far too big a task for me to address here. What is more, it is not directly related to the epistemic concerns of this book. For good discussions of the topic see Dummett (1984) and Poundstone (2008).

24   The view that elections are the essence of democracy has been endorsed by Huntington (1991, p. 9) and eloquently criticized by Sen (2009, pp. 326–8).

25   It is also regrettable that ordinary American citizens have little knowledge of their country's foreign policies. But this is regrettable, not so much because knowledge of foreign policy is vital to democracy as such, but because America has a global empire and so its foreign policies matter much more than the foreign policies of other countries. Goldman and others clearly think the solution to the ignorance of many American citizens on this subject is to better educate or inform them. While I have no objection to that, a more realistic (and moral) solution would be for the American government to scale back its empire, thus reducing the need for its citizens to be well-informed about foreign policy. This is one reason among many for thinking that empire is incompatible with democracy.

26   In Chapter Six, I will argue that a failure to recognize this leads Goldman and others into error about the role of the press in a democratic society.

27   Bertrand Russell (1928, pp. 130–4) characterizes civil servants as political experts. But he doesn't think they are all experts on a single subject, namely politics. Rather, he thinks of them as each having some expertise on some aspect or aspects of politics.

28   Much will depend on how broadly we construe the word "vote." Henry David Thoreau, for example, clearly uses the word very broadly when he exhorts his readers to "cast your whole vote, not a strip of paper merely, but your whole influence" (Thoreau, 1958/1849, p. 20).

29   Of course nothing compels them to state their actual opinions, but they will do so if they vote sincerely as opposed to tactically.

30   Posner's definition is inspired by Schumpeter's "second concept of democracy" (Schumpeter, 1992, p. 269).

4

Rumors and Rumor-Mongers

"Open your ears; for which of you will stop
The vent of hearing when loud Rumour speaks?"
(William Shakespeare, Prologue, *Henry IV Part II*)

In this chapter I will defend rumors and rumor-mongers. Although rumor itself has been largely ignored by philosophers, it is closely related to two phenomena, gossip and conspiracy theory, which have recently received a lot of philosophical attention. Like gossip and conspiracy theory, rumor has a bad reputation. Much of the philosophical literature on gossip and on conspiracy theory assumes that this bad reputation is deserved. But in both cases there is a small body of literature, which has come to the defense of the reviled subject matter.[1] In a similar spirit, I will argue that rumor does not deserve its bad reputation. Although I will concentrate on epistemic issues, moral issues will never be far away. The epistemology of rumors and the morality of rumor-mongering are closely related topics.

Any defense of rumors and rumor-mongering must, of course, be qualified. Rumors can be untrue or harmful; believing rumors or engaging in rumor-mongering is sometimes unwarranted. Nonetheless,

What To Believe Now: Applying Epistemology to Contemporary Issues,
First Edition. David Coady.
© 2012 David Coady. Published 2012 by Blackwell Publishing Ltd.

I will defend rumors against those who argue (or simply assume), that rumors are always, or typically, false, or that believing them is always, or typically, unjustified. I will also defend rumors against those who claim rumors are a threat to democracy. Far from being a threat to democracy, rumors are an essential part of the deliberative process, which, as we saw in the previous chapter, is an essential feature of democracy.

C. A. J. Coady (2006), one of the very few philosophers who has written about rumor,[2] provides a good example of the attitude I will argue against. He characterizes rumor as a kind of "pathological testimony," and says that once "we have reason to characterise some communication as rumor, then equally we have reason to treat it as lacking credibility" (p. 269). His only epistemic concession to rumor is the admission that, in some circumstances, one may deserve further investigation "just in case it is true, or with the prospect of discovering some truth that it distorts" (p. 269). This is faint praise indeed, since (as he says) outright lies may also deserve further investigation for similar reasons.[3] By contrast, I will argue that many rumors are credible (that is, it is rational to believe them), and that in general the fact that a proposition is rumored to be true is evidence in favor of its being true.

This does not mean, of course, that you should believe every rumor you hear. Whether you should believe a particular rumor (as well as the degree of credence that you should give it) depends on its antecedent plausibility, as well as the circumstances in which it was conveyed to you. These points are not, of course, distinctive of rumors; they apply to all forms of communication.

So what distinguishes rumor from other forms of communication? In each of the next two sections I will identify a necessary condition for characterizing a communication as a rumor. I will then argue that these individually necessary conditions are jointly sufficient. Neither condition justifies rumor's bad reputation, though they both help to explain why it has a bad reputation.

The Grapevine

To begin with, for a communication to be a rumor, it must have spread through a large number of informants (henceforth, the rumor-mongers). This is one difference between rumor and another form of communication with which it is often confused, gossip. Gossip may well be first-hand.[4]

By contrast, no first-hand account of an event can *be* a rumor, though it may later become one.[5] Furthermore, the number of informants through which a rumor has spread must be quite large. No second-hand account of an event can be a rumor, though it may be more of a rumor than a first-hand account. In general, the further a rumor has spread, the more fully it deserves the name.

Any acceptable account of rumor must allow for the possibility that a rumor may change as a result of this process. How much can a rumor change, and in particular how much can its content change, before it becomes a different rumor? I don't have any definitive answer to this question, but it seems clear that there must be some limits. To take an extreme and purely hypothetical example: if a rumor that *p* had changed so much in the telling that it came to be a rumor that *not p*, it would no longer be the same rumor. It seems that rumors are individuated partly by their causal ancestry, but also partly by their content.

The fact that the content of a rumor can change as it passes from person to person goes some way toward explaining why rumors are widely held to be unreliable. A natural way of thinking about the matter is as follows. Every time a rumor is passed on there is a real possibility of deliberate or accidental distortion, and no corresponding possibility of correction. Hence, it is natural to think, a second-hand account will inevitably be less reliable than an eyewitness account, a third-hand account less reliable than a second-hand account, a fourth-hand account less reliable still, and so on. Gordon W. Allport and Leo Postman, in their classic book *The Psychology of Rumor* (1947), took this to be an essential feature of rumors, which justifies their bad reputation. Allport and Postman conclude their book by saying that "so great are the distortions ... that it is never under any circumstances safe to accept rumor as a valid guide for belief and conduct" (p. 148).

Allport and Postman set out to study rumors experimentally in laboratory conditions. In their experiments, a volunteer was asked to describe a picture as accurately as possible to a second volunteer who had not seen the picture; the second volunteer was asked to repeat what he had heard to a third volunteer; the third volunteer would pass the message on to a fourth volunteer, and so on.[6] As a message passed from person to person Allport and Postman noted that its content tended to change in the following ways: (1) it would become increasingly inaccurate, (2) it would become increasingly simplified, and (3) it would increasingly conform to the prior beliefs and desires of the volunteers (for example, a picture of a white man mugging a black man became transformed in the telling to a picture of a black man mugging a white man). Allport and Postman concluded that these changes are characteristic of rumors in general.

It may appear that the distortions Allport and Postman observed constitute experimental confirmation of the thought Alexander Pope expressed in "The Temple of Fame":

> The flying rumours gathr'd as they roll'd,
> Scarce any tale was sooner heard than told;
> And all who told it added something new,
> And all who heard it made enlargements too.

Once you think of rumors in this way, the conclusion that they are fundamentally unreliable, and tend to become increasingly unreliable as they spread (and so become more fully rumors), is unavoidable.

There is a popular idea that the more steps away a communication is from an original eyewitness account the less warranted we are in believing it (whether or not that communication constitutes a rumor). It has been endorsed by numerous philosophers, including John Locke (1961/1690):

> *any testimony, the further off it is from the original truth, the less force and proof it has.* The being and existence of the thing itself, is what I call the original truth. A credible man vouching his knowledge of it is a good proof; but if another equally credible do witness it from his report, the testimony is weaker: and a third that attests the hearsay of an hearsay is yet less considerable. So that in traditional truths, each remove weakens the force of the proof: and the more hands the tradition has successively passed through, the less strength and evidence does it receive from them. (Locke, Bk. IV, Ch. XVI, s. 10)

Since rumors are by definition very far from an "original truth," it appears that they must all be highly unreliable.

Although this seems to be the reason many people think rumors should be treated with skepticism,[8] it cannot be the reason C. A. J. Coady thinks that rumors should be treated with skepticism. Elsewhere he has persuasively argued against the idea that there is an inevitable diminution in the reliability of testimony as it passes from person to person (1992, pp. 199–230). Not only can the reliability of such testimony be preserved, it can actually be enhanced. This can be brought out, in the case of rumors, by highlighting some of the differences between the Allport and Postman experiments and real rumors.

Although Allport and Postman concede that there are some differences, they insist that "nearly all [of them] may be expected to enhance the accuracy of the report in the experimental situation and to yield far less distortion ... than in real-life rumoring" (1947, p. 65). They themselves, however, mention one difference, that may be expected to *reduce* the accuracy of the report in the experimental situation and yield far *more* distortion than in real-life rumoring. Although those who hear rumors often have the opportunity to ask questions of their informants, the volunteers in the Allport and Postman experiments had no such opportunity. Allport and Postman dismiss the significance of this difference, claiming that people seldom take advantage of the opportunity to cross-examine their informants. However, they offer no evidence for this claim, and it is inconsistent with the findings of other rumor researchers (Caplow, 1947, p. 299; Shibutani, 1966, pp. 70–5). There are at least five other important differences between the experimental situation devised by Allport and Postman and real rumors, which when taken together imply there can be much less distortion in real rumoring than in their experiments. In fact, when taken together they imply that there need not be any distortion at all, and that any change in the content of a rumor can be in the direction of increasing accuracy. Allport and Postman, along with much of the rest of the literature on rumor, assume that any change in the content of a rumor constitutes distortion (i.e., reduced accuracy). But, as we shall see, this is unwarranted. Rumors can become more accurate as they spread.

First, people who hear real rumors, unlike the volunteers for the Allport and Postman experiments, will typically have some prior knowledge of the subject matter. Real rumors are not about pictures of imaginary events stripped of any context, but about real events, which are of interest to those spreading the rumor. Hence those who hear rumors may well be in a position to make reasonable judgments about the plausibility of what they are told based on whatever prior knowledge they have.

Second, real rumors are often spread among people who know each other. This means that those who hear a rumor may be in a position to make a rational judgment about whether or not to believe it, on the basis of their knowledge of their informant's reliability,[9] as well as the reliability of their informant's informant, their informant's informant's informant, and so on (to the extent that they know who all these informants are).

Third, real rumor-mongers can do more than merely relay the content of a rumor. They can also relay an "estimate of plausibility" of the rumor. For example, a rumor-monger may preface his or her account of a rumor with a qualification, such as "I'm not absolutely sure that this is true, but I heard … ."[10] An estimate of plausibility indicates the strength of a rumor-monger's endorsement of a rumor. In other words, it indicates roughly where he or she would place the rumor on a spectrum ranging from the highly plausible to the highly implausible. People who hear a rumor may use their informant's estimate of plausibility to make their own judgment about whether or not to believe it.

Fourth, people who hear real rumors, unlike the subjects of the Allport and Postman experiments, have the option of not passing on what they've heard. Those who hear a rumor may dismiss it as incredible and, as a result, decide not to spread it any further. Hence a rumor's success in spreading can be seen (to put the matter in academic terms) as success in passing a lengthy process of peer review.

Fifth, real rumors do not travel in the unilinear fashion of the Allport and Postman experiments. A person may hear a rumor through more than one channel, and this may constitute evidence that the rumor is true. Indeed a person who hears a rumor through more than one channel may well have more justification for believing the rumor than any of his or her informants had. If he or she in turn spreads the rumor, it would be natural to describe this as a situation in which the evidence that the rumor is true is increasing as the rumor spreads. Furthermore, if people hear different versions of the same rumor, they may well be able to transmit a new version of the rumor, which is more credible and/or accurate than any of the versions transmitted to them. It may even be more credible and/or accurate than the account of an eyewitness. In short, we have seen nothing so far that rules out the possibility that it could be rational for you to believe a rumor, even when it contradicts the "testimony" of your own senses.

Allport and Postman conceive of rumor-mongers as completely passive in the face of the information they are given. They are like imperfect recording and transmitting devices, through whom information, like noise, is gradually distorted. But each of the above points shows that people have resources available to them, if they are prepared to use them, to do more than merely produce an inferior version of what they have heard. They are able to use any or all these resources to get the story straight in their own mind, and thus minimize distortion. They are also able to evaluate the internal consistency of the story itself, as well as its consistency with other things they already know. This in turn can put them in a position to reject part or all of the rumor if it is unlikely to be true, modify parts of it that are unlikely to be wholly true, and alter the content of the rumor on the basis of plausible hypotheses about how it came to be modified in the telling. All this means that not only is it not inevitable that rumors will become increasingly distorted (i.e., less accurate) as they spread, there is a realistic possibility of them becoming more accurate as they spread.[11] What is more, even if a rumor doesn't become more accurate as it spreads, the very fact that it has spread may constitute evidence of its accuracy.

It might be objected to all this that although epistemically conscientious rumor-mongers would be able to do more than just mindlessly repeat what they hear to the best of their ability, rumor-mongers are, by definition, not epistemically conscientious. Rumor-mongers, so the objection goes, are by definition not interested in the "original truth," but only in parroting what they heard from the last link in the chain of transmission (or perhaps one of the last links, if they heard the rumor from more than one source). This seems to be what Jonathan Adler is suggesting when he claims that those who spread rumors are not offering genuine assertions (Adler, 2007, p. 76).[12]

But this cannot be right. It supposes that rumor-mongers necessarily have no interest at all in whether the rumors they spread are true. Of course, some rumor-mongers are like this. Rumor-mongers sometimes even know that a rumor they are spreading is false. But no rumor could survive *as a rumor*, as opposed perhaps to a myth or an explicit fiction, if most of those spreading it were completely indifferent to whether it was true. I take it to be an essential feature of a rumor that most of the people spreading the rumor are interested in whether it is true, and that many (an appropriately vague quantifier) of them believe that it is in fact true. If few people believed rumors, there would be little reason to warn people against believing them. This is why, of course, the staunchest opponents of rumor do not think of rumor in this way.[13] Opponents of rumor typically warn people against believing rumors. Many of them offer advice to governments and businesses about how to quash rumors by persuading people not to believe them. There would be little point to any of this if few people were in fact inclined to believe rumors. Fortunately for them, many people are inclined to believe rumors. Furthermore, there is reason to believe that rumors that are not believed by many people will rarely spread far or last long. In order to explain why this is so, it is necessary to develop another model of rumors, which avoids the flaws of the Allport and Postman model.

The sociologist Tamotsu Shibutani (1960) has suggested that rumors develop through a process analogous to natural selection in biology.[14]

This is a promising idea, since rumors have many of the features of biological organisms that led Darwin to invoke the concept of natural selection. Like biological organisms, rumors spread by making copies of themselves; these copies are similar in some respects, but different in others; there is "competition" between different rumors (as well as different versions of the same rumor), in the sense that some survive and spread at the expense of others which rapidly die out. Finally, which rumors (and which versions of rumors) survive and spread is not entirely arbitrary. In other words, there are selection pressures.[15]

Shibutani claims that *plausibility* is one such selection pressure, although its importance as a selection pressure is quite variable. He claims that plausibility will have less of a role in the construction and dissemination of rumors in periods of "collective excitement" (p. 178), because, in these circumstances, people's behavior tends to become "contagious." Rather than thinking about the plausibility of what they are told, they tend to think and act as those around them are thinking and acting.

Shibutani construes plausibility as a matter of consistency with "previously accepted beliefs" (p. 178). But, if taken at face value, this is open to obvious counterexamples. For example, a few years ago I heard a rumor that the Pope had died. That a man I knew to be old and sick should have died was not at all implausible, even though it was inconsistent with the beliefs I held at that point, one of which was that the Pope was alive.

Another problem with Shibutani's account of plausibility is that he characterizes it as if it were entirely a matter of content. This leads him to claim that transformations "in rumor content are always in the direction of greater harmony with shared assumptions" (1966, p. 179). Harmony with shared assumptions is certainly one factor that may be taken into account when assessing the plausibility of a rumor, but it is not the only one. Other factors include: the credibility of the immediate source of the rumor, as well as less immediate sources (if enough is known about them); whether there seems to be more than one source for the rumor, and if so, how many; and whether there is a plausible explanation of how the rumor could have begun and how it could have spread, if it were not true. Shibutani's unnecessarily narrow account of plausibility fails to do justice to the possibility that a rumor may be highly plausible, even though it conveys very surprising news.

Despite these problems, Shibutani's insight that plausibility is a selection pressure on the construction and dissemination of rumors is important. All else being equal, a person is more likely to pass on a rumor, and more likely to pass it on with a high estimate of plausibility, if he or she thinks it is true. All else being equal, a rumor accompanied by a high estimate of plausibility will be more likely to be passed further on. Consequently, all else being equal, the more confidence those who spread a rumor have that it is true, the more likely it is to survive and be widely disseminated.

Now, if you hear a rumor, that is *prima facie* evidence that it has been reasonably effective at surviving and spreading. After all, you are less likely to hear rumors that do not last long and are transmitted to relatively few people. So if you hear a rumor, that is *prima facie* evidence that a large number of people have found it reasonably plausible. Now, I would claim that this is *prima facie* evidence that it is true, and that the longer a rumor lasts and the greater the number of people who spread the rumor, the greater the *prima facie* evidence that it is true.

This is another example of "going by the numbers," a topic we discussed in each of the last two chapters. We saw that Alvin Goldman and others are skeptical of the rationality of believing something on the grounds that a lot of other people believe it (or have a high degree of confidence in it). In particular, they claim that the fact that a lot of people believe something means little when their beliefs are not formed independently of one another. Those who believe rumors do not form their beliefs independently of one another, so Goldman and others would presumably urge us not to be swayed by the fact that a lot of people believe a particular rumor. In fact, we don't have to wonder about Goldman's attitude to rumors, since he explicitly applies his skepticism about going by the numbers to the topic:

> Another example, which also challenges the probity of greater numbers, is the example of rumors. Rumors are stories that are widely circulated and accepted though few of the believers have access to the rumored facts. If someone hears a rumor from one source, is that source's credibility enhanced when the same rumor is repeated by a second, third, or fourth source? Presumably not ... (Goldman, 2001, pp. 98–9)

It should be clear by now what is wrong with Goldman's reasoning. It ignores the fact that each person who passes a rumor on could have decided not to, on the grounds that it was too implausible. To the extent that *plausibility* is a selection pressure which contributes to the survival and spread of rumors, the more a rumor is repeated the more likely it is to be true.

Of course, there may be selection pressures other than plausibility at work, such as *interest*, and it is possible for belief in rumors to become less justified, or at least for it not to become more justified, as a result of repetition. But there is certainly no *a priori* reason to believe that repetition cannot make us more justified in believing rumors.

This is not a mere theoretical possibility. There is empirical evidence that, at least in certain circumstances, rumors that survive and spread are more likely to be true, either because they were true all along, or because they became true (or more true) as they spread. During World War II, the United States military tried to limit the spread of rumors among its troops. It was worried, not because these rumors tended to be false, but because they tended to be true, and there was a danger they might spread to the enemy, giving them important military intelligence, especially about planned troop deployments. The military tackled this problem by regularly redeploying troops to break up the normal channels along which rumors passed. Theodore Caplow (1947), who studied these antirumor campaigns, found that they had the desired effect of inhibiting the spread of individual rumors. He also found that they had the – presumably undesired – effect of increasing the number of rumors that came into existence (I assume that many of these rumors concerned the motives behind the antirumor campaigns). A third, and in the current context most significant, effect of these antirumor campaigns was that they made rumors less accurate. This also seems to be have been desirable, from the military's point of view. Caplow accounts for this phenomenon in the following passage:

> Distortion in terms of wishes and avoidance seems to be an individual rather than a group characteristic. As channels solidified, this phenomenon became comparatively rare, because of the exclusion of persons associated with previous invalidity. When they were broken up, wish fulfillment again became conspicuous. (Caplow, 1947, p. 301)

So the survival and reproductive success of the rumors Caplow was studying appear to have been partly dependent on their being disseminated by people widely known to be reliable sources. Judgment about the reliability of one's source is part of an overall judgment about the plausibility of what one is told. Not only is there empirical evidence that rumor-mongers can make such judgments, there is also empirical evidence that they can be quite good at it. Caplow cites examples of rumors becoming increasingly accurate as they spread, and finds that there was "a positive and unmistakable relation between the survival of a rumor, in terms of both time and diffusion, and its veracity" (Caplow, 1947, p. 302).

It should be clear by now that the "distance" of rumors from an original eyewitness account does not constitute a general reason for skepticism about their veracity. On the contrary, such distance may make belief in rumors more warranted. It is common for those who are skeptical of rumors to point out that people who believe rumors have no "direct evidence" for doing so (Sunstein, 2009, p. 6). This is true, but indirect evidence is still evidence, and it may be as strong as direct evidence, or even stronger. A great deal of what we know, and of what we are most justified in believing, is based on indirect evidence. Almost all our knowledge of history, for example, is based on indirect evidence. Should we doubt that Napoleon existed, because all our evidence about him is indirect? Obviously that would be absurd.[16]

Rumors as Unofficial Communications

I have said that for a communication to be a rumor it must have spread through a number of informants. Although this is a necessary condition, it is not sufficient. Robert Knapp, a doctoral student of Allport, captured another important feature when he defined rumor as "a proposition for belief of topical reference disseminated without official verification" (1944, p. 22). Knapp draws our attention to the fact that rumors are essentially *unofficial* things. No public statement by a government or a government agency, for example, no matter how far removed it was from an original eyewitness account, could *be* a rumor, though it could confirm a pre-existing rumor (at which point it would cease to be a rumor) or be responsible for starting rumor.

C. A. J. Coady has criticized Knapp's definition on the grounds that it "would count every newspaper expose of government misdeeds or secrets that met with official silence or denial as rumour" (2006, p. 263). This objection seems to presuppose that "official verification" means "verification by government officials," and though this may be what Knapp means, there is a broader understanding of the concept of *officialdom*, which avoids this objection and leads to a better understanding of the nature of rumor. Elsewhere I have argued that to describe a communication as "official" is to say that it is endorsed by an institution with significant power (especially the power to influence what is widely believed) at the time and place in question (Coady, 2007b, p. 200). Government statements are one particularly obvious kind of official communication, but they are not the only kind. Since newspapers are institutions which typically have significant power to influence what is believed by many of their readers, their reports typically have official status, and so should not count as rumors, even if those reports are denied or ignored by the government of the day.

To characterize rumors as unofficial communications then is to say that they lack a certain kind of institutional endorsement. Does this feature of rumors imply that believing them is always or typically unjustified, or that we should adopt an attitude of *prima facie* skepticism toward them? Knapp clearly thinks so; he claims that "rumors are more subject than formal modes of transmission to inaccuracy" (Knapp, 1944, pp. 22–3). But this is clearly at best a contingent truth. Whether rumors are more or less subject to inaccuracy than formal modes of transmission will depend on what the available formal modes of transmission are. In some societies, rumor may well be more accurate than formal modes of transmission. For example, in the Soviet Union in 1953, Raymond Bauer and David Gleicher found that the majority of people believed that official information was less reliable than "word-of-mouth communication" (1953, p. 307), and that this belief was particularly widespread among the better-educated classes. Who could doubt that this preference for rumor over official information was justified?

Of course, the level of trust in official information in our society is much higher. What is more, a higher level of trust is clearly justified. Does that mean that, in our society at least, we should agree with Knapp and other critics of rumor, and that we will always (or at least typically) be more justified in believing official information than rumors? It seems to me that this view both exaggerates the reliability of official information and underestimates the reliability of rumor.

Neil Levy has argued that it is "almost always rational" to accept official information, where this is characterized as information "promulgated by the authorities" (Levy, 2007b, p. 181).[17] But Levy's position seems to trade on an ambiguity. There is a sense in which official information can be identified with information promulgated by the authorities, and there is a sense in which it is almost always rational to believe authorities. But they involve two quite different senses of the word "authority." We can call the former sense "institutional authority" and the latter sense "epistemic authority." In the institutional sense, being an authority just means being someone entitled to speak on behalf of a certain institution. In the epistemic sense, being an authority means (roughly at any rate) being an (objective) expert. Levy moves freely between talk of "epistemic authority" and talk of "expertise," and there can be no doubt, as we saw in Chapter 2, that (with some qualifications) it is usually rational to believe experts (on the topics on which they have expertise). But information promulgated by epistemic authorities obviously need not have any official status, since epistemic authorities are not always entitled to speak on behalf of institutions with significant power to influence opinion. What is more, although official information is by definition promulgated by authorities (in the institutional sense), there is no guarantee that those authorities will be epistemic authorities.

For Levy, epistemic authority emanates from "properly constituted structures":

> The right kind of structure is that exemplified by science: knowledge claims are the product of a socially distributed network of enquirers, methods and results are publicly available (especially, but not only to other members of the network), inquirers are trained in assessing knowledge claims according to standards relevant to the discipline, and rewards are distributed according to success at validating new knowledge *and* at criticizing the claims of other members of the network. (Levy, 2007b, p. 188)

These are generally admirable ideals. But they are no more than ideals. No actual structure, including science (that is, science as practiced by actual people in lab coats, as opposed to the idealized science that is often the subject of philosophy of science), has ever completely lived up to them. At best they have approximated them to one degree or another.

Levy's naivety about this issue is particularly apparent in his claim that the media is (or is a part of) a properly constituted epistemic authority (Levy, 2007b, p. 192, n.3). I will discuss the media in greater detail in Chapter 6, but it is worth briefly discussing the performance of the Western media during the build-up to the latest war in Iraq, to demonstrate how far short it falls of Levy's ideals. The methods of the media at this time were not in general "publicly available." The media's regular use of unnamed official sources to create the illusion of verification of official statements has been well-documented (Dadge, 2006, pp. 131–5).[18] Since then, rewards have palpably not been distributed according to "success at validating new knowledge" or "criticizing the claims of other members of the network." Many of those who uncritically accepted false official statements at that time have seen their careers go from strength to strength, while some of those who raised legitimate doubts about those statements appear to have been punished for doing so.[19]

It may be that in an ideal society official information would carry an epistemic authority such that it would almost always be rational to believe it. But that is not our society, nor, I suspect, is it any society that has ever been or ever will be. What is more, if such a society were to come into existence, it seems likely that it would be unstable, since it would likely lead to complacency about officialdom that would be exploitable by officials hoping to manipulate public opinion to advance their interests. To the extent that the view that we should place our trust in official information rather than rumor gains widespread acceptance, official information will be less subject to scrutiny and, as a result, less likely to be true.

Characterizing a communication as "official" should be seen as epistemically neutral. An institution can have the power to influence what is believed for epistemically good reasons. For example, its power might result from its having a well-known track record of accuracy, or from its being properly constituted in something like Levy's sense. On the other hand, an institution can have the power to influence what is believed for epistemically bad reasons. For example, it might have that power because it has a virtual monopoly on the dissemination of information, or because it seeks to confirm the irrational prejudices of consumers of its information.

Even if you did have good reason to trust the veracity of official information in your society, that would not automatically translate into a reason for adopting a skeptical attitude toward rumors, because rumors need not actually contradict any official communications. The absence of official verification is essential to a rumor, but that does not entail the presence of official refutation (or even denial). Quite often officialdom will have no interest in the content of a rumor and, even when it does have an interest in quashing a rumor, it may choose not to deny it, because there is evidence that denial (and even refutation) can be counterproductive (Shibutani, 1966, pp. 200–1).[20] So even if you are confident that you can trust officials to speak the truth, you may still reasonably believe rumors, because you do not trust them to speak the whole truth.

Have I Missed Something?

I have argued that two things are essential for a communication to be a rumor: first, it must have passed through many hands (or lips); second, it must not have been endorsed by an institution with official status at the time and place in question. Neither of these characteristics provide us with any general reason for being skeptical of rumors. Nor does there seem to be any compelling moral argument against believing rumors or engaging in rumor-mongering. Opponents of rumor often point out that rumors have been known to cause civil disturbances (Rosnow & Fine, 1976, pp. 115–17). But this is no reason to be opposed to the many rumors which have no such tendency. At any rate, as almost all political philosophers have long recognized, civil disturbance is not necessarily bad. It may be justified by government misdeeds.

Of course, I may not have fully understood the nature of rumor. There may be something else about it that justifies its bad reputation. I will consider some possible candidates for being that "something else."

Rumors are often transmitted by word of mouth. Perhaps this justifies their reputation for unreliability. It could be argued that the spoken word is less reliable than the written word, because written communication requires more thought, and is therefore less prone to error. The weakness of this argument should be apparent. Talk is often thoughtful, and writing is often thoughtless. Furthermore, there is more to the reliability of a communication than the absence of error. The issue of honesty must also be considered, and there seems no reason to think that written communication is generally more honest than spoken communication. At any rate, it was never an essential feature of rumors that they be transmitted by word of mouth and, in the information age in which rumors are often spread by email, text, Twitter, or Facebook, it may not even be the most common form of transmission.

C. A. J. Coady pursues another approach, stipulation. According to him, rumor, by definition, lacks a "strong justificatory base" (2006, p. 262). To illustrate his position, he considers a report, originating from the Peruvian Embassy, which reached the American Ambassador to Japan in January 1941, according to which the Japanese Navy was planning a surprise attack on Pearl Harbor. The Ambassador dismissed the report on the grounds that sources in the Peruvian Embassy were "not very reliable." Of course, we now know that the report was accurate. Coady considers two things we might say about this case:

> The ambassador could have been right in his assessment of the general reliability of sources in the Peruvian Embassy. On the other hand, it might have been his assessment of their credibility that was at fault and the communication may not have deserved the title "rumour". (C. A. J. Coady, 2006, p. 269)

On this view, we can only determine whether a communication is a rumor once we have determined whether or not it came from a reliable source. If it came from an unreliable source, then we may call it a "rumor," otherwise not. This seems unsatisfactory for two reasons.

First, there are many communications which come from unreliable sources, but which are clearly not rumors, for example eyewitness accounts by people with poor eyesight or in poor viewing conditions, or official statements by compulsive liars. If we make rumors unreliable by fiat, we face the challenge of explaining what distinguishes rumor from other unreliable communications in a way that leaves rumor as the interesting and important phenomenon it clearly is. I don't see how that can be done. If it can't be done, then stipulating that rumors are unreliable is entirely *ad hoc*, and can only be understood as a way of suggesting falsely that communications which have spread through a large number of informants and which have not been officially endorsed should not be believed.

Second, if rumors by definition come from unreliable sources, those who exhort others not to believe rumors are making a trivial semantic point. By definition one should not believe anything that comes from an unreliable source. Hence by definition one should not believe rumors. Of course, that is not how most opponents of rumor understand their position. They claim to be establishing the illegitimacy of rumor as a substantive fact (even as the kind of fact that can be demonstrated in a laboratory), not as a trivial definitional one.

Another approach opponents of rumor could take would be to stipulate, not that belief in rumors is by definition unjustified, but that rumors themselves are by definition false. I don't know of anyone who explicitly makes this move. C. A. J. Coady certainly thinks that some rumors are true, and even Allport and Postman concede that there are true rumors, although they are obviously loath to do so (1947, pp. 147–9). Nonetheless, the assumption that "rumor" is synonymous with "false rumor" is implicit in quite a bit of antirumor rhetoric. Cass R. Sunstein's recent book *On Rumors*, for example, is tellingly subtitled *Why Falsehoods Spread, Why We Believe Them, What Can Be Done*, as if we could just assume that all rumors are false. Although Sunstein occasionally seems to accept that rumors can be true, all the rumors he discusses are false (or at least they are clearly believed to be false by him), and he moves from trying to explain why people believe false rumors to trying to explain why people believe rumors, as if there is no difference between these tasks (e.g., Sunstein, 2009, p. 57). He certainly never considers the possibility that sometimes people believe rumors because they have good reason to believe they are true.

Stipulating that rumors are false would be just as *ad hoc* as stipulating that they are unjustified. It would also make nonsense of the ordinary concept of rumor. For example, we standardly think of rumors as things that can be confirmed. But one cannot confirm something if it is false by definition. As we have seen, Sunstein doesn't explicitly define rumors as false. In fact, he explicitly declines to offer his own definition of rumor (2009, p. 5). Nonetheless, he routinely assumes that rumors are false, and sometimes seems to be using the word "rumor," not merely as a synonym for "false rumor," but as a synonym for "falsehood." For example, he describes the official pretext for the invasion of Iraq, the claim that it possessed weapons of mass destruction, as a rumor (p. 47). The official status of this claim means that it is not a rumor on my definition, and it is not a rumor on any other definition I am aware of either. For the most part, however, Sunstein's concern about the dangers of rumor amounts to little more than a worry that people might accept unofficial rather than official sources of information. He is particularly concerned that people might wrongly lose faith in the government as a result of believing false rumors (p. 9). The possibility that they might rightly lose faith in the government as a result of believing true rumors is not considered.

Rumors, Democracy, Urban Legends, and Propaganda

C. A. J. Coady quite rightly criticizes Knapp's approach to rumors on the grounds that it invokes "an ideal of official control of information that is, to put it mildly, undemocratic" (2006, p. 263). But Knapp is not alone in having this ideal. Critics of rumor almost invariably, explicitly or implicitly, invoke an ideal of official control of information, where "official" is understood in the broad institutional sense I have explained. It is an ideal closely associated with the concept of guided democracy, which I criticized in the last chapter. If the dissemination of credible information were the exclusive province of institutions, then real political power would largely be concentrated in those institutions. Sunstein repeatedly characterizes rumors (or at least false rumors) as a threat to democracy.[21] The fact that some rumors are true is simply ignored, as is the fact that rumors, true or false, are an important check on institutional power. It is, I suppose, conceivable that a rumor, true or false, could constitute a threat to democracy. But rumor itself is not a threat to democracy; critics of rumor who want the state and other powerful institutions to have a monopoly on information are.

We have seen that two closely related and widespread views about rumor are unfounded. The first is that there is a presumption against believing rumors. The second is that belief in a particular rumor becomes less warranted the further it spreads. In fact, as we have seen, except in special circumstances, our warrant for believing a rumor will actually increase as the rumor spreads.

What are special circumstances? Our discussion suggests some answers. For example, belief in rumor will be less warranted when selection pressures other than judgments of plausibility are significantly affecting their development. A rumor may survive and spread, even though it is highly implausible, because it satisfies some deeply felt psychological or social need. This is often the case with one particular class of unwarranted rumors, urban legends.[22] Although some writers treat urban legends as distinct from rumors (C. A. J. Coady, 2006, pp. 266–7; DiFonzo & Bordia, 2007, pp. 25–6), they count as rumors on my definition, since they are unofficial communications which spread through many informants, most of whom are interested in whether they are true and many of whom believe they are true. Hence I say that urban legends are rumors; they are rumors with certain distinctive characteristics.

One of these characteristics is their habit of changing as they spread in such a way that their content becomes up to date and localized (Kapferer, 1990, p. 29; C. A. J. Coady, 2006, p. 267). This can sometimes help us recognize a rumor as an urban legend, and hence recognize that belief in it is unjustified. In December 2002, for example, I heard a rumor from several sources that a local truck driver had recently given a lift to a man of Middle Eastern appearance who left his wallet in the truck; the honest truck driver chased after the man and returned his wallet, where upon the man, in a rush of gratitude, warned the truck driver not to go to the local marketplace the following Saturday. This rumor spread quickly and, because I was known to have an interest in the topic, I was asked to comment by the local newspaper in Hobart, Tasmania.[23] I was able to tell them that the rumor was a version of a well-known urban legend, sometimes called "The Grateful Terrorist" by folklorists. Panic was averted, and applied epistemology was vindicated.

To say that a rumor is an urban legend is to say (among other things) that belief in it is unjustified. Nonetheless, we should not rule out the possibility that some urban legends may be true. Some certainly contain an element of truth. The urban legend known as "The Unsolvable Math Problem" (Brunvand, 1999, pp. 452–6), originated as an entirely true (though hard to believe) story, and retains elements of that truth in each of its many iterations.

Our discussion also suggests that our warrant for believing a rumor may depend, in part, on how well the rumor-mongers know each other. Belief in a rumor that is spreading through a crowd consisting of people who are mostly strangers to one another, for example, may well be unwarranted, because the rumor-mongers will be handicapped by being unable to judge the reliability of their sources. By contrast, belief in a rumor that is spreading through settled communities or stable institutional settings will, all else being equal, be more warranted.

This idea seems to be broadly consistent with the empirical literature. DiFonzo and Bordia recently surveyed a wide variety of rumor studies, and found that "rumor accuracy varied substantially, but certain field settings seemed to produce accurate rumors" (2007, pp. 145–6). In particular, they found that rumors which spread through "established organizational settings," such as workplaces, tend to be accurate (p. 146). This discovery surprised them:

> The reputation of the workplace rumor as inaccurate apparently is itself inaccurate! The reason for this disparity is puzzling. If the overwhelming majority of rumors that are recalled were true, why would the overall impression of rumor tend to be not credible? We have noticed this pattern repeatedly: When asked about rumor overall, people classify it as false or low-quality information. When asked to recall specific rumors people tend to report true or high-quality information. (DiFonzo & Bordia, 2007, p. 154)

DiFonzo and Bordia offer two explanations for this disparity. First, they suggest that it is partly explained by something they call "social desirability bias"; people are reluctant to endorse rumor, because doing so is considered socially undesirable. There is no doubt that this is true, but it just pushes the explanatory task one step further back. Why is it socially undesirable? What explains how rumor came to have its bad reputation in the first place? Second, DiFonzo and Bordia suggest that rumors probably constitute a minority of information, especially when compared to "news,"[24] and that, as a result, "false specimens of that minority may become relatively salient and then falsely correlated" (p. 154). There are two problems with this explanation. First, it is not at all clear that people do in fact get more of their information from news than from rumor (however precisely we draw that distinction). Second, even if it were true that rumor constitutes a minority of most people's information, the explanation remains incomplete until it is accompanied by an account of why false specimens of rumors, rather than (say) true ones, tend to become salient.

It seems to me that the real explanation for rumor's bad reputation is quite straightforward. Those responsible for the dissemination of official information, that is, institutions with considerable influence over what a lot of people believe, typically have a vested interest in maintaining or increasing that influence. Hence they have a vested interest in giving unofficial information, and especially rumor, a bad name. Given their power over what people believe, it should not be surprising that they have been quite successful at doing this. In short, it seems clear that rumor's bad reputation is a consequence of propaganda, and false propaganda at that.[25]

In fact, the propagandistic nature of official campaigns to discredit rumor has long been evident. During World War II, Robert Knapp was put in charge of the Division of Propaganda Research in the United States. In this capacity, he was responsible for setting up Rumor Clinics. His guidelines for these clinics included the need to "assure good faith in the regular media of communication," the need to "develop confidence and faith in leaders," and the need to "campaign deliberately against rumormongering by showing its harmful effects, its inaccuracies, and the low motives of the originators and liaisons of such tales" (Rosnow & Fine, 1976, p. 121). We have already seen that many American officials at this time were less concerned about inaccurate rumors than they were about accurate ones. It is perhaps understandable that officials should seek tight control of information, both true and false, in times of war. Nonetheless the antidemocratic nature of such campaigns should be clear. What is more, official campaigns against rumor did not end with the war. Knapp's Rumor Clinics developed into Rumor Control Centers, under the auspices of the US Department of Justice (Rosnow & Fine, 1976, pp. 120–3). Antirumor propaganda propagated by people in positions of official authority remains widespread. Cass R. Sunstein is not just an academic; he is a close advisor to Barack Obama, and head of the Office of Information and Regulatory Affairs, where his responsibilities include overseeing policies relating to "information quality."[26] It is not surprising that someone in his position should try to persuade people not to believe communications that have not been officially endorsed.

Conclusion

If rumor does not deserve its bad reputation, this fact has significant implications for the way we understand the practice of history. Many disputes about history involve one party criticizing another for their reliance on rumor. The revisionist Soviet historian J. Arch Getty, for example, once denounced fellow historian Robert Conquest for using rumor as his principal form of evidence for the Stalinist era (Getty, 1985, p. 5). Conquest responded to Getty's charge by pointing out that rumor is often the best available form of evidence, when trying to understand an era in which the official record was systematically falsified (Conquest, 1992).[27] Similarly, it is common for one side of the "history wars" in Australia to denounce their opponents for using rumor as a source of historical evidence.[28] If I am right, there is nothing wrong with historians or anyone else using rumor as a source of evidence.[29]

I have argued that belief in rumor will be less warranted when we are justified in believing that officials are being open and honest. If officials were generally open and honest, rumor-mongering would be more deserving of its bad reputation. In these circumstances, however, rumor would also be less prevalent, since it is, to a large extent, a response to insufficient or inaccurate official information. So rumor is not *in itself* a cause for concern. It is true that we should be worried when people are too reliant on rumor for their beliefs about important matters. But the principal reason to be worried is not the possibility that they might be wrong to trust rumors, but that they might be right not to trust either the accuracy or completeness of official sources of information. The fact that a large and growing minority of people turn to internet blogs for information is worrying, but not because these sources are less reliable than official sources. Rather, it is worrying because it is a symptom of failures on the part of both the publicly owned and corporately owned institutional media. I will have more to say about these failures in Chapter 6, but one of them is worth noting here. Journalists working in the institutional media are often highly reliant on information from contacts inside the government. Sometimes this reliance is so great that they adopt an attitude toward their informants which is like the attitude the volunteers for the Allport and Postman rumor experiments adopted toward their informants; rather than seek out an "original truth," they simply repeat to the best of their ability what they are told by an authorized source.

I should stress that I am not advocating a utopian ideal in which official information would be recognized as so trustworthy that rumor fades away or ceases to be an important source of information. Even if officials had a complete monopoly on information and always told the whole truth and nothing but the truth, we would not be warranted in believing they were telling us the whole truth and nothing but the truth. Rumor will always be an important check on government, media, and other institutional sources of information, and that is as it should be.

Notes

1   I will discuss conspiracy theories in the next chapter. However, I will not be discussing gossip in great detail in this book, since those who condemn gossip, unlike those who condemn rumor, are typically doing so for moral, rather than epistemic, reasons.
2   Alvin Goldman also discusses rumor, though much more briefly (Goldman, 2001, pp. 98–9). He gives an equally negative account of its epistemic credentials.
3   Here it is assumed that a lie need not actually be false, merely believed to be false by the liar. Even the most fervent opponents of rumor typically admit that some rumors are true.
4   Although rumor and gossip overlap to some extent, the concepts are quite different. Another difference is that gossip is essentially personal. There is always a person who is the subject of the gossip and who has not authorized it. By contrast the subject matter of rumor can be quite impersonal, for example earthquakes or inflation.
5   David Benfield and Mianna Lotz have objected (personal communications) that this requirement entails that it is impossible to start a rumor. I reply that it is possible to start something at one time even though it doesn't come into existence at that time. For example, it is possible to start a tradition, even though the tradition doesn't come into existence until much later. I thank Charles Pigden (personal communication) for bringing this analogy to my attention.
6   On this model rumors are like the children's game Telephone or Chinese Whispers.
7   Remember we are presently discussing a necessary but insufficient condition for being a rumor.
8   Of course a person's skepticism about rumors in principle may well be belied by his or her practice. If everyone who claimed that rumors should never be believed never believed rumors, rumors would not be so widespread.
9   Assessing an informant's reliability consists in assessing his or her general reliability and reliability in relation to the rumor's subject matter.

10   Alternatively, if the rumor-monger is confident the rumor is true, an explicit estimate of its plausibility may not be necessary.

11   We shall shortly see some empirical evidence of this phenomenon. When I speak of rumors becoming more accurate, I mean that they increasingly conform to a pre-existing reality. It is also possible that a rumor could become more accurate, because reality changes to increasingly conform to the rumor. Some rumors, for example rumors about stock market collapses or social conflict, can be self-fulfilling.

12   Adler says that "to recognize an assertion as rumor is thereby to undermine the speaker's claim to be offering an assertion." I have trouble making sense of this, since it seems to me that if someone claims to be offering an assertion, then they are, in virtue of that fact, offering an assertion. I don't see how one can wrongly claim (i.e., assert) that one is making an assertion.

13   More than one opponent of rumor defines rumor as "a proposition for belief" (Allport & Postman, 1947, p. ix; Knapp, 1944, p. 22).

14   This anticipates Richard Dawkins's (1976) concept of a *meme*.

15   Of course, we should not push this analogy too hard. The variations on which natural selection works in biology are not intended by anyone, but the variations that occur as rumors are spread may be intended. Nonetheless it is still appropriate to call the *process* natural, rather than artificial, selection, because, although individual changes may be intended, the overall development of a rumor is not.

16   Archbishop Whately wrote a very amusing satire of the idea that we should be skeptical of Napoleon's existence (Whately, 1985/1819). It was intended as a parody of Hume's argument against belief in miracles.

17   The expression Levy uses for official information is "official story," an expression he borrowed from me. See Coady (2006b).

18   The use of anonymous official sources to "confirm" the public statements of officials has become endemic in the media. This contrasts with the legitimate use of anonymity by the media to protect whistleblowers who *contradict* the official statements of an organization they belong to.

19   See Jebediah Reed "The Iraq Gamble: At the Pundits Table the Losing Bet Still Takes the Pot," http://www.fair.org/index.php?page=22&media_view_id=8331. Accessed December 11, 2010.

20   People sometimes confuse the denial with that which is being denied. Furthermore, denying a rumor can bring it to the attention of more people than would otherwise have become aware of it, and they may find the denial unconvincing.

21   He describes the market place of ideas (i.e., free speech) as an inadequate remedy for the problem (2009, pp. 10–11). Although he eschews "old-style" censorship, he thinks that legal measures may be necessary to stop the spread of false rumors (p. 12).

22 This now popular expression was popularized by the folklorist Jan Harold Brunvand (see Brunvand, 1981, 1999).

23 See *The Saturday Mercury*, December 21, 2002, "Dismiss Absurd Stories," p. 22.

24 This contrast between news and rumor is quite common in the psychology literature. By contrast, the sociologist Tamotsu Shibutani characterizes rumor as a form of news. Rumor, according to him, is improvised news.

25 Propaganda is an interesting topic in applied epistemology, but it is beyond the scope of this book. Propaganda can be true; however, it is typically characterized by indifference to the truth.

26 This information about Sunstein's position is available at http://www.whitehouse.gov/omb/inforeg_administrator. Accessed December 11, 2010.

27 I thank Charles Pigden (personal communication) for bringing this debate to my attention.

28 See, for example, Keith Windschuttle, "The Real Stuff of History," http://www.sydneyline.com/Real%20Stuff%20of%20History.htm. Accessed December 11, 2010.

29 The existence of a rumor can be evidence that what is rumored to be true is true, but it can also be evidence of other things. For example, the existence of a rumor will typically constitute evidence that the people spreading it are interested in its subject matter.

5

Conspiracy Theories and Conspiracy Theorists[1]

"While you here do snoring lie,
Open-eyed conspiracy
His time doth take."
(William Shakespeare, *The Tempest*, Act II, Scene 1)

I noted in the last chapter that the concepts of rumor and conspiracy theory are often linked, with the former being portrayed as a vehicle for the latter (e.g., Sunstein, 2009, p. 7; Sunstein & Vermeule, 2009, p. 203). They are also linked inasmuch as they are both widely regarded as bad things. I defended rumors and rumor-mongers against their detractors in the last chapter. In this chapter I will defend conspiracy theories and conspiracy theorists against theirs.

Several authors have claimed that there are more conspiracy theories and more conspiracy theorists now than in the past, that "conspiracism" or "conspiracy thinking" is on the rise (Keeley, 2006, pp. 45–6; Wilson, 1998, pp. 1–2). Typically these authors say or imply that this situation is undesirable, and some have been moved to offer solutions to this so-called problem (Sunstein & Vermeule, 2009, p. 203). This chapter will argue that this is all a mistake. If anything, there are *fewer* conspiracy

What To Believe Now: Applying Epistemology to Contemporary Issues,
First Edition. David Coady.
© 2012 David Coady. Published 2012 by Blackwell Publishing Ltd.

theories and theorists now than in the past (*less* conspiracism and conspiracy thinking), and it is *this* situation that should be deplored. Furthermore this deplorable situation has at least partly been brought about by the contemporary fashion for castigating certain people as "conspiracy theorists" and dismissing their beliefs as "conspiracy theories," a fashion which appears to have been started by fellow-philosopher Sir Karl Popper. These expressions were not widely used before Popper. Popper used them pejoratively, and they have retained those pejorative connotations to this day.[2]

The contemporary treatment of those accused of being conspiracy theorists is an intellectual witch hunt. Although those identified as "conspiracy theorists" are not literally subjected to an *auto da fé*, they are routinely sneered at, condescended to, or ignored. Of course some of them may deserve to be criticized or ignored (maybe even condescended to or sneered at), but there is no more justification for criticizing, ignoring, condescending to, or sneering at, people *because* they are conspiracy theorists than there was for punishing people *because* they were witches. One can denounce a witch hunt without defending everyone who has been accused of being a witch.

To many, this analogy will seem far-fetched. It will be objected that while there are no real witches, there are real conspiracy theorists. In fact, neither part of this claim is straightforwardly true. It all depends on how you define "witch" and on how you define "conspiracy theorist." If a witch is understood to be a person with magical powers derived from a relationship with Satan, then it would be objectionable to be a witch, but no one ever was one. If, on the other hand, a witch is understood to be a follower of a pre-Christian matriarchal religion, then there really were witches (and still are), but it is (and always was) an unobjectionable thing to be. The expression "conspiracy theorist" works in a similar way. On some definitions, there is something wrong with being a conspiracy theorist, but no one (or hardly anyone) is a conspiracy theorist. On other definitions, there really are conspiracy theorists (perhaps a lot of them) but there is nothing wrong with being one.

A definition of the first kind is suggested by Popper's approach to the issue. Suppose we define "a conspiracy theorist" as someone who believes what Popper called "*the* Conspiracy Theory of Society" (Popper, 1962, p. 94; 1972, p. 123). This is the theory that *everything* that happens (or at least everything big and bad that happens) is due to a *successful* conspiracy, that is, that the big bad thing that happens is due to a secret plan to bring about exactly that big bad thing.[3] There is no need for us to consider Popper's arguments that the conspiracy theory of society is false. He is obviously right about this. What is not so clear is whether anyone has ever thought otherwise. Although Popper claims that the conspiracy theory of society is "very widespread" (Popper, 1972, p. 123), he offers no argument or evidence for this claim. Pigden seems to be right when he says that, so far from being very widespread, the conspiracy theory of society is "a thesis that no one believes" (Pigden, 2006b, p. 20). Even if there are people who believe it, the vast majority of those castigated as conspiracy theorists do not. For example, those who think that the Bush administration conspired to deceive the American public into believing that Saddam Hussein was involved with 9/11 typically do not believe that every big bad thing that happens is due to a conspiracy, let alone a conspiracy to bring about that very thing. For many of them suppose that the war in Iraq (the result, in part, of Bush's conspiracy) has led to a net decline in American power and prestige, which may or may not be a bad thing, but which is definitely not a bad thing that Bush conspired to bring about. The consequence was almost certainly the reverse of what he intended.

A definition of the second kind can be found in Pigden (2006a, p. 157). According to Pigden, a conspiracy theory is just a theory – true or false, rational or irrational, well-confirmed or otherwise – which explains some event or events by positing a conspiracy (not necessarily a successful one), and a conspiracy theorist is simply someone who subscribes to a conspiracy theory, understood in this way. Now there is clearly nothing wrong with being a conspiracy theorist in this sense. Indeed there would be something wrong with not being one. In order to avoid being a conspiracy theorist, in this sense, one would have to be almost completely misinformed or ignorant of both history and current affairs (not to mention a great deal of one's immediate environment). On Pigden's definition, so far from being nonexistent, conspiracy theorists are a dime a dozen. Indeed, most, if not all, of the self-proclaimed foes of conspiracy theory are conspiracy theorists in this sense. After all, many events are, and are widely known to be, due to conspiracies – coups, "disappearances," kidnappings, assassinations, terrorist attacks (in many cases), acts of torture, and a great deal of fraud, bribery, and corruption. These things do not happen (or at least do not happen very often) without secret plans and covert actions on the part of some group. Thus anyone who believes that there are such things as coups, "disappearances," kidnappings, assassinations, secret torture chambers, or fraud, bribery, and corruption is pretty much bound to be a conspiracy theorist, in this sense.

So far we have considered two conceptions of what it is to be a conspiracy theorist. On one of them, the property of being a conspiracy theorist is an unobjectionable one, which applies to (almost) everyone. On the other, it is an objectionable property, which applies to (almost) no one. In what follows I will consider attempts to find a middle way, that is, a conception of what it is to be a conspiracy theorist, which makes it an objectionable thing to be, and which applies to some people and not to others. In particular, I will look for a conception of what it is to be a conspiracy theorist which makes it objectionable to be a conspiracy theorist and which applies to the people who are pilloried as such, but *not* to those who pillory them. As we shall see, such conceptions are hard to come by.

I have said that almost everyone is a conspiracy theorist, in Pigden's sense. But there do seem to be some exceptions. There are, that is, people who appear to think that conspiracies never happen, that no one ever conspires to do anything, and hence that conspiracy theorists are mistaken in the same way flat earth theorists are mistaken. Conspiracy theorists, on this view, are people who believe in something which just does not exist. I think we can safely ignore this view. Even Popper is at pains to stress that conspiracies do occur (1962, p. 95; 1972, p. 342), and most of his followers will concede the point, at least when pushed. On the face of it, that should be the end of the matter. Since conspiracies happen, it can't be irrational to believe they happen. Hence, it can't be irrational to be a conspiracy theorist. Yet many people accept the premise but balk at the conclusion. They agree that people conspire but insist nonetheless that conspiracy theorists are irrational, or in some other way misguided. When challenged to explain what they mean by the expression "conspiracy theorist" and what exactly is supposed to be the matter with being one, they typically respond with "Of course there are conspiracies, but … ." Much of the rest of this chapter will be devoted to different ways of filling in the but-end of this sentence.

Conspiracies Don't Happen Often

Perhaps conspiracy theorists are people who fail to recognize how rarely conspiracies occur. Popper provides some support for this way of understanding who conspiracy theorists are and where they go wrong, when he claims that conspiracies are "not very frequent" (Popper, 1972, p. 342). But Popper is just wrong about this. Conspiracy is a common form of behavior throughout history and in all cultures, a point that has been established very effectively in a series of articles by Charles Pigden (2006a, 2006b, 2007). Prior to Popper no one appears to have thought otherwise. Indeed, Popper himself does not appear strongly committed to the view that conspiracies are rare, admitting elsewhere that conspiracies are "typical social phenomena" (1962, p. 95). In other words, they are not rare.

You might think that the question of whether conspiracies are rare depends a great deal on how we define the expression "conspiracy." But in fact it doesn't make much difference. So far, I've been following Popper in thinking of a conspiracy simply as a secret plan on the part of a group of people. But some people have rightly noted that not all such secret plans seem to count as conspiracies. Hence Charles Pigden has suggested that we should add the requirement that the secret plan must be "morally suspect" (Pigden 2006a, p. 157).[4] I myself have come to think that a slightly different tweaking of the definition is called for. Secrecy is not enough for a collective plan to constitute a conspiracy: active deception on the part of the conspirators is required as well. Another possibility is to look at the legal concept of conspiracy and insist that no plan should count as a conspiracy unless it is a plan to do something illegal. There is no need to consider these moves in detail or adjudicate between them here. All of them narrow the extension of the word "conspiracy" somewhat, but not enough to make conspiracies rare (still less nonexistent). Very often secret plans are secret *because* they are plans to do something morally suspect. Very often secret plans involve deception, *because* deception is the only way to preserve secrecy. Very often secret plans are plans to do something illegal, *because* secrecy is required in order not to get caught and punished. On all definitions of conspiracy that have been seriously proposed (at least that I am aware of) conspiracies are common.

Of course, terms like "common," "rare," and "typical" are relative. Conspiracies are rare compared to some things and common compared to others. Presumably some people think conspiracies are more common than in fact they are, but they don't seem to be the people most likely to be castigated as conspiracy theorists. Someone who believed in very few conspiracies, but believed that they are of great importance would be much more likely to attract the pejorative label "conspiracy theorist" than one who believed in more conspiracies, but considered them to be of little moment. This suggests another way of understanding what is supposed to be wrong with being a conspiracy theorist.

Conspiracies Tend to be Insignificant

Several authors have suggested that conspiracy theorists go wrong, not by overstating the frequency with which conspiracies occur, but by overstating their significance when they do occur. On this view, you can believe in as many conspiracies as you like, so long as you do not believe that they are particularly important. Again, Popper provides some support for this way of understanding who conspiracy theorists are, and what is wrong with being one. He claims that conspiracies do not "change the character of social life" and that, were they to cease "we would still be faced with fundamentally the same problems which have always faced us" (Popper, 1972, p. 342).

But Popper himself effectively admits that conspiracies can be important when he says that "Lenin's revolution, and especially Hitler's revolution and Hitler's war are, I think, exceptions. These were indeed conspiracies" (Popper, 1972, p. 125). With exceptions like these it's hard to put much faith in the rule. Just to be clear, "Lenin's revolution" was The October Revolution, which brought the Bolsheviks to power and created the Soviet Union; "Hitler's revolution" was the revolution which brought the Nazis to power in Germany, and "Hitler's war" was World War II (or at least the European theater of that war). All of these conspiracies have had an enormous impact on "the character of social life" in every country in the world ever since. And it's not as if the "exceptions" Popper mentions are the only ones. Those interested in the enormous impact conspiracies have had just on the twentieth century should consult Pigden (2006b, pp. 34–6). So it is simply not true that we would be faced with "fundamentally the same problems" without conspiracies.

Conspiracies Tend to Fail

Machiavelli once said that "experience demonstrates that there have been many conspiracies, but few have been concluded successfully" (Machiavelli, 1979/1532, p. 62). In a similar vein, Popper claimed

115

that few "conspiracies are ultimately successful. Conspirators rarely consummate their conspiracy" (Popper, 1962, p. 95). More recently, Daniel Pipes has run a similar line, claiming that "familiarity with the past shows that most conspiracies fail" (1997, p. 39). This suggests that the problem with conspiracy theorists is that they are people who postulate mainly successful conspiracies and that this is irrational. This objection is sometimes conflated with the previous one,[5] but the two objections should be distinguished. A successful conspiracy can be unimportant, and a failed conspiracy can be quite momentous. The failed conspiracy by Soviet generals against Gorbachev in 1991 brought about, or at least hastened, the break-up of the Soviet Union. Likewise the failed conspiracy by Richard Nixon and his associates to cover up a burglary at the Watergate Hotel led to his resignation. The collapse of the Soviet Union and the resignation of Richard Nixon are both, by any standards, momentous historical events.

The idea that conspiracies tend to fail is very widespread and seems to be what a lot of people are getting at when they object to conspiracy theories and conspiracy theorists. Conspiracy theories are often contrasted with cock-up theories, with the suggestion that the latter are always, or at least typically, preferable to the former.[6] But, popular though it is, this idea is wrong in two respects. First, conspiracies and cock-ups are not incompatible. A cock-up is a plan or endeavor which fails through incompetence (if I am not trying to do something, I can't cock it up). And since conspiracies are plans of a certain kind, it is perfectly possible to cock them up. Second, although conspiracies have been known to fail, there is no reason to think that they are more prone to failure than other kinds of human endeavor (such as starting a business, making oneself attractive to the opposite sex, or promoting growth in Third World countries). Indeed it's hard to see why people would continue to conspire if the historical record really shows that the activity tends to be pointless or counterproductive. Are conspirators particularly stupid? There seems no reason to think so.

In fact the historical record shows that conspiracies are quite often successful. The conspiracy to assassinate Julius Caesar was successful, as was the conspiracy to assassinate Abraham Lincoln. So too, the coup of Thermidor which struck down the terrorist regime of Robespierre, the 18th Brumaire of Napoleon Bonaparte, and the October Revolution of 1917. The history of the Byzantine Empire (as of Tsarist Russia) is punctuated with successful palace revolutions, most of them the products of conspiracy.

Perhaps the argument is that such conspiracies are not ultimately successful, since they often have consequences that are neither intended nor wanted by the conspirators. This may be the line Popper and others are running when they accuse conspiracy theorists of ignoring the unintended and/or unwanted consequences of social action. But the fact that conspiracies have unintended and/or unwanted consequences (from the point of view of the conspirators) does not entail that they are peculiarly prone to failure. For *most* (and perhaps all) human actions have unintended and/or unwanted consequences (from the point of view of the actors), but that surely does not entail that most (and perhaps all) human activity is doomed to failure. To suppose that it does would be to lose our grip on the distinction between failure and success.

Is there any reason to suppose that conspiracies are more likely to fail than other things people do? Well you might argue that since secrecy is essential to most definitions of conspiracy,[7] all the conspiracies I have mentioned failed, in as much as they are not secret (after all we know about them); these examples show that there are conspiracies, indeed that there are lots of them and that many of them are important, but they also show that conspiracies tend to fail because they tend to be exposed *in the end*. This seems to be Pete Mandik's reasoning when he denies that the belief that Al-Qaeda blew up the World Trade Center is a conspiracy theory on the grounds that it isn't a secret (Mandik, 2007, pp. 213–14).

The argument that conspiracies tend to fail because they always or usually end up being exposed is mistaken in two ways. First, there is no reason to believe the premise is true. Second, the conclusion does not follow from the premise.

Why accept the premise that conspiracies always or usually end up being exposed? The argument is that all the conspiracies *we know of* are no longer secret, therefore it is reasonable to conclude that conspiracies tend not to remain secret. This is closely parallel to an argument of Berkeley's that nothing exists without thought, because everything you can think of is (at the time in question) being thought of (Berkeley, 1965/1710, p. 75). In both cases there is a clear selection effect operating on the available data. I can't provide you with any examples of objects which are not being thought about, because the process of trying to find examples inevitably involves my thinking about them. Similarly, I can't provide you with any examples of conspiracies that are still completely secret, because if they were still completely secret (and I wasn't in on them), I wouldn't know about them. But this does not support the claim that there are no such conspiracies, or even the claim that there aren't very many of them.

Even if it were true that conspiracies tend not to remain secret, the conclusion that they tend to fail would not follow. To suppose that it would is to interpret the secrecy required for successful conspiracy in far too strict a way; in such a way in fact that a conspiracy will count as a failure if anyone other than the conspirators ever finds out about it. But conspirators (at least the ones we know about) typically have much more limited aims than that with respect to secrecy. They want to keep their activities secret from some people (usually the targets of the conspiracy and those who might sympathize with them) for some period of time (often only until the deed they are conspiring to do has been done). Indeed many conspiracies *need* to be widely publicized (once the deed is done) if the conspirators are to succeed in their long-range plans. This appears to be the case with the Al-Qaeda conspiracy to blow up the twin towers. The object of the exercise was not just to strike a blow against the Great Satan, but to publicly be seen to have done so. It was certainly the case with the conspiracy to kill Julius Caesar. Brutus and Cassius' plans were secret up to the point where they stabbed Caesar, after which they publicized the deed far and wide (Plutarch, 1999, pp. 356–7).

It is of course possible that there are conspiracies whose success requires permanent secrecy from everyone not involved in the conspiracy. But these are not the kind of conspiracies that those who are castigated as conspiracy theorists believe in. Certainly they don't believe in conspiracy theories of this kind that have been completely successful. They do not believe that the conspiracies they subscribe to have successfully been kept secret from everyone *including them*. To characterize their position in this way would be to suppose that they are straightforwardly inconsistent. And there is no reason (or at least I have never seen any reason) to suppose that even the most irrational of those who are castigated as conspiracy theorists make *this* mistake.

Governments and Government Agencies of Western Countries Don't Conspire Often, Successfully, or Significantly

Just believing in lots of significant and/or successful conspiracies is not usually *on its own* enough to get you accused of being a conspiracy theorist. A great deal depends on whom you attribute the conspiracies to.

No matter how many conspiracies you believe the North Korean regime is involved in, and no matter how important and successful you believe those conspiracies are, no one is likely to call you a conspiracy theorist, unless you also think that Western governments or Western government agencies are involved. So perhaps the error of conspiracy theorists is that they fail to recognize that neither Western governments nor their agents conspire, or that they rarely do, or that it doesn't much matter when they do, or that they rarely achieve their aims when they do.

The US is the most important Western government, and it is typically people's belief in conspiracies by American governments or American government agencies that leads them to be accused of being conspiracy theorists. So we will use the US as a case study. Robert Anton Wilson, who is a fairly typical and widely cited conspiracy baiter, begins his book *Everything Is Under Control: Conspiracies, Cults and Cover-ups* by citing a survey according to which 74 percent of Americans "believe that the U.S. government regularly engages in conspiratorial and clandestine operations." He says that this statistic is significant, because it means that most Americans "now believe what only embittered left-wing radicals believed a century ago" (Wilson, 1998, p. 1).[8] The rest of his book is premised on the assumption that his readers are among the 26 percent who don't believe their government is regularly conspiring and that no argument for this position is required. It is simply assumed that the majority of Americans have become susceptible to "strange" and "paranoid" conspiracy theories.

The statistic Wilson cites is disturbing, but not for the reason he thinks. It is an indictment of the American media and of the American educational system that 26 percent – over a quarter of its citizens – appear to be unaware that their government engages in conspiratorial and clandestine operations on a regular basis. They have obviously never heard of the CIA, or perhaps they think it is a fictional entity regularly used as a plot device on television. Certainly they cannot have read its mission statement, which describes its role as (among other things) "conducting covert action at the direction of the President."[9] What kind of covert action? Since it is covert, our knowledge is limited, but we do know it has included assassination and torture programs in the not too distant past, including the notorious Phoenix Program (Hersh, 1972). We also know that the CIA has played a covert role in the overthrow of several democratic governments, including the government of Iran in 1953 (Weiner, 2007, pp. 81–92), Greece in 1967 (Weiner, 2007, pp. 330–1), and Chile in 1973 (Weiner, 2007, pp. 306–16).

But it is not just the CIA. The 26 percent are presumably also unaware that their government lied to them about the so-called Gulf of Tonkin Incident in 1964, which was used as a pretext to escalate the war in Vietnam, or the fact that their government regularly lied to them about the strength of the enemy throughout that conflict (Ellsberg, 2002).

Moving right along (and skipping over the Menu bombings, Watergate, and the Iran-Contra affair), it is no longer a secret that the American government regularly kidnaps terrorism suspects and sends them abroad to be tortured (Thompson & Paglen, 2006). But although this is not a secret *now*, it is an operation that was originally planned and conducted in secret, since it contravenes national and international laws. Does "the U.S. government regularly engage in conspiratorial and clandestine operations"? No one familiar with US history could think otherwise.[10]

Conspiracy Theory and the Open Society

It is true, as I have argued elsewhere (Coady, 2006a, p. 10), that in open societies government conspiracies are likely to be both less common and less significant, and there is no question that the US and other Western countries are much more open than some other countries, such as North Korea. But this should not lead us to conclude that governments and government agencies of Western countries don't conspire often, successfully, or significantly, for three reasons. First, openness is a matter of degree. There is no such thing as a completely, or even highly, open society. Second, openness, such as it is, is not the exclusive province of the United States and other Western societies. Some non-Western societies seem to be more open than some Western societies.[11] Third, even in the most open of actually existing societies, conspiracy (including conspiracy by government) is common, important, and often successful.[12]

Cass Sunstein and Adrian Vermeule describe the United States, along with Britain and France, as open societies, and deride conspiracy theorists for being unaware of "the abundant evidence that in open societies government action does not usually remain secret for very long" (2009, pp. 208–9). What does this "abundant evidence" consist in? Sunstein and Vermeule cite two, once secret, facts which have been reported in the American media: first, that the Bush administration illegally spied on American citizens without court orders,[13] and second that, since September 11, the CIA has been torturing prisoners in secret "black sites."[14]

These examples hardly establish that government conspiracies in America and other putatively open societies don't remain secret very long. The article in the *New York Times*, which revealed the Bush administration's warrantless wire-tapping program, came out approximately four years after that program began. What is more, a careful reading of the article reveals that "after meeting with senior administration officials to hear their concerns, the newspaper delayed publication for a year." It has since emerged that the delay was considerably longer than that; the *New York Times* had the story before the 2004 presidential election.[15] So this is hardly evidence that secretive government action does not stay secret very long. On the contrary, it seems to have stayed secret for as long as the government wanted it to stay secret. Jane Mayer's revelation of a CIA torture program also came out long after, in fact almost six years after, that program began.

You might try arguing that at least these examples constitute evidence that, in open societies such as our own, government secrets will *eventually* be exposed. But these examples do not support even this, much more limited, claim. As we have seen, there is an inevitable selection effect operating on our available data about conspiracies. To argue that conspiracies in Western societies will eventually be exposed, because this or that conspiracy has been exposed, is like arguing, as some criminologists have, that there is a correlation between being a criminal and having a low IQ, based on the fact that prisoners tend to have low IQs. This data is inevitably drawn from a subset of criminals who may well be unrepresentative, the ones who get caught, that is, the unsuccessful ones. Similarly, to the extent that long-term secrecy is essential to the success of conspiracies, the ones we know about will tend to be the unsuccessful ones.[16] We have no reason to believe these are representative.

We have seen that, at least on some readings of what it is to be a conspiracy theorist, the more open one's society is the less one will be justified in being a conspiracy theorist. How can one tell how open one's society is? A range of factors may be taken into consideration. All else being equal, a society will be more open if it has little or no government censorship, if it has effective freedom of information legislation, if it has diversity of media ownership, if it has freedom of internet usage, if the public service is independent of the government and the branches of government are independent of one another, and if it is rarely in a state of war (since war is commonly used to justify closing a society's channels of communication).

One final factor merits particular attention. All else being equal, a society will be more open to the extent that "conspiracy theorist" and cognates, such as "conspiracist" are not used as terms of abuse. As we've seen, despite the bewildering variety of uses of these expressions, they are standardly used to deride those in Western countries who believe their governments are engaged in conspiracies (or important conspiracies or successful conspiracies, etc.). This usage serves to intimidate and silence such people, whether or not their beliefs are justified, and whether or not they are true. Hence this usage makes it less likely that government conspiracies will be exposed (or exposed in a timely manner), and more likely that the perpetrators will get away with it. So there is reason to think that pejorative uses of these expressions have the effect of making societies in which they occur less open. There is a sad irony in the fact that Popper, the author of *The Open Society and Its Enemies*, should have started a practice (the witch hunt against conspiracy theorists) which has made it less likely that conspiracies will be exposed, and so made it easier for conspiracy to thrive at the expense of openness.

My account of the different things people are getting at when they accuse others of being conspiracy theorists was not meant to be complete. Those interested in the variety of uses of the expressions "conspiracy theory" and "conspiracy theorist" should consult my two edited collections on the topic (Coady, 2006a, 2007a). But behind the heterogeneity of uses there is a clear common thread; a person who is accused of being a conspiracy theorist believes, or is interested in investigating, something which conflicts with a view that has achieved a certain status, that of being an officially sanctioned or orthodox view in his or her society. Indeed, the expression is sometimes used of such people, even when their so-called conspiracy theory does not involve a conspiracy (e.g., Coady 2006b, p. 125). Understood in this way, the relationship between conspiracy theories and officialdom is like the relationship between rumors and officialdom, with the difference that rumors are defined as merely lacking official endorsement, whereas conspiracy theories, on this way of understanding them, must actually contradict some official version of events. What if we accepted a definition of "conspiracy theory" along these lines? Would that justify adopting a dismissive attitude toward conspiracy theories? No. As we saw in the last chapter, to say that a version of events has official status should be seen as epistemically neutral. Hence to say that a conspiracy theory by definition contradicts an official version of events is to say nothing about whether it is true, or whether a person who believes it is justified in doing so. The expressions "conspiracy theory" and "conspiracy theorist" are the respectable modern equivalents of "heresy" and "heretic" respectively; these expressions serve to castigate and ridicule anyone who rejects or even questions orthodox or officially endorsed beliefs.

Conspiracy Baiting as Propaganda

The propagandistic nature of campaigns against conspiracy theories and conspiracy theorists is at least as evident as the propagandistic nature of campaigns against rumors and rumor-mongers. Both forms of propaganda serve to herd opinion, or at least "respectable opinion," within limits set by governments and other powerful institutions.

Cass R. Sunstein and Adrian Vermeule's "Conspiracy Theories: Causes and Cures," which was published in *The Journal of Political Philosophy*, is a particularly clear example of this. Sunstein and Vermeule tentatively define a conspiracy theory as *"an effort to explain some event or practice by reference to the machinations of powerful people, who attempt to conceal their role (at least until their aims are accomplished)"* (Sunstein & Vermeule, 2009, p. 205). They concede that some conspiracy theories are true (p. 206), and that some are justified (p. 207). Nonetheless, they propose to focus on the ones that are "false, harmful, and unjustified" (p. 204). Not only do they focus on such "bad conspiracy theories," they repeatedly refer to conspiracy theories as if we could simply assume that they have some or all of these undesirable characteristics. They claim, for example, that "conspiracy theories are a subset of the larger category of false beliefs" (p. 206), and that they are a product of "crippled epistemologies" (p. 224). Hence they not only ignore, but implicitly define out of existence, when it suits them, conspiracy theories that are true, beneficial, and/or justified. Talking about conspiracy theories as if we could just assume they are false, harmful, and unjustified, is, given their definition, tantamount to assuming that explanations which posit secretive behavior on the part of powerful people are false, harmful, and unjustified. We have already seen that not only some, but many, such explanations are both true and justified.

They may still, of course, be harmful. Sunstein and Vermeule are concerned that conspiracy theories can "have pernicious effects from the government's point of view, either by inducing unjustifiably widespread public skepticism about the government's assertions, or by dampening public mobilization and participation in government-led efforts, or both" (2009, p. 220). Is there a point of view, other than that of the government, which might be worth considering, such as that of the citizen? They do not say. Nor do they consider the possibility that widespread public skepticism about the government's assertions might be justified, or that the public might be right not to want to participate in government-led efforts (e.g., efforts to persecute minorities, or attack foreign countries without provocation).

Putting these concerns aside for the moment, what should the government do about the problem of people being unjustifiably skeptical about what it says and unjustifiably reluctant to do what it wants? You might have though that the solution lies in greater openness, honesty, and accountability on the part of government. Sunstein and Vermeule adopt a somewhat different approach. They say their "main policy claim" is that "government should engage in *cognitive infiltration of the groups that produce conspiracy theories*" (2009, p. 218). In this way, government will be able to "undermine the crippled epistemology of believers by planting doubts about the theories" (p. 219). Of course, government agents cannot be entirely open about their participation in such programs; hence Sunstein and Vermeule recommend that "government officials should participate anonymously or even with false identities" (p. 225). In other words, they recommend that government should engage in conspiracies[17] in order to undermine belief in conspiracy theories. Of course, there is a danger that the targets of these proposed government conspiracies will find out about them. Sunstein and Vermeule can hardly dismiss this possibility, since, as we saw, they claim that in open societies, such as the United States, "government action does not usually remain secret for very long" (pp. 208–9). If the targets of Sunstein and Vermeule's proposed conspiracies were to find out about them, they would then believe even more conspiracy theories[18] (albeit true ones) than they did before. This would of course be counterproductive, from government's point of view (which is the only point of view they consider). So what should the government do in these circumstances? It's not absolutely clear what Sunstein and Vermeule would recommend. They do say that "as a general rule, true accounts should not be undermined" (p. 206).

Nonetheless, they regard it as an "interesting question" whether "it is ever appropriate to undermine true conspiracy theories" (fn. 17).

There appears to be a glaring inconsistency between Sunstein and Vermeule's assurances that government can't get away with secrecy in open societies like ours, and their advocacy of government secrecy (and indeed deception). I assume they don't mean to suggest that the cognitive infiltration they recommend is doomed to failure. But mere inconsistency is the least of the worries raised by their paper. Shouldn't we be worried by the prospect of government officials secretively and deceptively manipulating public opinion? Shouldn't we be especially worried when someone like Sunstein, who, as we saw in the previous chapter, is himself an extremely powerful government official, recommends that government officials behave that way? Isn't it possible that government officials might try to undermine, not just false, unjustified, and harmful conspiracy theories, but also true, justified, and/or beneficial ones? Sunstein and Vermeule say that they "assume a well-motivated government that aims to eliminate conspiracy theories, or draw their poison, if and only if social welfare is improved by doing so" (2009, p. 219). But why should we assume government is "well-motivated" or that it will seek to improve "social welfare," rather than its own welfare? What reason can we have for abandoning the defining insight of liberal political thought, namely, that we can't just assume that governments are well-intentioned and will act in our interests rather than their own, especially when it comes to actions that are carried out in secret? All Sunstein and Vermeule have to say in defense of their assumption is that it is "a standard assumption in policy analysis" (p. 219). It is indeed a standard assumption of a certain kind of policy analysis, that known as "government propaganda".

So What Should be Done?

In looking at different ways of understanding what people are getting at when they accuse others of being conspiracy theorists, we have seen that the expression "conspiracy theorist" (like its close relative "conspiracy theory") is multiply ambiguous. What is more, reflection on each of the standard ways of understanding what it is to be a conspiracy theorist shows that there is nothing wrong with being one. In fact, in each case it is those who accuse others of being conspiracy theorists who are guilty of irrationality (or at least error). What should someone who recognizes this do about it?

The first and most obvious response would be to stop using the expressions, and to discourage others from using them as well. The goal would be to create a world in which the expressions "conspiracy theorist," "conspiracy theory," "conspiracism," and so on, would be recognized as products of an irrational and bigoted outlook. In this world, people would be as ashamed to dismiss a view on the grounds that it is a conspiracy theory, or a person on the grounds that he or she is a conspiracy theorist, as they would be to dismiss a view on the grounds that it is heretical, or a person on the grounds that he or she is a witch.

Of course, attempts to create such a world may not be successful. We can expect them to be resisted by those who find it easier to dismiss people and their views with sound bites than to argue with them or consider the evidence. An alternative strategy should therefore be considered, that of retaining the expression, but without the negative connotations. The words "witch" and "queer" have both come to be used quite widely in nonderogatory ways. In fact, these words have come to be embraced by many of the people who in the past would have been most likely to be maligned as witches or queers. Perhaps the expression "conspiracy theorist" could be transformed in a similar way. Along these lines, I have suggested (Coady, 2007b, 194–6) that it could reasonably be applied to people who have a particular interest in investigating and publicizing conspiracies (when they occur, who is responsible for them, and so on). This conception fits in well with the way we think of other kinds of theorists (e.g., number theorists) as people who have an interest in a particular field of research, rather than as people with particular kinds of beliefs. Conspiracy theorists, in this sense, serve a vitally important social function. In fact, being a conspiracy theorist, in this sense, is an important aspect of the job description of political journalists.[19]

Those who resist either of the strategies I have suggested so far (getting rid of the expression "conspiracy theorist," or retaining it without the negative connotations) will point out quite rightly that some theories which are criticized as conspiracy theories and some people who are criticized as conspiracy theorists deserve to be criticized. We've seen that conspiracies are common, but some people presumably think they're more common than in fact they are. We have seen that conspiracies often succeed, but some people probably think they succeed more often than in fact they do. We've seen that conspiracies are important, but some people may think that they're more important than in fact they are. Finally, we've seen that conspiracies by governments and government agencies of Western countries, such as the United States, are common, often successful, and often important. But some people almost certainly think they are more common, successful, and/or important than in fact they are.

All these people are making errors, and some of these errors have been arrived at irrationally. What is more, some people sometimes characterize some of these errors as "conspiracy theories" and the people who are most prone to irrationally making these errors as "conspiracy theorists." But this use of nomenclature is extremely misleading. In the first place, we are not talking about a single form of irrationality or error here, but several, and it can only promote confusion to conflate them. In the second place, each of these forms of irrationality or error has an opposite, that is, the irrationality or error of believing that conspiracies are rare, the irrationality or error of believing that conspiracies rarely succeed, the irrationally or error of thinking that conspiracies are unimportant, and so on. We have seen in each case that it is the latter form of irrationality or error that is most widespread and most troubling. Hence it seems that, at least as long as the witch hunt against conspiracy theorists goes on, we need to popularize pejorative expressions to denote those who, in various ways, irrationally dismiss evidence of conspiracy (or evidence of its importance, or evidence of its success, and so on).

To that end, I have suggested (Coady, 2007b, pp. 196–7) popularizing the expression "coincidence theorist," to denote those who, like Hume, are skeptical about inferences "beyond the present testimony of our senses or the records of our memory" (Hume, 1966/1748, p. 26), but who, unlike Hume, do not confine their skepticism to theoretical philosophy. Coincidence theorists are people who fail, as it were, to connect the dots; who fail to see any significance in even the most striking correlations. To give you a sense of the influence of coincidence theory on our political culture, consider the theory that terror alerts in the United States were manipulated for domestic political advantage by the Bush administration. This theory got a lot of publicity when the early Democratic Party front-runner for the 2004 presidential election, Howard Dean, publicly suggested that it might be true. He was immediately denounced as a (you guessed it) "bizarre conspiracy theorist" by President Bush's campaign spokesman Terry Holt.[20] This way of dismissing Dean and those who agreed with him was immediately picked up, amplified, and repeated uncritically by a variety of voices in the media. As a result, there was no public debate (in the conventional media at least) during that election campaign about whether this conspiracy theory was in fact true. Instead there was a debate about how much the Democratic Party's chances in the election would be hurt by conspiracy theorists like Dean. More than one journalist called on John Kerry, the party's eventual nominee, to denounce Dean's conspiracy theory, which he dutifully did.[21]

Now we know that Dean's conspiracy theory was true. Tom Ridge, former Homeland Security Secretary, has admitted that the Bush administration manipulated the system for domestic political advantage.[22] Pointing to cases like this in which those who posited a conspiracy have been proven right and the coincidence theorists who sneered at them have been proven wrong may go some way to providing some much needed balance to our public debates. But it is a frustrating business. The conventional media silence that has followed Ridge's admission has been almost deafening. One of the very few journalists in the conventional media to make any reference to it at all, Marc Ambinder has said that although journalists, including himself, "were very skeptical when anti-Bush liberals insisted that what Ridge now says is true, was true. We were wrong."[23] But despite admitting that his skepticism and that of his colleagues was factually mistaken, he nonetheless insists that it was warranted, and that those who thought otherwise were unwarranted in their suspicions. The evidence on which this particular conspiracy theory was based before Ridge's confession (for example, the number of occasions bad political news for the Bush administration was followed by a raising of the terror alert, and the regularity with which this in turn was followed by improved Republican polling) does not count. It can all safely be dismissed as coincidence. It appears that on Ambinder's view, conspiracy theories should not be believed, or even investigated, until the conspirators themselves confess. Conspiracy baiters often accuse those they castigate as conspiracy theorists for believing that "There is no such thing as a coincidence" and they are of course right that there is such a thing as being too willing to postulate what Hume called "secret powers" (1966/1748, p. 33) behind observed phenomena. But there is also such a thing as being too reluctant to make inferences beyond what we immediately perceive. Popularizing the expression "coincidence theorist" to denote people who make this error would go some way toward promoting rational public debate.

Coincidence theorists have an irrational tendency to reject clear evidence of conspiracy, but not everyone so inclined is a coincidence theorist. Some people, particularly on the Left, have an irrational tendency to reject clear evidence of conspiracy for quite different reasons. I call them "institutional theorists."[24] A typical example of institutional theory at work can be found in the preface to *Manufacturing Consent*, where Edward S. Herman and Noam Chomsky, anticipating the "accusation" that they are conspiracy theorists, respond pre-emptively with the claim that they "do not offer any kind of 'conspiracy' hypothesis to explain mass-media performance." Instead, they use "a propaganda model," which seeks to explain mass-media performance in impersonal institutional terms, and as "largely an outcome of market forces" (Herman & Chomsky, 1989, p. xii).[25]

The main problem with this line of thought is that impersonal explanations in terms of institutions and market forces are not inconsistent with conspiratorial explanations. Many institutions owe their existence, at least in part, to conspiracies (think of the United States government's debt to the conspiratorial activities of the founding fathers) and many institutions themselves regularly conspire. Indeed, many institutions do little but conspire (think of the CIA or the KGB). What is more, market forces are not inconsistent with conspiracy. Indeed, as Adam Smith recognized, market forces frequently lead to conspiracy.[26] More generally, institutions and impersonal social forces are not disembodied or abstract entities. They are the result, although not always the intended result, of a lot of intentional activity, much of which is conspiratorial. So an explanation can be, and often is, both conspiratorial and institutional.

At the root of the institutional theorists' critique of conspiracy theorists is a concern not to offer excessively easy solutions to social problems. The worry is that conspiracy theorists encourage the idea that the road to societal improvement consists in the removal of bad people from positions of power, while ignoring the underlying structures that are the real cause of most of our problems (problems which may well include the presence of bad people in positions of power).

While there is certainly something to this concern, the alternative strategy of concentrating on systematic or institutional change comes with its own dangers. First, it can be unrealistic, at least in the short term where most of us live our lives. Second, as history has often demonstrated, the new institutions may be worse than the ones they replaced.

The debate between conspiracy theorists and institutional theorists is reminiscent of the debate George Orwell discussed in his essay on Charles Dickens between "moralists" and "revolutionaries":

> The moralist and the revolutionary are constantly undermining one another. Marx exploded a hundred tons of dynamite beneath the moralist position, and we are still living in the echo of that tremendous crash. But already, somewhere or other, the sappers are at work and fresh dynamite is being tamped in place to blow Marx at the moon. Then Marx, or somebody like him, will come back with yet more dynamite, and so the process continues, to an end we cannot yet foresee. The central problem – how to prevent power from being abused – remains unsolved. Dickens, who had not the vision to see that private property is an obstructive nuisance, had the vision to see that "If men would behave decently the world would be decent" is not such a platitude as it sounds. (Orwell, 1961, p. 48)

We cannot stop power from being abused just by investigating and exposing conspiracies. But we also cannot stop power from being abused if we ignore the fact that much of that abuse is, and probably always will be, conspiratorial.

Conclusion

It has sometimes been suggested that conspiracy theories should be dismissed, because they are "just theories." On this view, conspiracy theories are epistemically suspect because theories are epistemically suspect; by definition one cannot be justified in believing them and one cannot know that they are true. There is no doubt that the word "theory" is sometimes used in a dismissive way, according to which theories are contrasted with facts. On this usage "theory" is roughly synonymous with "speculative hypothesis," but this doesn't seem to be what people who dismiss conspiracy theories mean by the word "theory." If it were, their objection would have nothing to do with conspiracies, and there would be no need to mention them. What is more, they would presumably adopt equally dismissive attitudes to other kinds of theories, such as scientific theories. Typically they don't. Several authors have claimed that intellectuals are particularly likely to be dismissive of conspiracy theories (Clarke, 2006, p. 77; Levy, 2007b, p. 181; Räikkä, 2009, p. 197).

But intellectuals are not likely to be dismissive of theories just for being theories, nor think of theories as things which are by definition unjustified or as things which cannot be known to be true. On the contrary, they typically think of "theory" as an epistemically neutral term, and think that we are justified in believing some of them and that we can know that some of them are true. In this sense, theories are not contrasted with facts, because some theories are facts.

A standard ploy on the part of those who deride conspiracy theories and theorists is to pick a conspiracy theory, argue that it is false and/or that the conspiracy theorists who believe it are irrational or in some other way misguided, and conclude that what is true of this conspiracy theory and these conspiracy theorists is true of conspiracy theories and theorists in general. This is obviously a fallacious form of argument. What needs to be shown is not that there are conspiracy theories and theorists with certain undesirable characteristics, but that there is a connection between being a conspiracy theory or theorist and these undesirable characteristics. What needs to be shown, in other words, is that the theories or theorists have the undesirable characteristics *because* they are conspiracy theories or theorists.

Jill LeBlanc (1998, pp. 192–4), for example, argues (in a critical thinking text book of all things) that people who believe that the United States government is conspiring to keep the public unaware of contact with alien species at Roswell, New Mexico, are committing certain identifiable reasoning fallacies. Whether or not she is right about this, she is certainly wrong when she goes on to assert without argument that these fallacies are characteristic of conspiracy theorists. This is no different from arguing that a certain foreigner is irrational and concluding from this that irrationality is characteristic of foreigners. In a similar way, Steve Clarke (2007) argues against the "controlled demolition theory" of the collapse of the World Trade Center on September 11, and simply assumes that the flaws of this particular conspiracy theory are characteristic of conspiracy theories in general. This is like assuming that the flaws of phlogiston theory (for example the fact that it is false) are characteristic of scientific theories in general.

The invalidity of this species of reasoning in the case of theories about the collapse of the World Trade Center should be particularly evident, because all theories of this event are inevitably conspiracy theories, at least on most definitions of "conspiracy theory," including Clarke's.

After all, the World Trade Center clearly collapsed because of some conspiracy or the other. As Pigden has noted, it's hard to imagine what it would be like not to believe a conspiracy theory in this case:

> you would have to suppose that the perpetrators assembled in the planes quite by chance and that, on a sudden, by coincidence, it struck them all as a neat idea to hijack the planes and ram them into the Twin Towers, the Whitehouse and the Pentagon, with the aid of other perpetrators who, presumably, they had never met before. (Pigden, 2006a, p. 158)

When all accounts of an event are conspiracy theories, why should we assume that false and unjustified ones are characteristic of the kind, rather than (say) true and justified ones?

Of course, many people will be reluctant to describe the theory which Clarke calls "the Al Qaeda Theory" as a conspiracy theory. But it's not at all clear that they can justify their reluctance. They cannot justify it on the grounds that this so-called theory is a fact rather than a theory, for, as we have seen, being a theory is compatible with being a fact. They could try justifying their reluctance by pointing out that the Al Qaeda Theory has official status, and stipulating that this means it cannot be a conspiracy theory. But, whatever you think of this semantic move, it doesn't give us a reason for preferring the Al Qaeda theory to the controlled demolition theory. As we have seen, to say that a theory contradicts an official version of events is to say nothing about whether it is true, or whether it should be believed. I happen to think that Clarke makes a good case against controlled demolition theory and those who believe it. But the case has nothing to do with it being a conspiracy theory or them being conspiracy theorists. They are not wrong because they believe in the existence of conspiracies, or lots of conspiracies, or important or successful conspiracies, or because they believe in conspiracies by the United States government or its agents, or because they believe something which contradicts an official version of events. They are wrong, because they believe in something (something which in this case just happens to be a conspiracy), which is not supported by the available evidence.

I am not alone in defending conspiracy theories.[27] However, some authors who present themselves as defenders of conspiracy theories have internalized some of the presuppositions of the conspiracy baiters. I will conclude with a discussion of how my position differs from theirs.

Lee Basham defends conspiracy theories against many criticisms, but he also ends up rejecting conspiracy theories, albeit on pragmatic, rather than epistemic, grounds:

> A more solid ground for the rejection of conspiracy theories is simply pragmatic. *There is nothing you can do.* While it would be speculative (but reasonable) to conclude that this is why many people dismiss conspiracy theory, it is a considerable reason why we *should.* (Basham, 2006a, p. 74)

In another article, Basham appeals to "the 'get a life' principle" (2006b, p. 104) in support of this position. But Basham surely cannot mean to dismiss *all* conspiracy theories on these grounds. There are often things we can do about conspiracies (depending to some extent of course on who "we" are). For example, we may be able to expose one; we may, that is, be able to persuade others that a true conspiracy theory is true. This is something good investigative journalists do for a living. But it is also something all concerned citizens should be prepared to do in cases of heinous conspiracies that they have good reason to believe in.

It is possible that Basham's pragmatic rejection of conspiracy theories is only meant to apply to the most extreme imaginable conspiracy theories, those that postulate what he calls "malevolent global conspiracies" (Basham, 2006b). These conspiracy theories postulate conspirators who are so powerful that it is impossible for anyone who is not a co-conspirator to know there is a conspiracy. Now Basham is certainly right that there is nothing one could do about malevolent global conspiracies, understood in this way. You can't foil conspiracies if you can't know they exist. Conspiracy theories of this kind are a form of radical skeptical hypothesis, like the evil demon and brain-in-a-vat hypotheses that philosophers have been grappling with for centuries. Whatever you think of these hypotheses, they are not conspiracy theories as we know them. The conspirators of actual conspiracy theories, justified and unjustified, true and false, are not omnipotent. Their conspiracies can be seen through (that is what the conspiracy theorists believe themselves to have done), and thwarted (that is often what the conspiracy theorists hope to do). Hence our impotence in the face of Basham's malevolent global conspiracies cannot be the reason many people reject conspiracy theories, because few people have heard of any such conspiracies. Even the examples of conspiracy theories which Basham uses to illustrate his argument do not postulate malevolent global conspiracies in the required sense. For example, Basham asks us to imagine that we are told that we are told that a group of Freemasons, or the Council of Foreign Relations, is secretly ruling the planet. The conspirators of these theories are not omnipotent beings, but flesh-and-blood humans, and there would inevitably be limits to their ability to keep their activities secret in the face of determined investigation. Most of the readers of this book either have, or could easily find, evidence that these theories are false.

Juha Räikkä also defends conspiracy theories, or at least a class of conspiracy theories he calls "political conspiracy theories," against a variety of criticisms, and concludes that "political conspiracy theories may not be much weaker than standard non-conspiratorial explanations of political events" (Räikkä, 2009, p. 198). But this "defense" of political conspiracy theories wrongly presupposes that political conspiracy theories are weaker (albeit not necessarily by much) than their rivals. As we have seen, political conspiracy theories, like other conspiracy theories, are often much stronger than their nonconspiratorial rivals; indeed their nonconspiratorial rivals are often obviously false, while they are obviously true. It's not clear to me what Räikkä means by describing the rivals to political conspiracy theories as "standard," but I suspect he means something like "official." It is quite common to contrast conspiracy theories with their official nonconspiratorial rivals, but, as we have seen, the official version of events can be just as conspiratorial as its rivals (indeed it can be more so). When this is the case, it is the unofficial explanation that will inevitably attract the label "conspiracy theory," with all its undeserved negative connotations.

The association between conspiracy theorizing and irrationality is so deeply entrenched in our culture that when people hear that I defend conspiracy theorists and theories they often assume that I must be defending irrationality. I am not. I am defending conspiracy theorists and theories against accusations of irrationality (along with a variety of other accusations). Unfortunately, some would-be defenders of conspiracy theorizing have embraced a form of irrationalism. This is evident in the following passage from an academic collection on conspiracy theories:

> these authors treat conspiracy ideas, near and far, as discourses that construct truths in contradistinction to the (also constructed) truths of discourses of transparency. Although recognizing that those making the transparency argument often hold considerably more power than

those left to suspect these claims the authors level the epistemological playing field between these truth-asserting endeavors. (West & Sanders, 2003, p. 15)[28]

I also want to "level the epistemological playing field." But it is misguided to think that the way to do this is by adopting the relativist position that conflicting social explanations are "constructed truths," equally valid for different communities of believers. If a conspiracy theory contradicts another theory, then at least one of the two theories is false. Nothing can be said *a priori* about which it is. The only way to find out is by listening to arguments and examining evidence.

Notes

1 This chapter began as a collaborative project with Charles Pigden. We had intended to write a joint paper which for various reasons never came to fruition. My thanks to Dr Pigden for his permission to incorporate many of his thoughts and words into this chapter. I am, of course, responsible for any errors.

2 John Ayto (1999, p. 15) cites a use of the expression "conspiracy theory" from 1909. It appears that it did not, at that time, have negative connotations. Apart from this single example, I have been unable to find any uses of the expression which predate Popper.

3 I thank Charles Pigden for this pithy and accurate way of characterizing the conspiracy theory of society.

4 On Pigden's account something can be morally suspect without actually being immoral.

5 Pipes, for example, does not clearly distinguish these objections.

6 Bernard Ingham, Chief Press Secretary to Mrs Thatcher, is the classical source for this contrast: "Many journalists have fallen for the conspiracy theory of government. I do assure you that they would produce more accurate work if they adhered to the cock-up theory" (quoted in the *Brisbane Times*, September 1, 1999).

7 The *Oxford English Dictionary* lists an archaic usage, which makes no reference to secrecy. According to it, a conspiracy is simply a "union or combination (of persons or things) for one end or purpose."

8 I doubt whether Wilson is right that a century ago only "embittered left-wing radicals" believed that their government was engaged in regular conspiratorial and covert operations. But if he is right and the majority did have more faith then that their government was open and above-board, then the majority was wrong and the embittered left-wing radicals were right.

9   https://www.cia.gov/about-cia/cia-vision-mission-values/index.html. Accessed December 11, 2010.

10 I do not mean to imply that the US is unique or even unusual in this way.

11 The 2010 Press Freedom Index, compiled by Reporters Without Borders, which ranks countries on the basis of their respect for freedom of the press, rates the United States 20th, behind Estonia, Japan, Lithuania, and Malta. France is ranked 44th, well behind Namibia, Ghana, Mali, and many other non-Western countries.

12 I will not address the question of whether a completely open society in which we could be sure governments could not get away with conspiring would be desirable, since we can be sure that no actual society is or ever will be that open.

13 James Risen and Eric Lichtblau, "Bush lets U.S. spy on callers without courts," *New York Times*, December 16, 2005, p. A1.

14 Jane Mayer, "The black sites: a rare look inside the C.I.A.'s secret interrogation program," *New Yorker*, August 13, 2007, p. 46.

15 http://www.salon.com/news/politics/war_room/2006/08/14/times. Accessed December 11, 2010.

16 I have made a closely related point before (Coady, 2006a, p. 5).

17 Sunstein and Vermeule's proposals constitute conspiracies on any of the definitions considered so far, and any definition that I have ever come across. The cognitive infiltration they recommend not only involves secrecy and deception, it is obviously "morally suspect," to put it very mildly, since it involves dishonestly manipulating people's opinions. What is more, it appears to be illegal, under statutes which prohibit the government from engaging in "covert propaganda" which is defined as "information which originates from the government but is unattributed and made to appear as though it came from a third party." See http://www.prwatch.org/node/7261. Accessed December 11, 2010.

18 To believe that the government is engaged in secretive and deceptive cognitive infiltration is to believe a conspiracy theory, on Sunstein and Vermeule's own definition and also on every other definition that I'm familiar with.

19 This is meant as a normative claim. Too often political journalists do not see their role this way. I will have more to say about the role of political journalism in the next chapter.

20 http://swampland.blogs.time.com/2009/08/20/color-coded-con-job/a Accessed December 11, 2010.

21 http://www.cbsnews.com/stories/2004/08/02/politics/main633561.shtml. Accessed December 11, 2010.

22 http://politics.usnews.com/news/blogs/washington-whispers/2009/08/19/tom-ridge-on-national-security-after-911.html. Accessed December 11, 2010.

23 http://www.theatlantic.com/politics/archive/2009/08/dont-cry-for-
    tom-ridge/23574. Accessed December 11, 2010.
24 This is a deliberate echo of the concept of "institutional analysis," which is
    often explicitly contrasted with "conspiracy theory." Institutional analysis
    of course has positive connotations, at least among those who practice it.
25 Despite their attempts to assure their readers, many were not convinced.
    Nicholas Lemann in a review in *The New Republic* insisted that "*Manu-
    facturing Consent* really is a conspiracy theory" (Lemann, 1989, p. 36). The
    truth is that *Manufacturing Consent* does offer numerous "conspiracy
    hypotheses" (many of which are very plausible and some of which are
    obviously true). However, it is not itself a conspiracy theory.
26 "People of the same trade seldom meet together, even for merriment and
    diversion, but the conversation ends in a conspiracy against the public"
    (Smith, 1910/1776, Book I, Chapter X).
27 Charles Pigden is a particularly good ally in this campaign.
28 Jodi Dean (1998) seems to adopt a similar position.

6

The Blogosphere and the Conventional Media

"Freedom of the press is guaranteed only to those who own one."
(Abbott Joseph Liebling)

In this chapter, I will defend bloggers and the blogosphere in much the same way that I defended conspiracy theorists and theories in Chapter 5, and rumor-mongers and rumors in Chapter 4. With the notable exception of Alvin Goldman (2008), this topic has been almost completely ignored by epistemologists. Although I will be criticizing Goldman's approach in some detail in this chapter, I will try to do more than merely respond to one person's argument. As usual, Goldman has identified a vitally important and philosophically neglected issue, and discussed it with clarity and intelligence. His errors are important, not only because of his influence in academic philosophy, but because he gives a particularly clear voice to a set of arguments which are widely accepted, and which are particularly popular in the conventional media.

Goldman claims that declining newspaper readership in the United States, as a result of the growing influence of the internet, is a sign that "the conventional media" has less influence than it once did.[1] He sees this as cause for concern, and worries that it is a "bad sign for the

What To Believe Now: Applying Epistemology to Contemporary Issues,
First Edition. David Coady.
© 2012 David Coady. Published 2012 by Blackwell Publishing Ltd.

epistemic prospects of the voting public" (2008, p. 113). Although he initially sets up a contrast between the internet and the conventional media, the substantive content of his article (as well as its title) make it clear that the contrast he's really interested in is between one particular application of the internet, "namely blogging and its associated realm, the blogosphere" (p. 115), and the conventional media. This is just as well, because the putative contrast between the internet and the conventional media is really no contrast at all. After all, many people consume what are by most standards conventional news sources, such as the BBC, CNN, or the *New York Times*, on the internet. Indeed, it could be argued that declining newspaper readership is not symptomatic of a decline in the influence of the conventional media at all, but merely a sign that more and more people are accessing conventional news sources on the internet. On this view, the conventional media is simply embracing a new technology, just as it once embraced radio and television.

A great deal will depend of course on how we define the terms "blogosphere" and "conventional media." Although Goldman doesn't explicitly define either of these terms, his understanding of the contrast emerges in the course of his critique of the blogosphere.

Before we look at the detail of that critique, however, we should note some restrictions on its scope. First, it is restricted to epistemic considerations. Goldman is not engaged in an *all-things-considered* evaluation of the blogosphere. Rather, he is evaluating it specifically as a source of knowledge, where knowledge is understood in the purely *veritistic* way we have come to associate with him, that is, as nothing more than true belief. Goldman holds that knowledge, understood in this way (at least when it is on a topic of interest), is intrinsically valuable (e.g., Goldman, 1999b, p. 87), but in his critique of the blogosphere he concentrates on its instrumental value, its value as a way of helping voters identify the candidates or options that are *right for them*. Goldman endorses a variant of epistemic democracy, which we discussed in Chapter 3. On Goldman's version of epistemic democracy, outcomes are characterized as right for individual voters rather than right *simpliciter*. Hence democracy is thought of as a way of achieving outcomes that are right for the majority of voters, rather than as a way of achieving outcomes that are right for the community as a whole, and knowledge, in this context, is treated as a means to that end. I have already criticized some aspects of Goldman's approach to democratic theory in Chapter 3, but I certainly agree with him about the importance of knowledge (i.e., true belief) to democracy and specifically about the importance of voters being suitably well-informed. Because democracy is a political concept, it will be appropriate for us to restrict our discussion, in most of what follows, to evaluating the blogosphere as a source of knowledge (i.e., true belief) about political issues.

Filtering

Goldman characterizes the blogosphere as "unfiltered."[2] Filtering involves "a gatekeeper," that is, a third person, in addition to a prospective sender and a prospective receiver of certain messages, who has the power to select which proffered messages are sent via a certain channel of communication and which are not (Goldman, 2008, p. 116). Goldman notes that long before the internet there were unfiltered mediums, such as the postal service or telegraph wires, but that these were typically only able to reach small audiences. The internet has changed all that, allowing unfiltered messages, and especially unfiltered political messages, to reach almost anyone in the world with access to a computer. Later on, we will see that this characterization of messages on the internet is not quite accurate. But for now I will proceed as if it were accurate, because it contains an element of truth, and because it is central to the rhetoric of both defenders and critics of the blogosphere.

Richard Posner (2005) has claimed that the development of this unfiltered medium is a good thing, on the grounds that filtering is a form of censorship and hence an infringement of free speech. Goldman responds with a defense of filtering which appeals to two examples of it which don't seem to constitute censorship and which don't seem to violate anyone's right to free speech. First, he notes that conventional scientific journals engage in a form of filtering when they submit proffered articles to the process of peer review, and says that "nobody considers the process of peer review to be 'censorship'. Nor does anyone, to my knowledge, consider it an 'infringement' of speech" (2008, p. 116). Goldman's second example of "good filtering" is that employed in the common-law court system. In this system the judge acts as a gatekeeper, determining who may speak and which messages the jury will be allowed to hear during a trial. Goldman says that this is "a massive amount of filtering. But nobody describes such filtering as 'censorship', nor is it generally called an 'infringement' of speech" (p. 116).

Of course, Goldman is right that the filtering practices of scientific journals and the common-law court system are rarely criticized on these grounds. But it is not immediately obvious what this has to do with the epistemic issues that are Goldman's professed concern. As we have seen, Goldman's stated concern is not with whether the filtering practices of the conventional media constitute censorship or an infringement of free speech, nor whether they are good, all things considered, but whether they are an epistemic good.

The real point of these analogies becomes clear when he goes on to say that the filtering practices of scientific journals and the common-law system "are commonly rationalized in terms of (something like) helping the relevant audience determine the truth" (p. 116). His argument then is that just as we regard certain scientific and legal filtering practices as desirable, insofar as they promote true belief, we should have the same attitude to the filtering practices of the conventional media. Understood in this way, the question of whether any or all of these filtering practices constitute a form of censorship or an infringement of free speech is beside the point.

Now, it seems correct (or at least I will assume that it is correct for the purposes of this chapter) that, despite some well-documented failures,[3] the filtering practices of scientific journals and the common-law court system are reasonably good, in the sense that we are epistemically better off with them than we would be with none at all (which is not to say that we couldn't have epistemically better filtering practices in both cases). In general, it should be conceded that filtering can be beneficial and specifically that it can be epistemically beneficial. The question remains open, however, whether the filtering practices of the conventional media are epistemically beneficial.

This is, to a large extent, an empirical issue. It is striking therefore that Goldman does not refer to any empirical work on media performance. Such work is clearly relevant. Goldman is not claiming (or at least should not be claiming) that the epistemic benefits of filtering can be established *a priori* or that filtering is *in itself* epistemically beneficial, no matter who is doing it or why. I am sure he would not claim, for example, that the state-run media of Iran, Saudi Arabia, or China have epistemically beneficial filtering practices, nor, I am sure, would he deny that blogging has greatly improved the veritistic quality of the beliefs of many citizens of those countries.[4] Inevitably empirical data is relevant. I will concentrate on data from the United States and Britain, partly because these countries are likely to be of particular interest to readers of this book,[5] but mostly because arguments for filtering seem particularly strong in these countries, because of the relatively open nature of their societies (see Chapter 5) and the existence of vigorous debates about media performance within them. If conventional media filtering does not have the epistemic benefits Goldman claims in the United States or Britain, it is unlikely to have them anywhere.

Goldman's analogies between the filtering of the conventional media and the filtering of scientific journals and the common-law court system are both illuminating, though not in the way he intends. In both cases, they reveal epistemic failings on the part of the conventional media that are being actively addressed in the blogosphere.

Journalism as a Profession

Goldman supports his analogy between the filtering of scientific journals and the filtering of the conventional media by characterizing the gatekeepers of both as professionals. "Presumably" he says, "the advantage of having the news delivered by dedicated, well-trained professionals in a rigorous journalistic enterprise is that the filtering performed before dissemination generates a high level of reliability among stories actually reported" (2008, p. 118). It is a common complaint within the conventional media that the blogosphere is undermining journalistic *professionalism*. I will argue that, although the blogosphere is undermining journalistic professionalism, concerns that this is harming the epistemic prospects of the voting public are overblown. If anything, the voting public is benefiting epistemically from this development.

The term "professional" is ambiguous. There is a sense in which anyone who is paid to do something is a professional. That is the sense in which being a professional is contrasted with being an amateur.[6] Conventional journalists are paid for what they do, whereas many bloggers are not.[7] Does this give us a reason to suppose that the reports of conventional journalists will have "high levels of reliability" compared to those of bloggers? There seem to be two arguments to this effect, which are more or less implicit in Goldman's article.

The first is that because conventional journalists don't have to earn a living doing something else, they have more time to thoroughly research their stories. This is typically true, but the lack of time available for research by individual bloggers is more than made up for by the number of bloggers engaged in research. The total amount of time devoted to researching stories in the blogosphere is likely to be much greater than the total amount of time devoted to researching stories in the conventional media. Furthermore, the speed with which bloggers can correct errors decreases the likelihood that their readers' epistemic states will be adversely affected by any errors. Here is Richard Posner on the subject:

> The blogosphere as a whole has a better error-correction machinery than the conventional media do. The rapidity with which vast masses of information are pooled and sifted leaves the conventional media in the dust. Not only are there millions of blogs, and thousand of bloggers who specialize, but, what is more, readers post comments that augment the blogs, and the information in those comments, as in the blogs themselves, zips around blogland at the speed of electronic transmission. (Posner, 2005, pp. 10–11)

The speed with which errors can often be corrected, and the number of people willing to work on such corrections, would appear to be good news for the epistemic prospects of the voting public.

The second argument that paid journalists will tend to be more reliable than unpaid journalists claims that the former have an incentive to be reliable that the latter lack. Paid journalists, it is argued, face the prospect of getting sacked if they get it wrong, and being retained and promoted if they get it right. Unpaid bloggers, by contrast, have no such incentives. This argument is very weak. The history of pamphleteering and citizen journalism shows that the desire to seek out and write the truth about politics has never been confined to those who are paid to do it.

If payment provides journalists with an incentive for seeking truth and avoiding error, it does so indirectly. The *direct* incentive payment gives journalists is the incentive to please their employer. Hence whether payment produces epistemic benefits depends on the nature of the employer and the incentives faced by that employer. It is true of course that employers in the conventional media will be motivated by (among other things) the desire to attract and retain an audience, and that the reporting of falsehoods or the failure to report truths *can* undermine that goal.[8] But bloggers are also motivated by the desire to attract and retain an audience, though some critics of the blogosphere don't seem to recognize this fact (e.g., Figdor, 2010, p. 160). If bloggers did not want readers, they would confine their thoughts to a private diary. Bloggers are just as motivated by the desire to attract and retain an audience as paid journalists.

There are reporters in the conventional media who have been financially rewarded for reporting truths and reporters who have been sacked for reporting falsehoods (or being reckless with respect to the truth of what they report). But there are also reporters whose careers have flourished despite (and sometimes, it appears, as a result of) having repeatedly reported falsehoods (or repeatedly being reckless with respect to the truth of what they report). What is more, there are reporters who appear to have been sacked (or had their careers stall) for reporting the truth.[9]

A "professional," in the sense we have considered so far, is simply someone who is paid to do something. But there is reason to suppose that Goldman and others who are concerned about the blogosphere's impact on professional journalism has a different concept of *professional* in mind, one in which being a professional is contrasted, not with being an amateur, but with being a tradesperson. In recent decades journalism has increasingly come to be seen, especially by some of its practitioners, as a profession, rather than a trade. However, there are still a number of journalists who consider this to be a bad development.[10] Although I am sympathetic with their view, I will not try to defend it here.[11] I will confine myself to arguing that political journalists should not be thought of as professionals in the same sense that paradigmatic professionals such as doctors, lawyers, and especially scientists, are professionals, and that this is enough to undermine Goldman's analogy between the filtering of scientific journals and the filtering of political news in the conventional media.

We accept the filtering of scientific journals (and for that matter of medical, legal, and philosophical journals), partly because the gatekeepers of those journals have been accredited by certain professional bodies as experts on the subject matter in question. But there is an important difference between the subject matter of these journals and the subject matter of political journalism. As we saw in Chapter 3, the guiding idea behind epistemic approaches to democracy is that political questions, unlike scientific questions, legal questions, and so on, are best left to the "wisdom of crowds."[12] To the extent that there is such a thing as expertise in politics it is extremely limited because political information is distributed widely and reasonably evenly across political communities.[13] It is striking, therefore, that the starting point of Goldman's argument, the epistemic approach to democracy (i.e., the claim that democracy is superior to other systems of government in its ability to "track the truth"), is so palpably inconsistent with his elitist conclusion about the public's inability to sort through unfiltered information on its own. If people without the proper accreditation really cannot be relied on to distinguish truth from falsehood about political matters, why should we suppose that they can be relied on to identify and vote for the right candidate (or even the one who is "right for them"[14])? If we really could trust a class of professional political journalists to filter out falsehoods about politics for us, then we could trust them to do the voting for us as well. And we can't.

In an earlier work, Goldman claims that ideally the press would comprise a set of political experts who would filter information about politics for us, just as physicians filter information about medicine for us (1999b, p. 340). But this ideal is clearly undemocratic. I am not saying that journalists shouldn't be experts on something (after all, as we saw in Chapter 2, everyone is an expert on numerous things). Nor am I denying that political journalists may have expertise on a variety of political issues, personalities, and/or processes. What I am denying is that journalists are (or ideally should be) experts on politics itself. They are not, and should not aspire to be, experts on which policies or candidates voters should vote for, or on what information voters need in order to work out who or what they should vote for. Journalists should have a distinctive form of expertise, but it is principally a form of skill expertise, rather than cognitive expertise; journalists should be experts at gathering and disseminating information which the public has a right to know.

The Value of "Balance" in Journalism

We have seen why one of Goldman's analogies fails. But we also saw that he deploys another analogy, one which involves the Anglo-American common-law trial system. It fails too, though for somewhat different reasons.

Goldman points out that the blogosphere and the Anglo-American trial system are similar, in some respects. They are both "adversarial systems," which allow "zealous advocates" of differing points of view to argue their case, leaving the decision about whom to believe in the hands of the reader in the former case and the jury in the latter case. Goldman suggests that this could be seen as an argument in favor of the blogosphere:

> Maybe it's a good global system that allows these different advocates to argue for their respective points of view and lets the reader decide. Maybe this is good even in terms of truth-determination. Isn't that, after all, a primary rationale for the adversary process in the British-American trial system? (Goldman, 2008, p. 119)

Having made this suggestion, however, Goldman goes on to reject it because of a difference between the blogosphere and the Anglo-American trial system, which makes "very dubious the truth-determining properties of the adversarial system exemplified by the blogosphere" (p. 120).

Before looking at this difference, it is worth noting that no advocate of the blogosphere appears to have deployed this analogy. Rather, Goldman has suggested it as a *possible* analogy, before rejecting it. So let's grant him, at least for the sake of argument, that the adversarial system of the Anglo-American trial system does have better truth-determining properties than the adversarial system of the blogosphere. This would not be surprising, and it is presumably part of the reason we would disapprove of trial by blogging. But our disapproval of trial by blogging is surely part of a broader disapproval of any kind of trial by media. Trial by media is deplorable, whether the media in question is the conventional media or the blogosphere, and we have been given no reason to think that one is worse than the other. Remember that we are not trying to make an *absolute* evaluation of the epistemic merits of blogosphere, but a *comparative* one. We are not asking whether the blogosphere is good *simpliciter*. Rather, we are asking how it compares to its rival, the conventional media. Presumably the point of Goldman's analogy then is to suggest that the conventional media and the Anglo-American trial system share some veritistic virtues, and that these virtues are absent (or present to a lesser degree) in the blogosphere. With that in mind, consider the following passage:

> a crucial difference between jurors and blog readers is that jurors are required to listen to the entire legal proceeding, including all arguments from each side. Since the litigants are systematically offered opportunities to rebut their opponents' arguments, jurors will at least be exposed to a roughly equal quantity of arguments on each side. The analogue is dramatically untrue in the case of blog users. Quite the opposite. ... Nothing constrains them to give equal time to opposing positions. (Goldman, 2008, p. 120)

Of course, nothing *necessarily* constrains consumers of conventional news to give equal time to opposing positions either. Nonetheless, it is true that most conventional news services at least give lip service to this ideal in their presentation of the news. It is an ideal which often goes by the name "balance." The conventional media has embraced this ideal to a great extent and, in this respect, it is more like the Anglo-American trial system than is the blogosphere, and this is presumably Goldman's point.

But although balance, understood as giving "equal time to opposing positions," is often presented as a (or even the) central journalistic virtue in the conventional media, a little reflection shows there is nothing inherently valuable (epistemically or otherwise) about it. Here is Stephen Klaidman and Tom Beauchamp on the topic:

> Fairness does not always require giving equal weight to the views of those on either side of an issue; some views might be absurd, uninformed, framed and calculated to political ends, and so on. If the preponderance of thoroughly assembled evidence overwhelmingly supports the conclusion that the earth is an oblate spheroid, this view deserves more weight than the tenuously supported opinion that the earth is flat. (Klaidman & Beauchamp, 1987, p. 46)

Let's apply this reasoning to a real political dispute. Should the media give equal time to holocaust deniers and their disputants? Obviously not, since doing so would imply that each side of this debate is equally worthy of consideration and (at least roughly) equally well-evidenced. Furthermore, even if such "balance" were justifiable on grounds of fairness, it would obviously not be justifiable on veritistic grounds. I am not denying, of course, that there is a sense in which "balance" is a journalistic value. Balance, if it is understood as giving consideration to both the evidence for and against a proposition, where both kinds of evidence exist, can be justified on veritistic grounds. But that is quite a different thing.

In fact, Goldman's analogy with the Anglo-American trial system, so far from giving us a reason to prefer the conventional media to the blogosphere, does just the opposite. There are exactly two sides to every case put before a jury in the Anglo-American trial system. The jury may decide for one party or for the other, or (in some cases) decide that the correct answer lies somewhere between the contending positions.[15] But it is utterly misguided to think that there are precisely two sides to every political issue. Sometimes there are more (i.e., there are more than two positions, each supported by some of the available evidence) and sometimes there are fewer (i.e., there is only one position supported by the available evidence).

The idea that there are precisely two sides to each political issue which should each be given equal time (or space, in the case of newspapers), is closely associated with the fact that political power in most Western countries, including the United States and Britain, takes the form of a duopoly (i.e., there are two dominant political parties or coalitions). In these countries, the conventional media treat their viewers, listeners, or readers as if they were members of a jury. Equal time is offered to the arguments of "each side" (i.e., the two main political parties or coalitions) and little time, if any, to the arguments of anyone else. In the lead-up to the 2003 invasion of Iraq, arguments that Saddam Hussein did not possess significant quantities of WMD were almost totally absent from the conventional media of Britain and the United States. This can, to a large extent, be explained by the fact that the leaders of both major political parties in both countries were in agreement that the weapons were there. As David Ignatius of the *Washington Post* proudly noted, "In a sense, the media were victims of their own professionalism. Because there was little criticism of the war from prominent Democrats and foreign policy analysts, journalistic rules meant we shouldn't create a debate on our own."[16] This conception of the role of the political journalist is endemic in the conventional media, though it is rarely so explicitly acknowledged. According to it, political journalists should report what "the two sides" of the political establishment are saying and leave it at that. It is not their role to investigate whether what they are told is true. Whatever else may be said of the journalistic rules Ignatius cites, they can hardly be commended on veritistic grounds. One prominent blogger, Glenn Greenwald, has summarized this approach to journalism in the United States in the following passage:

> There are two sides and only two sides to every "debate" – the Beltway Democratic establishment and the Beltway Republican establishment. If those two sides agree on X, then X is deemed true, no matter how false it actually is. If one side disputes X, then X cannot be asserted as fact, no matter how indisputably true it is.[17]

This veritistically harmful conception of "balance" is even more pervasive in public broadcasting than in commercial broadcasting.[18] We have already seen one case of the conventional media treating a falsehood as true, because it was accepted by both sides of the political establishment. A good example of it refusing to report a truth because it is disputed by one side of the political establishment is the refusal of National Public Radio to report that the Bush administration practiced torture. Alicia C. Shepard, the NPR ombudsman, defends NPR's refusal to report this, not on factual or semantic grounds (that is, not by reference to what Bush did or what the word "torture" means), but on the following grounds:

> It's a no-win case for journalists. If journalists use the words "harsh interrogation techniques," they can be seen as siding with the White House and the language that some U.S. officials, particularly in the Bush administration, prefer. If journalists use the word "torture," then they can be accused of siding with those who are particularly and visibly still angry at the previous administration.[19]

This is indeed a "no-win" situation for journalists if winning consists in keeping everyone (or everyone who matters) happy. But it is not a no-win situation for journalists whose goal is to report the truth.

Journalists in the conventional media often justify this approach to their reporting on the grounds that it is "objective," as if by following this practice they are keeping their own judgments or opinions out of their reporting. This outlook is explicit in the following interview with one of America's most influential journalists, Jim Lehrer:

> LIZ COX BARRETT: At CJR Daily, we spent a lot of time during the 2004 presidential campaign criticizing ... stories that "highlight the controversy," report this claim versus these competing claims, rather than providing facts for the reader and helping them navigate toward the truth. What are your thoughts on this? How do you approach reporting when a public official has said something that is blatantly untrue?
> LEHRER: I don't deal in terms like "blatantly untrue." That's for other people to decide when something's "blatantly untrue." ... My part of journalism is to present what various people say about it the best we can find out [by] reporting and let others – meaning commentators, readers, viewers, bloggers or whatever ... I'm not in the judgment part of journalism. I'm in the reporting part of journalism.[20]

Lehrer's conception of "the reporting part of journalism" clearly cannot be justified on veritistic grounds. By failing to tell his viewers that blatant untruths are untrue, he reduces his viewers' chances of being able to know that they are untrue. Of course, Lehrer's claim that he is not in the "judgment" part of journalism is disingenuous, to put it mildly. He is after all making judgments about which people have opinions that are worth hearing. This point is central to the critique of the conventional media's role as "stenographer" for the political establishment, a role which has been brilliantly parodied in the following interview on *The Daily Show*:

> STEWART: Here's what puzzles me most, Rob. John Kerry's record in Vietnam is pretty much right there in the official records of the U.S. military, and hasn't been disputed for 35 years.
> CORDDRY: That's right, Jon, and that's certainly the spin you'll be hearing coming from the Kerry campaign over the next few days.
> STEWART: That's not a spin thing, that's a fact. That's established.
> CORDDRY: Exactly, Jon, and that established, incontrovertible fact is one side of the story.
> STEWART: But isn't that the end of the story? I mean, you've seen the records, haven't you? What's your opinion?
> CORDDRY: I'm sorry, "my opinion"? I don't have opinions. I'm a reporter, Jon, and my job is to spend half the time repeating what one side says, and half the time repeating the other. Little thing called "objectivity" – might want to look it up some day.
> STEWART: Doesn't objectivity mean objectively weighing the evidence, and calling out what's credible and what isn't?
> CORDDRY: Whoa-ho! Sounds like someone wants the media to act as a filter! Listen, buddy: Not my job to stand between the people talking to me and the people listening to me.[21]

The idea that reporting should consist in balance between two sides (Democrat/Republican, left/right, liberal/conservative) is so deeply ingrained in our political culture that even those who exhibit intermittent awareness of its absurdity often fall back into it. For example, Michael Massing (2009, p. 31) praises the blogosphere for its rejection of "reflexive attempts at 'balance'," but then goes on to criticize it, citing a study according to which bloggers rarely link to, and even more rarely show respect for, bloggers on "the other side" of the political divide. He seems entirely oblivious to the fact that this study presupposes that bloggers can be divided into two sides, and that balance, understood as giving both of them the same attention and respect, is desirable.

Of course failure to acknowledge the existence of opinions that differ from one's own is (at least typically) a bad thing. But it is not a bad thing which is particularly distinctive of the blogosphere. A lot of the blogosphere is devoted to media criticism. As Jane Singer notes, "bloggers have taken to heart the self-appointed role as watchdogs of the watchdogs" (Singer, 2010, p. 125). This means that bloggers often link to media outlets (conventional and otherwise) that they are criticizing. No doubt there are some bloggers who rarely link to people who disagree with them, just as there are people who rarely talk to people who disagree with them. But it should be clear that failure to acknowledge or respect a diversity of opinion is at least as characteristic of the conventional media as it is of the blogosphere. As we have seen, the conventional media routinely fail to respect, or even acknowledge the existence of, views which are not endorsed by the major political parties in their country.

Some Conventional Media Filtering Practices

We have seen why the analogies Goldman deploys in defense of conventional media filtering fail. But Goldman does more than merely point to these analogies. He also discusses certain specific "filtering practices" which he thinks of as characteristic of the conventional media:

> Newspapers employ fact checkers to vet a reporter's article before it is published. They often require more than a single source before publishing an article, and limit reporters' reliance on anonymous sources. These practices seem likely to raise the veritistic quality of the reports newspapers publish and hence the veritistic quality of their readers' resultant beliefs. At a minimum, they reduce the number of errors that might otherwise be reported and believed. Thus, from a veritistic point of view, filtering looks promising indeed. Isn't that an argument for the superiority of the conventional news media over blogging, so long as knowledge and error-avoidance are the ends being considered? (Goldman, 2008, p. 117)

There are several points to note about this passage. One concerns the relationship between knowledge and error avoidance. Another concerns Goldman's assumption that reducing the number of errors reported will reduce the number of errors believed.

I will address both of those points later. For now the main thing to note about the above passage is that while things may "look promising" to Goldman, we can't really say whether that promise is being fulfilled until we look at some of the details of how these filtering practices actually work, and consider whether they do in fact raise the veritistic quality of the conventional media's reports or the veritistic quality of readers' beliefs. Again it will be necessary to look at this issue empirically. In what follows, I will look at some data from the United States and Britain about each of the three conventional media filtering practices Goldman refers to – employing fact checkers, requiring that (some) stories have multiple sources, and limiting the use of anonymous sources – before discussing another filtering practice which the conventional media tend to be more quiet about. I will argue that none of them provide any reason for supposing that the conventional media is epistemically superior to the blogosphere.

Fact checkers

Goldman clearly assumes that stories in the conventional media are "fact checked" by people other than the journalists who write them (i.e., the fact checker will be a gatekeeper). But this is often not the case. The "Guidelines on Integrity" for *The New York Times*, for example, state that "writers at *The Times* are their own principal fact checkers and often their only ones."[22]

This might seem to be a picayune point. It would be natural to respond that it doesn't really matter whether journalists fact check their own stories or someone else does. What matters is that someone is doing it, and doing it reasonably thoroughly. This response only works, however, if we have reason to believe that conventional news stories are more likely to be thoroughly fact checked by someone than stories in the blogosphere, and it is not clear whether we have any reason to believe that. A recent survey by Cardiff University of over 2,000 stories from the most prestigious newspapers on Fleet Street found that in only 12 percent of them was there evidence that the "facts" had been thoroughly checked (Davies, 2008, p. 95).[23] Now 12 percent is better than nothing, but of course bloggers also sometimes check their facts and sometimes do it thoroughly, and so far we have seen no reason to suppose that bloggers check their facts any less often or any less thoroughly than journalists or editors in the conventional media.

Requiring multiple sources

Is Goldman right that conventional news sources "often" require more than one source before going ahead with a story? Typically they are publicly committed to such a policy. For example, the BBC specifically instructs journalists that as a general rule they must have at least two sources for every story. However, there is a very important exception to this rule. A special notice issued by the BBC journalism board of December 1, 2004 told staff: "The Press Association can be treated as a confirmed, single source" (Davies, 2008, p. 75).

The BBC is far from alone in making an exception of the Press Association. Nick Davies has argued persuasively that it is the practice, if not the policy, of every major British media outlet to treat the Press Association as a single confirmed source (Davies, 2008, pp. 75–94). This attitude toward the Press Association is not a trivial exception to the rule, because the Press Association is, as Davies says, "the primary conveyer belt along which information reaches national media of Britain" (p. 74). The above mentioned Cardiff study found that 70 percent of news stories from quality British newspapers were "wholly or partly rewritten from wire copy, usually the Press Association" (p. 74).

Now most journalistic codes of ethics recognize that it would be unrealistic to do away with single-source stories altogether. In general, the rule is (or at least should be) that more than one source is required to the extent that the following conditions are met: (1) there is reason to doubt the reliability of the first source, (2) the story is of great importance (or at least it would be if were true). With that in mind we will consider one typical story, from a paradigm of the conventional media, the *New York Times*, called "U.S. Ties Iranians to Iraq Attack that Killed G.I.s," from July 2, 2007. This was a lengthy (23 paragraph) article, filled with claims that the Iranian government was orchestrating attacks on American forces in Iraq (not merely the one mentioned in the article's title). There was precisely one source for the claims mentioned in the article, a certain US military spokesman, Kevin J. Bergner.

It should be clear that both criteria for requiring multiple sources are met here. First, there is good reason to doubt the reliability of the single source for this story. US military spokesmen have recently been the sources for many false stories about relevantly similar topics, especially false stories about the activities of governments of oil-rich Middle-Eastern countries with which the US government has unfriendly relations (Mitchell, 2008).[24] Second, the story is clearly of great importance, given the article is effectively accusing the Iranian government of committing an act of war against the United States, and that false reports, not only from this newspaper, but even from this journalist, Michael R. Gordon, its chief military correspondent, have been used as a pretext for war before.[25]

So it seems, with respect to the issue of multiple sources, Goldman is again overly optimistic about the reliability of conventional media filtering practices. Some conventional news outlets have good policies about requiring more than one source, some don't. Even when they have a good policy, they often ignore it in practice, especially when their initial source is a government official, or is in some other way invested with institutional authority. Of course, the conventional media *sometimes* requires more than one source before going ahead with a story. But this does not distinguish it from the blogosphere. Bloggers, like anyone else seeking to collect and disseminate information, sometimes require more than one source for a story before they believe it themselves or try to get others to believe it. This requirement will not be the kind of formal, institutionally sanctioned, requirement found in the conventional media, because bloggers are, almost by definition, not working as part of a formally structured institution. I will have more to say about what difference this might make later on, but, so far at least, we have seen no reason to suppose that the conventional media is more scrupulous than the blogosphere in requiring stories to be supported by multiple sources.

Restrictions on the use of anonymous sources

Some limitations on the use of anonymous sources are epistemically desirable for at least three reasons. First, anonymity can be used as a cover for making false statements. Second, all else being equal, the public is less able to judge the veracity of a statement if they don't know who made it. Third, anonymity is, in and of itself, an epistemic harm to members of the public since it denies them knowledge of the identity of a source. Nonetheless, there are circumstances in which using anonymous sources clearly raises the veritistic quality of media reports and (in the process) raises the veritistic quality of readers' or viewers' beliefs. The classic example of such a veritistically beneficial anonymous source is Deep Throat, whose revelations helped expose the Watergate scandal.

So what limitations should be placed on the use of anonymous sources? Those who write on media and journalistic ethics have given a wide variety of answers to this question (not all of which are based on purely epistemic considerations).[26] Journalists are sometimes warned that, although they sometimes have an obligation to respect their sources' desire for confidentiality, this obligation is very different from the confidentiality obligations of other "professionals,"[27] such as doctors or lawyers (Chadwick, 1996). A journalist's primary obligation should be to his or her readers (or viewers), not to his or her sources. Journalists should allow a source to go off the record only if doing so will benefit their readers or viewers, especially if it benefits them epistemically. Sources should only be granted anonymity if it is clear that neither they, nor anyone else, will speak truthfully on the record. What is more, the promise of anonymity should always be conditional on the source's report being true (or at least on the source not lying or bullshitting).[28]

Anyone who pays close attention to the conventional media knows that it often does not adhere to principles of this kind. After the anthrax attacks inside the United States in 2001, for example, ABC News claimed that according to "four well-placed and separate sources" the anthrax involved contained bentonite, which is "a trademark of Iraqi leader Saddam Hussein's biological weapons program" and "only one country, Iraq, has used bentonite to produce biological weapons."[29] It turns out that no tests ever indicated any bentonite in the anthrax in question.[30] This means that the claims of four well-placed, and allegedly independent, sources were utterly false. What is more, it is clear that they were lying, or at the very least bullshitting. How could four well-placed people separately come to believe the same completely fabricated story in an epistemically responsible way? Yet ABC News continues to shield the identity of its sources to this day.

This is one particularly important example, but its general character is fairly typical. The conventional media often protect the identity of their sources in ways which lower the veritistic quality of their reports, especially when their sources are government officials, or people who are in some other way invested with institutional authority.[31]

Although granting anonymity to whistleblowers, that is, people who are saying something true which someone in a position of power over them (roughly speaking, their boss) would not want them to say, is an important practice which can be justified on veritistic grounds, granting anonymity to people who are saying something that the boss would approve of is a quite different matter. Unfortunately the latter practice is so widespread that it can be found in almost every newspaper almost every day. It takes a number of forms: praising the boss anonymously, confirming something the boss has publicly said anonymously, or saying something anonymously that advances an agenda the boss wants to advance. In each case, there is reason to think that such sources want anonymity, not because they are frightened of retaliation for speaking the truth, but because they either don't want to be publicly associated with a falsehood or because they want people to believe that what they are saying is supported by stronger evidence than in fact it is.

There are many reasons this veritistically unjustified use of anonymous sources is so common; many reporters enjoy the flattery of powerful people, the feeling of being a privileged insider, or the conspiratorial thrill of secret meetings. Political reporters in the conventional media tend to be highly dependent on their relationships with government officials, as well as officials of other powerful institutions, such as the military.[32] Bloggers typically do not have this kind of relationship with those in power. Although it is possible for conventional political journalists to "keep their distance from power," it is very difficult and it rarely happens. Consider the words of I. F. Stone, a man who, though he lived and died before the age of the internet, is widely considered to be the patron saint of blogging:

> I made no claims to inside stuff. I tried to give information which could be documented, so the reader could check it for himself. I tried to dig the truth out of hearings, official transcripts and government documents ... Reporters tend to be absorbed by the bureaucracies they cover; they take on the habits, attitudes, and even accents of the military or the diplomatic corps. Should a reporter resist the pressure, there are many ways to get rid of him ... But a reporter covering the whole capital on his own – particularly if he is his own employer – is immune from these pressures. (Stone, 1973, p. 312)

Stone's approach to journalism required rare skills and a prodigious appetite for hard work.[33] He was an epistemic saint,[34] profoundly committed to the public's right to know. The research and outreach potential of the internet has now given millions of much more ordinary people the opportunity to follow his example. What is more, blog readers have epistemic resources available to them that Stone's readers did not. Although Stone's readers *could* check the documentary evidence supporting the claims he made for themselves, a variety of practical obstacles meant that in fact they rarely would. By contrast, it is often easy for blog readers to access the evidence supporting claims made by bloggers via hyperlinks inserted in the text.

National security

One of the most important, but least discussed, filtering practices in the conventional media is the appeal to national security. It almost stopped the *New York Times* from publishing the Pentagon Papers, and for more than a year it stopped the same newspaper from publishing the story that President George W. Bush had authorized warrantless wiretapping on American citizens.[35] Even if you think this filtering technique is desirable on prudential grounds, it is clearly not desirable from an epistemic point of view, since it prevents members of the public from forming true beliefs.[36]

The Blogosphere as a Parasite

I have appealed to blogs as well as the conventional media in support of my argument. Goldman would clearly not approve of my use of blogs. When Richard Posner refers to an example of a conventional media outlet admitting a mistake after having it pointed out on a blog, Goldman claims that this actually supports his position:

> But this points precisely to the necessity of using a mainstream medium, a filtered medium! If we are trying to compare the veritistic credentials of a *pure* blogosphere with a *pure* set of mainstream media, this hardly vindicates the pure blogosphere because without the mainstream media to appeal to for validation, Posner implicitly concedes, the reader can't know whom to trust. (Goldman, 2008, p. 119)

This is a highly uncharitable interpretation of what Posner is doing. Posner is not (or at least should not be) appealing to the mainstream media because *he* thinks the mainstream media is more reliable than the blogosphere, but because those with whom he is arguing think it. The people Posner is trying to persuade (people like Goldman) are predisposed to dismiss blogs as unreliable, so, quite rightly, Posner appeals to sources that *they* will have more antecedent faith in. Compare it with the following situation. Suppose someone is predisposed to think that popes are a more reliable source of truth about the motion of heavenly bodies than astronomers. When arguing against this view, it would be perfectly legitimate to cite the recent example of a pope conceding that a pope was wrong and an astronomer was right about this topic.[37] This would not be an implicit concession that, without the pope to tell us, we can't know whom to trust.

Goldman's assumption that only the conventional media can truly validate a news story appears to be based on his acceptance of a widely held view that the blogosphere is a parasite on the conventional media:

> The blogosphere (in its current incarnation, at least) isn't independent of the conventional media; it piggy-backs, or free-rides, on them. Whatever credit is due to the blogs for error correction shouldn't go to them alone, because their error-checking ability is derivative from the conventional media. (Goldman, 2008, p. 114)

It is true of course that the blogosphere is not entirely independent of the conventional media; in this sense there is no such thing as a *pure* blogosphere. But it is also true that the contemporary conventional media is not entirely independent of the blogosphere; there is no longer any such thing as a pure conventional media either. In what follows I hope to make it clear that the blogosphere no more free rides or piggybacks on the conventional media than the conventional media free rides or piggybacks on the blogosphere.

There is ample evidence that the conventional media is heavily (and increasingly) dependent on the blogosphere. A 2008 survey of 1,231 conventional journalists found that just under 73 percent of them sometimes or always use blogs in their research.[38] There are numerous well-documented cases of the conventional media picking up important stories from the blogosphere,[39] and even of the conventional media plagiarizing the blogosphere.[40]

How extensive is the blogosphere's dependence on conventional media? To start with, it should be clear that the dependence is not complete. If bloggers offered nothing original, few people would read blogs and conventional media would not be threatened. Those, like Goldman, who accuse the blogosphere of being a parasite are typically not claiming that it is *completely* parasitic on the conventional news, rather they are claiming that it is parasitic with respect to *one* of the conventional news's traditional functions, namely "original reporting" or the provision of "primary data," as opposed to "opinion" or "analysis." Sometimes it is claimed that the blogosphere is not only a parasite in this respect, it is a parasite that is destroying its host, and hence, in the long run, undermining itself. Even Richard Posner, who is generally optimistic about the blogosphere, is worried by this possibility (2005, p. 11). By way of comparison, imagine there was a danger of theoretical physicists taking the jobs of experimental physicists, and ending up without the data they need to construct their theories.

The problem with this critique of the blogosphere is not its insistence on a distinction between news and analysis (the latter is often misleadingly called "opinion"). This is a distinction which, like the similar distinction in science between observation and theory, is vague and contestable, but nonetheless real and important. Rather, the problem is with the underlying conception of what the primary data of political news is, and of how that data should be gathered. Bloggers allegedly don't have access to the primary data of political reporting, because they don't have access to those in the corridors of power. We have already seen some of the dangers and limitations of this approach, as well as some of the possibilities of an alternative approach based largely on careful examination of documentary evidence.

I am not denying that interviews and other forms of first-hand contact with people in power have a legitimate role in political reporting. But it is not as if there is any serious danger that powerful people will be unable to get their message across to the public. If newspapers and other conventional media outlets collapse because of competition from the blogosphere, then the powerful will turn to bloggers to get their message out. Indeed we have perhaps seen the beginning of this process in the furore over President Obama fielding a question from a blogger from the *Huffington Post*.[41]

Another Analogy

We have seen why Goldman's two analogies fail. It would be nice if we could find a better one. I suggest that the emergence of the blogosphere as a competitor to the conventional media, which has been brought about by contemporary internet technology, is strikingly similar to the emergence of the printed book as a competitor to the manuscript, which was brought about by printing technology in the fifteenth century. Both phenomena led to an epistemic panic.[42] These epistemic panics have both been based on the thought that a significant increase in the number of things people can read will lead to a significant increase in the number of falsehoods they can read, and that this in turn will lead to an increase in the number of falsehoods they believe. Then as now, there were people who thought of filtering as a desirable way of protecting people from these falsehoods. In the fifteenth century this took the form of, ultimately unsuccessful, attempts by the Vatican to license the printing of all books (Eisenstein, 1983). Now they take the form of attempts by a variety of governments to restrict what people can access on the internet.[43]

It is true, in both cases, that access to more information has meant access to more falsehoods. But there is no justification for Goldman's assumption that when people have *access* to more falsehoods, they will inevitably *believe* more falsehoods. To think that this is inevitable is to assume that consumers of information are completely passive in the face of what they are told, unable to make choices about what to believe. This is an assumption we challenged in our discussion of rumors in Chapter 4.

What is more, even if it were true that the blogosphere leads people to believe more falsehoods than they otherwise would, it would not follow that its overall impact on them would be harmful, even from a narrowly epistemic point of view. In Chapter 1 we saw that William James (2007/1897, Part VII, pp. 17–18) was right to argue that the value of falsehood avoidance is distinct from, and can come into conflict with, the value of truth acquisition. We also saw that Goldman was wrong when he argued that these two values can be blended "into a single *magnitude* or *quantity*" (Goldman, 2002, p. 58).

How does this apply to the issue at hand? Remember that Goldman makes two claims about the benefits of conventional media filtering practices: first, that they seem likely to raise the veritistic quality of reports and hence the veritistic quality of readers' beliefs; second, more modestly, that they reduce the number of errors that are reported and believed. Now, the first part of the more modest claim should be uncontroversial. Almost any filtering practice is likely to reduce the number of errors reported. The only filtering practices that wouldn't do this would be filtering practices that only filter out truths. And not even the most ardent critics of the conventional media believe things are that bad. Even Noam Chomsky would concede that the conventional media occasionally filters out falsehoods.

If our only concern were to reduce the number of errors reported, the best filtering practice would be not to report anything that has any chance, no matter how small, of being false. In deference to Descartes, we might call this the Method of Doubt Filtering Practice. While it is certainly a good way of reducing error (since it would be certain to eliminate all error), it doesn't seem to be a good filtering practice, since it would also eliminate (almost) all reporting altogether, since (virtually) every newsworthy report has *some* chance of being false. Whatever merits the Method of

Doubt may have had for Descartes's special purposes, it is clearly not good methodology for political journalists. If error avoidance were all that mattered, the best strategy would be to never report anything at all.

This should make it clear that we can distinguish between the goals of trying to report the truth and trying to avoid reporting falsehoods. What is more, these two praiseworthy goals can come into conflict. So, even if you are unmoved by my examples of the conventional media failing to filter out falsehoods, and remain convinced that confining yourself to the conventional media is the best way to avoid error, it does not follow that confining yourself to the conventional media is the best way of acquiring truth. The blogosphere includes many more reports than the conventional media.[44] Inevitably the blogosphere reports falsehoods that the conventional media filters out, but equally inevitably, it reports truths that the conventional media filters out.

Although Goldman sometimes seems to acknowledge the distinction between the goal of promoting true belief (or knowledge) and the goal of avoiding error (or falsehood),[45] his actual arguments for the benefits of filtering are entirely focused on the latter goal. This is not surprising, since what filtering does, when it is working as it should, is stop falsehoods from being reported. But, as William James recognized, falsehood avoidance is not the only value at stake. Excessive concern with falsehood avoidance is an epistemic vice. It constitutes a form of epistemic timidity or incuriosity. People who confine themselves to a filtered medium may well avoid believing falsehoods (if the filters are working well), but inevitably they will also miss out on valuable knowledge.

It is true that a lot of people can now access falsehoods that they otherwise would not be able to access, and inevitably some of them will believe falsehoods that they otherwise would not believe. But it is equally true that a lot of people can now access (and believe) truths of which they would otherwise remain ignorant. The concerns of Goldman and others about this are likely to appear as quaint one day as do the concerns of those who worried about the epistemic consequences of printing technology in the fifteenth century.

Conclusion

Goldman expresses concern about the epistemic consequences of the internet. But the real issue is not the internet itself, but a kind of journalism which has flourished as a result of the internet. We have seen three characteristics of this journalism. First, it is largely carried out by nonprofessionals, in one or the other of the senses we have considered. Second, these nonprofessionals are not part of any large, formally structured, institution. Third, their principal form of research consists in examination of documentary evidence, rather than interviews (and other forms of contact) with people in positions of power. Each of these characteristics make it easier for bloggers to resist efforts by those in power to shape the news. By contrast, the conventional media's willingness to go along with those efforts is so pronounced that many people working in the conventional media clearly feel they have no choice. For example, Karen DeYoung, journalist and editor for the *Washington Post*, has said, of her profession, that "we are inevitably the mouthpiece for whatever administration is in power."[46] Likewise, *Time* journalist Andrew Sullivan dismisses the "volunteer army of bloggers who are engaged in a guerrilla war against the mainstream media," not on the grounds that they are unscrupulous or unreliable, but rather on the grounds that "they stay on the margins – because, like all insurgents, they're about sniping, not governing."[47] This suggests that he has internalized the outlook of his subject matter (the political class) to such an extent that he has come to think that the role of the media is to govern, rather than to provide a check on government.

Now I am not suggesting that there is no place for journalists who are professionals, in the sense that they are paid to do what they do. What I am suggesting is that we should not think of journalism as a profession, on the model of paradigmatic professions, such as medicine or law. There are two reasons for this. One is that it encourages the idea that there should be legal constraints on who can engage in journalism, or institutional constraints on who is regarded as a real journalist. To the extent that such constraints exist, we will have a guided democracy, rather than a genuine democracy (see Chapter 3). It is a mark of a genuine democracy that anyone can call himself or herself "a journalist," and anyone who succeeds in informing the public of things they have a right to know is a journalist. Several governments, along with some of their conventional media allies, have recently taken to denying that the founder of Wikileaks, Julian Assange, is a journalist. But it is not their role to determine who the real journalists are, any more than it is their role to determine which presses are to be accorded freedom of the press. It was relatively easy for governments to support, or at least tolerate, press freedom when there were relatively few presses, most of which were owned by people whose interests (in both senses) converged, to a great extent, with their own. As Abbott Joseph Liebling said in 1960, "freedom of the press is guaranteed only to those who own one."[48] Now, because of the emergence of the blogosphere, anyone with access to the internet can own a press, and freedom of the press has become a widely distributed right, like other freedoms associated with democracy, such as freedom of speech, freedom of association, and freedom of assembly.

The second problem with thinking of journalism as a profession, in the way in which medicine and law are professions, is that it encourages the idea that journalists have obligations to their sources which are analogous to the obligations which doctors have to their patients or which lawyers have to their clients. In particular, it encourages the idea that journalists have almost unconditional confidentiality obligations to their sources. Journalists don't work for their sources; they work for the reading, viewing, or listening public.[49] Hence their primary obligation is to their public, rather than to their sources. Many political journalists in the conventional media have come to value their insider status so highly that they seem to have lost sight of this. One of America's most prominent and prestigious journalists, Tim Russert, for example, testified that when any senior government official calls him, "they are presumptively off the record."[50] His refusal to tell us what senior government officials said to him, without first getting their permission, meant that he was effectively working for them, not for us.

I am not suggesting that filtering is necessarily a bad thing, or even that filtering political news is necessarily a bad thing. Up until now I have not challenged the contrast between a filtered conventional media and an unfiltered (gatekeeperless) blogosphere. This contrast is generally accepted by both critics of the blogosphere, such as Goldman, and proponents of it, such as Jane Singer in the following passage:

> Bloggers embody the idea that democratic power is essentially distributed and that the pursuit of truth works best as a collective enterprise. They personify the marketplace of ideas with a vengeance: put it all out there, and the truth will emerge. For the first time, the capability to put it all out there actually exists. That is what happens when there are no gates and no gatekeepers. (Singer, 2010, p. 125)

Although the internet as a whole is largely unfiltered, plenty of filtering goes on within it. Many websites act as hosts for bloggers and are, as a result, gatekeepers of the information produced by those bloggers.

So the idea that the blogosphere is an unfiltered medium is not really accurate. Even if newspapers and other noninternet sources of news cease to exist (which I think is highly unlikely), gatekeepers, and hence filtering, would not cease to exist. The internet does not eliminate gate-keepers; it merely gives us a wider range of gatekeepers to choose from.

Christopher Meyers is skeptical of Jane Singer's sanguine attitude to the blogosphere. He asks: "Why should we conclude truth will emerge, as opposed to merely the ideas of whomever has the loudest voice or the deepest pockets?" (Meyers, 2010, p. 88). There are of course no guarantees that truth will emerge. What I hope to have made clear, however, is that truth has a better chance of emerging through the blogosphere, precisely because those who have the deepest pockets (often assisted by those with the loudest voices) have to compete for attention with everyone else (including the impoverished and softly spoken).

One of the great virtues of blogging is that it is interactive. The blogosphere encourages consumers of news to be producers as well. Goldman dismisses this virtue on the grounds that it "obviously has little or nothing to do with the kind of epistemic good that interests us" (Goldman, 2008, p. 115). But this is not obvious at all. In fact, it is not true. All else being equal, people are more likely to arrive at the truth through an engagement with their sources of information, rather than through passive acceptance (or rejection) of what those sources say. As we have seen, the blogosphere inevitably leads to more false reports. But, as we have also seen, it is not inevitable that it leads to more false beliefs overall. Goldman's assumption that consumers of information are entirely passive in the face of what they are told may have been more acceptable when people had to rely on a limited range of sources for their news. But because of the internet many people have access to a range of news sources, saying mutually incompatible things. As a result they are able to develop their critical faculties, which in turn helps them make better choices about what and whom to believe. This is a good thing from an epistemic point of view as well as from the point of view of their general well-being.

Notes

1 Goldman sometimes refers to "mainstream media," rather than "conventional media."
2 To be precise, it is unfiltered at the "reporting stage," as opposed to the "reception" or "acceptance" stages. Even in the blogosphere, Goldman

notes, there is a sense in which filtering still takes place, because people have some choice about what news they read or listen to (as well as whether they read or listen to the news at all) and they also have some choice about what to believe and disbelieve (Goldman, 2008, p. 118).

3   We should, as C. D. Broad (1925, p. viii) noted, be careful of those who "confuse the Author of Nature with the Editor of *Nature*; or at any rate suppose that there can be no productions of the former which would not be accepted for publication by the latter." It has certainly not been obvious to everyone that the filtering of the common-law system is epistemically beneficial. The British barrister C. G. L. DuCann, for example, denounced rules of evidence which prevent jurors from hearing about a defendant's criminal record in the following terms: "suppression of truth in courts professing to seek 'the truth, the whole truth and nothing but the truth' should not be tolerated even in the fancied or real interest of the prisoner" (1960, p. 268).

4   Anyone disposed to doubt this should read Loewenstein (2008).

5   These are also presumably typical of the countries Goldman has in mind.

6   Professional athletes are professionals in this sense.

7   Goldman thinks it is characteristic of bloggers that they are unpaid (2008, p. 121). But it is possible to make money out of blogging. Popular bloggers can make money by advertising, asking for donations, or selling books based on their blogs.

8   It can also promote that goal. There are some things people don't want to know, and there are some things people would like to believe regardless of whether they are true.

9   See Jebediah Reed, "The Iraq Gamble: At the Pundits Table the Losing Bet Still Takes the Pot," http://www.fair.org/index.php?page=22&media_view_id=8331. Accessed December 11, 2010.

10   For more on this issue see Christopher Tollefson (2000).

11   Much of the contemporary literature on professionalism characterizes professionals in terms of their (alleged) commitment to certain moral ideals. I think these approaches are mistaken, since they tend to associate economic and social privilege with moral virtue. Contemporary debates about the true nature of "a professional" often resemble debates in 18th- and 19th-century literature about the true nature of "a gentleman" (with the difference that women can aspire to being professionals, but they can never be gentlemen).

12   Of course, there is not always a clear demarcation between political and scientific questions. This is particularly evident at the moment in the climate change debate.

13   Although I defended democracy in epistemic terms in Chapter 3, I don't think that's the only way to defend democracy. Democracy is still desirable (at least presumptively) if and when voters democratically pick the wrong candidate. This is because widespread participation in politics is desirable in and of itself.

14 I noted earlier that Goldman's version of epistemic democracy differs from others, in that Goldman envisions people voting for the candidate (or option) that is "right for them," rather than the candidate (or option) that is right *simpliciter*. This doesn't make any difference to the current argument, so I won't dwell on it. Nonetheless, I think Goldman's position involves a mistake about both the psychology of voting and the value of voting, a mistake I discussed in some detail in Chapter 3.

15 This third option exists where juries are allowed to determine sentencing in criminal trials or damages in civil trials.

16 David Ignatius, *The Washington Post*, April 27, 2004, p. A21.

17 Glenn Greenwald, http://www.salon.com/news/opinion/glenn_greenwald/2009/07/02/npr. Accessed December 11, 2010.

18 Goldman (1999b, p. 342) claims that public broadcasting is veritistically superior to commercial broadcasting. It's not clear to me whether he is right about this or not.

19 Alicia C. Shepard, "Harsh Interrogation Techniques or Torture?" http://www.npr.org/ombudsman/2009/06/harsh_interrogation_techniques.html. Accessed December 11, 2010.

20 *Columbia Journalism Review*, http://www.cjr.org/behind_the_news/jim_lehrer_on_billy_bob_report.php. Accessed December 11, 2010.

21 *The Daily Show*, http://www.thedailyshow.com/watch/mon-august-23-2004/kerry-controversy. Accessed December 11, 2010.

22 http://www.nytco.com/company/business_units/integrity.html. Accessed December 11, 2010.

23 This book is full of evidence, not only that the conventional media rarely thoroughly checks its facts, but also that these "facts" are often in fact false.

24 I don't give specific page references, since the book is almost entirely about false stories of this kind.

25 Michael Gordon and Judith Miller claimed in an article on the front page of the *New York Times* headed "US Says Hussein Intensifies Quest for A-Bomb Parts" on September 8, 2002, that "Mr Hussein's dogged insistence on pursuing his nuclear ambitions ... has brought Iraq and the United States to the brink of war." The only evidence presented for this claim were false statements by US administration officials to the effect that certain aluminum tubes could only be used to enrich uranium. We now know that what had really brought Iraq and the US to the brink of war (and beyond) was, among other things, newspaper articles like this.

26 One example of a restriction on the use of anonymous sources which does not seem to be based on purely epistemic considerations is the *New York Times*'s warning to its journalists not to grant anonymity to people who use it as "a cover for a personal or partisan attack." See http://www.nytco.com/company/business_units/sources.html. Accessed December 11, 2010.

27 As we saw earlier, it is very far from clear whether journalists are professionals.

28 Lying involves deliberate falsehood. Bullshitting *merely* involves indifference to the truth of what one is saying (Frankfurt, 2006). There is room for
legitimate debate about precisely what the standard should be. My own
view is that the onus should be on the source asking for anonymity to
make sure that what he or she is saying is true. Hence journalists should
not respect the confidentiality of sources who give them false stories, even
if those sources are not lying or bullshitting.

29 See www.salon.com/opinion/greenwald/2008/08/01/anthrax/. Accessed
December 11, 2010.

30 ABC News finally acknowledged this in 2007 in response to the efforts of a
blogger, Glenn Greenwald. See http://www.salon.com/opinion/greenwald/
2007/04/11/abc_response/. Accessed December 11, 2010.

31 Another example of this kind was the Jessica Lynch story. Reporters Susan
Schmidt and Vernon Loeb writing in the *Washington Post* wrote an article
called "She Was Fighting to the Death" on April 3, 2003, in which unnamed
army sources are used to fashion a heroic and almost entirely fabricated
story about Private Lynch's capture and escape.

32 This dependence is so great that some of them seem to think that their job
consists entirely in reporting the views of these officials. Judith Miller,
arguably the journalist most responsible for promoting widespread belief
in the falsehood that Saddam Hussein had significant stockpiles of WMD,
said "my job isn't to assess the government's information and be an
independent intelligence analyst myself. My job is to tell readers of the
New York Times what the government thought about Iraq's arsenal"
(Massing, 2004, p. 48). Of course, readers of the *New York Times* were entitled to think, and presumably did think, that she was endorsing the claims
which she repeated without question in her reports, and not that she was
merely reporting that the government was endorsing them.

33 He founded and ran his own newspaper to which he was almost the sole
contributor.

34 I borrow the term from Bernstein (1986).

35 See "Bush Lets U.S. Spy on Callers Without Courts," *New York Times*,
December 16, 2005, which was discussed in Chapter 5.

36 In fact, there is ample reason to think that such appeals to national
security are often motivated, not by a concern for the security of the
nation, but rather by a concern for the welfare of the government of the
day. For example, as we saw in Chapter 5, the Bush administration
managed to persuade the *Times* to delay the wire-tapping story until after
Bush had been re-elected.

37 See "A Papal Apology," http://www.pbs.org/newshour/bb/religion/jan-
june00/apology_3-13.html. Accessed December 11, 2010.

38 See Mike Sachoff (March 27, 2008), "Journalists Working Online More
and Using Blogs More," http://www.webpronews.com/topnews/

2008/03/27/journalists-working-online-more-and-using-blogs-more. Accessed December 11, 2010.

39 Perhaps the best known case of this occurred when former US Senate Majority Leader Trent Lott praised Senator Strom Thurmond, at a party in Thurmond's honor, in a way which suggested that Lott endorsed segregation. Despite the presence of several reporters from the conventional media at the party, no major media outlet picked up the story until long after it had been extensively reported in the blogosphere. Another, less well known example, was the story of US troops firing white phosphorus shells in order to burn insurgents alive during the storming of Fallujah in 2005, in breach of international laws against the use of chemical weapons. This story was started in the blogosphere and based on evidence obtained from a US Army magazine called *Field Artillery* (Davies, 2008, p. 395).

40 See, for example, http://tpmcafe.talkingpointsmemo.com/talk/blogs/ thejoshuablog/2009/05/ny-times-maureen-dowd-plagiari.php. Accessed December 11, 2010.

41 http://www.huffingtonpost.com/2009/06/23/huffposts-nico-pitney-ask_n_219865.html. Accessed December 11, 2010.

42 These epistemic panics are quite similar to the moral panics that tend to accompany any significant technological development. In fact I would argue that an epistemic panic is a form of moral panic.

43 Goldman does not argue for censorship (unless you consider filtering itself to be a form of censorship), nor does he draw any other conclusions about social policy. Nonetheless he does provide an argument which, if it were sound, would constitute a consideration in favor of censorship.

44 Most conventional media reports can be found in the blogosphere but relatively few reports in the blogosphere make it to the conventional media.

45 For example, he says the "question remains open whether communication systems that filter or those that don't have superior epistemic properties, specifically, are better at promoting true belief and/or avoiding error" (2008, p. 115). He also refers to the epistemic values of "promoting knowledge and avoiding error" (p. 116) as if these are distinguishable things.

46 See August 12, 2004, "The *Post* on WMDs: An Inside Story," http://www. washingtonpost.com/ac2/wp-dyn/A58127-2004Aug11?language= printer, Accessed December 11, 2010.

47 Andrew Sullivan, December 30, 2004, "Year of the Insurgents," http:// www.time.com/time/magazine/article/0,9171,1009920,00.html. Accessed December 11, 2010.

48 "Do You Belong in Journalism?" *New Yorker*, May 4, 1960.

49 Of course, there is also a sense in which they work for their employers.

50 Dan Froomkin, February 8, 2007, "Washington Journalism on Trial," http://www.washingtonpost.com/wp-dyn/content/blog/2007/02/08/ BL2007020801013.html. Accessed December 11, 2010.

7

Conclusion

This book has made no attempt to be exhaustive. Any attempt to cover all the important and interesting epistemic issues raised by the world we now live in would be doomed to failure. I will conclude by briefly discussing a selection of these issues and indicate in very general terms how they might be dealt with from the perspective of principles defended in this book, and, in the process, draw some general lessons about the project of applied epistemology.

Wikipedia and Traditional Encyclopedias

Wikipedia claims to be an encyclopedia,[1] so it is natural to wonder how it compares with traditional encyclopedias. A study in *Nature* comparing *Wikipedia* with *Encyclopedia Britannica* found that although the latter tended to be more accurate "the difference in accuracy was not particularly great" (Giles, 2005, p. 900). Nonetheless, there was apparently a difference and it did apparently favor *Encyclopedia Britannica*; does that mean *Encyclopedia Britannica* is epistemically superior to *Wikipedia*? By now it should be clear why we should resist this conclusion.

What To Believe Now: Applying Epistemology to Contemporary Issues,
First Edition. David Coady.
© 2012 David Coady. Published 2012 by Blackwell Publishing Ltd.

First, false reports do not necessarily lead to false beliefs. To suppose that they do is to suppose readers have an entirely passive relationship to what they read. This supposition is clearly illegitimate in the case of *Wikipedia* because *Wikipedia* itself provides resources which readers can use to assess the plausibility of its entries. In the first place, *Wikipedia* leaves a virtual paper trail, which allows any user to trace the steps by which an article has got to be the way it is. Readers can use this virtual paper trail to assess the integrity and competence of the process by which an entry has come into existence, which can in turn shed light on the plausibility of what it says. Furthermore, *Wikipedia* has rules requiring that sources (from outside *Wikipedia*) be provided for all claims; these sources can also be used by readers to help them assess the plausibility of what they read.

Second, even if false reports do lead to false beliefs, falsehood avoidance is not the only value at stake. This is a point we have seen in several places in this book. If encyclopedias were only concerned to avoid falsehood, they would have no entries at all, or at most they would have a small number of entries that they could be certain were completely accurate. As we have seen, truth acquisition is a value to be considered in addition to the value of falsehood avoidance; if an encyclopedia is to be serious about the value of promoting truth, it must have a large number of entries, with the inevitable consequence that it will include some errors, perhaps quite a lot of them. *Wikipedia* has more than 10 times as many entries as *Encyclopedia Britannica* (Runciman, 2009), and it is at least arguable that more errors (in both absolute terms and as a ratio to the total number of entries) is a price worth paying for this enormous quantity of information. Furthermore, it is at least arguable that we should be willing to accept an increase in the amount of falsehood we believe (in both absolute and relative terms) in return for a significant increase in the amount of truth we believe on topics in which we take an interest.

Because anyone with access to the internet can contribute to *Wikipedia*, it is tempting to treat it as a kind of large-scale rumor, and hence to see my qualified defense of *Wikipedia* as entailed by the qualified defense of rumor that I gave in Chapter 4. Nonetheless, I will resist this temptation. *Wikipedia* is an institution (albeit a nonprofit one) and rumors, as we have seen, by definition do not pass along institutionally sanctioned channels of communication. Most contributors to *Wikipedia*, unlike most rumor-mongers, see themselves as engaged in a single collective enterprise. This enterprise is governed by rules, and *Wikipedia* has a hierarchy that seeks to enforce those rules (Broughton, 2008). So, when P. D. Magnus characterizes the claims made in *Wikipedia* as "more like 'claims made in New York' than 'claims made in the *New York Times*'" (Magnus, 2009, p. 84) he is mistaken. Though there are obvious differences between *Wikipedia* and the *New York Times*, they are both institutions which gather and disseminate information widely, and their reliability depends, not only on their structure (e.g., the rules governing who can contribute and what they can contribute), but also on their culture. *Wikipedia* is a reasonably reliable source for a reasonably wide range of subjects because of the contingent fact that it has a reasonably good culture at the moment. Most of its contributors are reasonably well-informed on the topics they write about, and most of them are committed to the epistemic ideals of *Wikipedia*. I will not delve into those ideals here, partly because the culture of *Wikipedia* changes rapidly, and anything I say about it may no longer be true by the time this book goes to print, and partly because it would take me away from the political issues that have been my main focus in this book.

Torture

One political issue I have not discussed, which has recently been addressed in epistemic terms, is torture. Alan Dershowitz (2002) has influentially argued in favor of the state institutionalizing the practice of torture for interrogational purposes. Roger Koppl (2005) has argued against interrogational torture on the grounds that any information gained from it will be unreliable. Although this debate is of some theoretical interest, the question of whether the state should engage in torture is not, in my opinion, fundamentally an epistemic issue. The state should not torture because it is immoral, whether or not it works. If we reject torture because it is an unreliable source of information (supposing for the sake of argument that it is), then we are rejecting torture for the wrong reason. Koppl presents his argument as an example of veritistic social epistemology (VSE), which, as we have seen, is modeled on utilitarianism, with knowledge taking the place of happiness. Once again, an analogue of a criticism of utilitarianism seems applicable to VSE. Utilitarianism treats happiness as a good, no matter who is experiencing it or what is causing it. If torturers gain sadistic gratification from their work, then that counts, from the utilitarian perspective, as a consideration in favor of torture (albeit one which may be overridden by other considerations). But this kind of happiness is not a good of any kind and should not count, even a little bit, as a consideration in favor of any policy. Similarly, VSE treats knowledge (or at least knowledge of interesting or important subjects) as a good, no matter who gets the knowledge or how they got it. If torturers gain accurate information on a topic of interest from their work, then that counts, from the perspective of VSE, as a consideration in favor of torture (albeit one which may be overridden by other considerations). Once again, this seems to be wrong. VSE is wrong to treat knowledge (even interesting or important knowledge) as though it is always a good, just as classical utilitarianism was wrong to treat happiness as though it is always a good.[2]

I am not, of course, denying that knowledge is often very valuable (or that in some contexts it is intrinsically valuable). But I do deny that social epistemology (or applied epistemology in general) should be exclusively concerned with the question "How should we promote knowledge (or interesting or important knowledge)?"[3] It should be at least as interested in the question "How can we promote an environment in which people can draw their own conclusions about what to believe through free communication with others (testimony, debate, discussion, and so on)?" This is partly because free communication is intrinsically valuable, but it is also because experience shows that, in the long run, it is the best way of acquiring the truths that we should acquire.

Institutional Gullibility and Political Skepticism

A closely related theme that emerges from this book, especially from Chapters 4, 5, and 6, is about the nature of a certain epistemic vice, the vice of excessive willingness to believe institutional (as opposed to epistemic) authorities. This vice is closely related to (and arguably a form of)[4] a moral vice, the vice of excessive willingness to obey institutional authorities. It has been widely recognized, especially since the end of World War II, that obedience to orders from those in authority does not always excuse us for our deeds. It should be equally widely recognized that the fact that we weren't told something, or were lied to about it, by people in authority, does not always excuse either ignorance or error. We may have had an obligation to find out the truth. The communication revolution of the last two decades has dramatically widened the scope of this obligation. In *Henry V* (Act 4, Scene 1) a soldier laments that he and his comrades, who are about to fight in the battle of Agincourt, cannot know whether the cause for which they will fight is just. Another soldier reassures him that there is no need for them to know, "for we know enough, if we know we are the King's subjects. If his cause be wrong, our obedience to the King wipes the crime of it out of us." No one with access to the internet could justify unconditional obedience to the state in this way.

This book has had little to say about a problem that has dominated much of the history of epistemology, the problem of skepticism. Applied epistemologists should feel free to ignore this problem, and assume the correctness of the commonsense view that knowledge and justified belief are possible (just as applied ethicists typically ignore paradoxical metaethical views). The problem of skepticism has a special resonance, however, when it comes to politics. Skepticism about the possibility of political knowledge is not a mere classroom exercise designed to hone the wits of aspiring philosophers, but a widespread condition with real-world consequences. It is, as we have seen, frequently cited as an excuse for political inactivity or as an excuse for unquestioning obedience to the orders of our political masters. Political skepticism has a certain *prima facie* plausibility, because the subject matter of politics,[5] unlike the subject matter of natural science, for example, does have an interest in, and, to a greater or lesser extent, the power to influence, what is believed about it. In the natural realm, knowledge and/or justification may be hard to come by, but that is not because atoms (say) care what we believe about them.

Attractive though political skepticism is, we have a duty to resist it. Of course, we should be concerned when people are too confident of their political beliefs. But we should also be concerned when people are so scared of error that they fail to form political beliefs at all. When Bertrand Russell wrote an essay called "The Need For Political Scepticism" in which he claimed that any "well-intentioned person who believes in any strong political movement is merely helping to prolong that organized strife which is destroying our civilization" (Russell, 1928, p. 142), he may have been right. But now the greatest danger to our civilization comes from well-intentioned people who have no strong political beliefs at all and who, as a result, can be safely ignored by those in power who are not so well-intentioned.

Notes

1 This claim has been challenged. See P. D. Magnus (2009).
2 Some contemporary utilitarians, such as Peter Singer, talk of maximizing or promoting "preference satisfaction" rather than "happiness." The above argument applies equally to this form of utilitarianism. The fact that torture satisfies the preferences of torturers is not a consideration in its favor.
3 This point is meant to apply whether, like Goldman, you construe knowledge as just true belief or whether you give a thicker account of what it is.
4 Stanley Milgram's "obedience experiments" (Milgram, 1974) are a good example of the relation between these vices. In these experiments, many seemingly normal people were induced to commit (apparently) brutal acts, after being told to do so by a man wearing a laboratory coat. Many of the obedient subjects of these experiments justified their behavior by saying that they assumed that this "scientist" knew what he was doing.
5 Here I am thinking of the political class, that is, politicians and those who have the greatest influence on their decisions.

Postscript
Government Surveillance and Privacy

"You already have zero privacy – get over it."
Scott McNealy, CEO, Sun Microsystems

In Chapter 1, I noted that applied epistemology, like applied ethics, can be used to address questions of social policy. In particular, it can address questions about who is, and who is not, entitled to various kinds of knowledge. The presumptive right to know what one's government is doing is particularly important to the concerns of this book. It is, for example, central to the epistemic conception of democracy, which was discussed in Chapter 3; if we don't know what the government is doing, we cannot make reliable judgments about whether its mandate should be renewed. This right is also central to the ideal of an open society, which has been another important theme in this book. An open society is not a society in which there are no secrets. It is a society in which citizens have a right to know what government is doing, but government has no right to know what citizens are doing.[1] The ideal is of society as a one-way mirror, through which the citizen can observe the state, but the state cannot look back. Increasingly, this one-way mirror is pointing in the wrong direction. We know less and less about what the state is

What To Believe Now: Applying Epistemology to Contemporary Issues,
First Edition. David Coady.
© 2012 David Coady. Published 2012 by Blackwell Publishing Ltd.

doing,[2] while the state knows more and more about what we are doing.[3] I have already said enough about the importance of our being able to know what the state is doing. This epilogue is about the importance of limiting and regulating what the state can know about what we are doing. In other words, it is an argument against extensive and/or unregulated government surveillance.

Since criticisms of extensive and/or unregulated government surveillance (henceforth "the surveillance state") usually involve an appeal to privacy rights, it is tempting to explain the asymmetry in knowledge rights between people and their government by saying that people, unlike governments, have a right to privacy. But although I think it is true that people have a right to privacy and that governments have no such right, I don't think this is the best way to critique the surveillance state. In the first place, there are good reasons for thinking that the right to privacy cannot be the basis for an adequate critique of the surveillance state. In the second place, there are good reasons for opposing the surveillance state which have little or nothing to do with privacy considerations.

One reason for thinking that the right to privacy cannot be the basis of an adequate critique of the surveillance state is simply that this right seems too easily overridden. Even people who base their opposition to unrestricted government surveillance largely or entirely on considerations of privacy will sometimes concede that the right to privacy is not a particularly "strong" right. Andrew von Hirsch (2000), for example, while arguing that we have a right to privacy and that this right entails that there should be "significant" restrictions on government surveillance, nonetheless concedes that the right to privacy is not as stringent as certain other rights. Invoking Ronald Dworkin's influential idea that a right is a kind of "trump" (Dworkin, 1977, Ch. 7), which can override ordinary societal objectives such as crime prevention, von Hirsch describes the right to privacy as follows:

> Its "trumping" effect is not so strong as the right against torture (which should bar torture-based investigations entirely) or the right to free speech (which should permit prosecutions only when immediate and serious risk of criminal harm is involved). However, privacy should retain a significant protective effect in limiting how surveillance is carried out. (von Hirsch, 2000, p. 68)

But if the right to privacy is so weak that it can be overridden without the presence of any immediate and serious threat of criminal harm, it is not clear that, on its own, it provides significant grounds for restricting the state's powers to engage in surveillance of its citizens.

A second, closely related, reason to be cautious of appeals to privacy rights in general, and of their centrality to debates about government surveillance in particular, is that privacy rights are arguably (to use the Marxist language) "bourgeois rights" which promote the interests of the wealthy and powerful at the expense of the poor and powerless. Of course, some Marxists will claim that this is true of all rights (or at least all individual rights), but the view that individual rights are bourgeois in the Marxist sense is much more plausible in some cases than others. It is easy to see, for example, why one might think of property rights as bourgeois rights; but it is much harder to see how there could be anything particularly bourgeois about free speech rights (in fact I would argue that free speech rights are particularly important for the poor and powerless). Privacy rights seem much closer to property rights than free speech rights in this respect. Privacy rights are well suited to those who live in spacious houses surrounded by high fences. But for those who are homeless or who, for economic reasons, are compelled to live in close proximity to others, talk of a right to privacy is about as meaningful as talk of a right to caviar. For this reason, attempts to critique the surveillance state by appealing to the right to privacy cannot be expected to carry much weight with large sections of the population. Instead, such appeals tend to confirm widespread stereotypes to the effect that liberal political philosophy is elitist and out of touch with the concerns of ordinary people.

A third reason to be cautious about appeals to privacy rights in general, and the role of such appeals in the surveillance debate in particular, comes from feminist concerns about the way such appeals have historically been used to shield the domestic sphere from state action. Catharine MacKinnon has put the point as follows:

> The legal concept of privacy can and has shielded the place of battery, marital rape, and women's exploited labor; has preserved the central institutions whereby women are *deprived* of identity, autonomy, control, and self-definition. ... This right to privacy is a right of men "to be let alone" to oppress women one at a time. (MacKinnon, 1987, pp. 101–2)

Of course, appeals to privacy rights don't always lead to the oppression of women. Indeed such appeals have sometimes been used to liberate women in ways that feminists (generally) will support. Perhaps the most notable example of this is to be found in the abortion debate, and especially in the American Supreme Court decision *Roe v. Wade*, in which a woman's right to an abortion was defended as an aspect of her right to privacy.

Nonetheless it is not clear that an adequate account of women's rights (including their abortion rights) must include a right to privacy. Judith Jarvis Thomson (the author of one of the most influential defenses of abortion rights) has argued that anything that can legitimately be defended in terms of a right to privacy can just as well be defended in terms of some other right, or, as she puts it, "the right to privacy is everywhere overlapped by other rights" (Thomson, 1975, p. 310). A similar position has been endorsed by the legal theorist Frederick Davis in the following passage:

> If truly fundamental interests are accorded the protection they deserve, no need to champion a right to privacy arises. Invasion of privacy is, in reality, a complex of more fundamental wrongs. Similarly, the individual's interest in privacy itself, however real, is derivative and a state better vouchsafed by protecting more immediate rights. (Davis, 1959, p. 20)

I do not have the space to defend the Davis/Thomson view here (I do not think I could do a better job than they do themselves). I will, however, insist on two things. One is that, as MacKinnon and many other feminists have noted, appeals to privacy rights have often been used to harm the interests of women. The other is that where appeals to privacy rights have benefited women, it is plausible to think that the same outcomes could have been achieved without reference to the concept of privacy.

A fourth reason to think that privacy rights are an inadequate foundation for a critique of the surveillance state is based on the fact that our privacy can be, and often is, violated by entities other than the state. Indeed, it has been plausibly argued (e.g., Rosenblum, 1987; Kymlicka, 1990) that the emphasis on privacy that characterizes much contemporary liberal thought arose, not out of concerns about the power of the state, but out of concerns about the power of society, and the pressure toward conformity that society brings with it. As Hannah Arendt has observed, the modern concept of privacy "was discovered not as the opposite of the political sphere but of the social" (Arendt, 1959, p. 38). In an age in which the internet and other advances in information technology have made it almost inevitable that a wide variety of people and organizations will have access to information about us which we have not authorized them to have and which we would prefer them not to have, it is not clear whether unregulated surveillance by the state adds significantly to the privacy violations we have to endure anyway. What is more, so long as we are focused on privacy as the pre-eminent value at stake, state surveillance can be, and has been, defended, more or less plausibly, as a way of protecting our privacy rights against nonstate violators of those rights.

The lesson I take from all this is not that state surveillance is unproblematic or that it should be unregulated, but rather that many critics of the surveillance state have made a mistake by making privacy the central issue. There has been a growing tendency in recent decades, especially among American philosophers and legal theorists of a liberal bent, to defend any and all claims that individuals have against state power by appealing to the language of privacy and privacy rights. We've seen this in the abortion debate and we see it in the surveillance debate.

I hope I have said enough to at least *motivate* the search for a critique of the surveillance state, which is not presented in terms of privacy rights. I will develop such a critique through a discussion of a recent debate about one aspect of the surveillance state, the ever expanding and largely unregulated use of CCTV cameras in public places in many Western societies.

CCTV Cameras

Jesper Ryberg (2007) started a debate in the pages of the philosophy journal *Res Publica* when he compared being watched by a CCTV camera with being watched by a lonely old lady whom he calls Mrs Aremac (camera backward). Mrs Aremac is presented as someone who is incapable of participating directly in the life of her community because of a disability, and who makes up for her loss by spending her days gazing out the window at the passing parade. Ryberg presents Mrs Aremac as someone who is essentially helpless and harmless and whose life would have very little meaning if not for her innocent "voyeurism." He then asks the following questions:

> If Mrs Aremac is not in any way acting wrongly, then why and when does a CCTV camera placed at the third floor of a building monitoring daily life in the streets constitute a moral problem? Why does this sort of surveillance violate people's privacy rights if Mrs Aremac is not a rights violator? (Ryberg, 2007, p. 130)

Notice that in running these two questions together Ryberg conflates two issues, (1) whether there is anything wrong with the surveillance in question (Mrs Aremac's or the CCTV camera's), and (2) whether that surveillance is a violation of people's privacy rights. Although Ryberg elsewhere insists that he is not arguing that CCTV monitoring "does not constitute a moral problem," and that he is confining himself to what he sees as the more "limited" project of arguing that it does not constitute "a moral problem *in terms of privacy rights*" (p. 142), it should be clear that he considers his limited project to be a significant contribution to a defense of the state's use of CCTV cameras in public places.

His attitude is understandable, given the nature of the extant debate about this issue. Most critics of the unregulated use of CCTV cameras make an appeal to privacy rights central to their case. For this reason, Annabelle Lever and Benjamin Goold, the two authors who responded to Ryberg in the pages of *Res Publica*, were not content to argue that there are disanalogies between the surveillance of Mrs Aremac and that of a CCTV camera in virtue of which the latter, but not the former, is morally problematic (though they *do* argue that); they *also* argue that these disanalogies are such that the latter, unlike the former, is morally problematic *because* it involves a violation of people's privacy rights.

As we shall see, this latter conclusion is quite unconvincing. The lesson I take from this is not that Ryberg has succeeded in giving even a partial defense of the state's use of CCTV cameras in public places, but rather that those who find the state's use of CCTV cameras in public places objectionable have been wrong to express their objections in the language of privacy rights. This is not because these rights don't exist or shouldn't be legally protected, but because the objectionable features of CCTV camera use (and especially unregulated and widespread CCTV camera use) are best brought out without reference to the concept of privacy.

Now the most obvious difference between CCTV camera surveillance and Mrs Aremac's "surveillance" is that the former, unlike the latter, is carried out on behalf of the state. Benjamin Goold, in his response to Ryberg, takes this to be crucial:

> Unlike Mrs. Aremac, the state has a monopoly on the use of legitimate force and can, under certain circumstances, deprive me of both my liberty and my property. As a consequence, we seek to limit the things that may be done by the state in an effort to protect individuals from the dangers that are attendant with the existence of such power. (Goold, 2008, p. 45)

This is absolutely right. Unfortunately Goold immediately goes wrong by characterizing those dangers as dangers to privacy:

> If I know that the information being gathered by a camera might be passed on to the police or security services, I may decide that *my privacy is at risk* and choose to change my behaviour in public, particularly as regards who I choose to talk to or associate with. This is not to say that I consider myself to be doing anything wrong, but rather because I fear that the state may – incorrectly – view my actions as criminal and take action against me. Such concerns do not, however, arise in relation to Mrs. Aremac. (2008, p. 46, emphasis mine)

The first thing to note about this passage is that if Goold were really worried that the state might wrongly regard something he does as criminal and take action against him, any danger to his privacy would be the least of his concerns. In these circumstances, his liberty, his physical well-being, his very life, might well be at risk. His privacy would also be at risk (especially if he were to end up in prison) but that is only one risk among many, and a relatively minor one at that. Of course it would be possible to characterize these other risks as risks to his privacy. But to do so would obviously be to stretch the English language out of all recognizable shape.

The second thing to note about the above passage is that it is very far from clear that Goold is right that his concerns about having to alter his behavior in response to the danger of the state mistakenly thinking he is engaged in criminal activity do not "arise in relation to Mrs Aremac." After all, Mrs Aremac might incorrectly form the opinion that someone in the street has done something criminal and inform the agents of the state (presumably the police), who might in turn take action against that person. What is more, people might very well change their behavior because they are concerned that someone like Mrs Aremac is watching them. Presumably Goold thinks that people are more likely to feel the need to change their behavior in response to CCTV cameras than in response to the Mrs Aremacs of this world. But it's not clear why he would think that, given that the only reason he gives for people changing their behavior in response to CCTV cameras is fear that some innocent action on their part may wrongly be construed by the state as criminal. Of course CCTV cameras *might* cause the state to make such mistakes. But they also *might* help the state avoid making such mistakes (by providing alibis for the innocent, identifying the real perpetrators, and so on). What Goold would need, to make this argument persuasive, is some reason for thinking that the dangers of the former outweigh the benefits of the latter. He doesn't provide any such reason and it is hard to see how he could. After all, there is no suggestion (as far as I am aware) that CCTV cameras are particularly unreliable as tools for gathering information. Although CCTV cameras *could* presumably lead agents of the state to think that an innocent act was in fact criminal, it's hard to imagine *any method* police (or other agents of the state) could use to gather information which does not involve that risk. Presumably Goold would not want to argue that the state should not investigate crime, because investigating crime *could* result in innocent people being arrested or even convicted.

At this point it is worth pausing to note that there seems something paradoxical about supposing that the use of CCTV cameras *in public areas* could violate people's privacy rights. How can people have a right to privacy in public? Don't they give up whatever claims they have to privacy when they go out into public places? Liberal critics of CCTV camera surveillance in public places, including Goold (2002, 2006), von Hirsch (2000), and Slobogin (2002), have responded to this difficulty by conceding that although we do give up some of our privacy rights when we are in public places, we do not give up our right to a particular form of privacy which they identify with *anonymity*. It is privacy in this sense, privacy as anonymity, which, they claim, is at issue in the CCTV camera debate. Goold puts the position this way:

> The widespread use of CCTV represents a significant threat to anonymity – and therefore privacy – in public spaces. Although the presence of a surveillance camera may not in and of itself destroy anonymity, the fact that that CCTV systems are capable of taking pictures that can later be used to identify particular individuals undoubtedly does. Under the gaze of CCTV, it is simply impossible to blend into the situational landscape, or be confident that one is acting anonymously. (Goold, 2006, p. 5)

But this kind of argument plays directly into Ryberg's hands. Is Mrs Aremac violating my right to privacy if she recognizes me (and hence deprives me of my anonymity) as I walk down the street? That seems pretty implausible. Is she violating my right to privacy if she goes out of her way to identify me after I have walked by? Well, maybe, but there doesn't seem to be anything very objectionable about it, unless she uses the information to cause me some harm (or further harm, if you think that any intrusion on privacy is in itself a harm).

Goold is right that "little old ladies in windows are not the same as CCTV cameras, and we clearly have good reasons to object to the latter even if we are willing to accept or tolerate the former" (Goold, 2008, p. 46). He is wrong to explicate the differences in terms of privacy or privacy rights. In trying to explain the difference between the state and Mrs Aremac, Goold comes very close to claiming that privacy rights can only be understood as rights against the state.[4] He does explicitly suggest that "privacy rights in public spaces" are such that they "can only be rights against the state" (p. 46). But this position is extremely counterintuitive. There are all kinds of ways that nonstate agents could behave toward me in public, which I would naturally describe as violations of my privacy (this becomes even clearer if you accept the idea that anonymity is a form of privacy, since that would mean anyone who recognizes me in public is *eo ipso* violating my privacy). Of course, Goold *could* claim that although my privacy can be violated in public spaces by nonstate agents, I have no *right* to my privacy in those cases. But this would seem to be an entirely *ad hoc* move. If we really have privacy rights in public spaces (as Goold and other liberal critics of CCTV surveillance suppose), there is no more reason to think that those rights are only rights against the state than there is to think that our privacy rights in private spaces are only rights against the state. As I have already argued, to the extent that our privacy stands in need of protection, it needs to be protected against the intrusions of our fellow-citizens as well as (and perhaps as much as) against the intrusions of the state.

Annabelle Lever, the other author who responded to Ryberg in the pages of *Res Publica*, also claims that CCTV cameras violate our privacy in a way that Mrs Aremac's "surveillance" does not. She offers a slightly different argument, however. She claims that because CCTV cameras indiscriminately survey everything that takes place within a given area, they treat all people within that area as potential criminals. She goes on to say that "it strikes me that there is something seriously wrong with treating people as incipient criminals, whilst providing no evidence and no grounds for them to rebut the presumption" (Lever, 2008, p. 39).

But this is not very persuasive. In the first place, as Ryberg points out in response (Ryberg, 2008), it is not clear that treating everyone within a given area as potential criminals is necessarily objectionable. If it were, it would seem to be objectionable to put a lock on your bike when you leave it in public. In the second place, even if it were wrong to treat everyone within a given area as a potential criminal, it is very unclear why it should be regarded as a violation of their right to privacy. Lever claims that "as privacy is one of the first things to go when we do not trust each other to behave lawfully, the threat to privacy is intimately, not contingently, related to the supposition that we are potential criminals" (Lever, 2008, p. 39). But, as Ryberg points out, this argument seems to put Lever in an untenable position:

> In order to sustain the overall claim that CCTV monitoring violates people's right to privacy, it seems that Lever has to commit herself to a view along the lines of: "if X does not trust Y, then X has violated the privacy right of Y". (Ryberg, 2008, p. 54)

Clearly such a view would be absurd. No one has the right to be universally trusted.

The Real Problem with the Surveillance State

So what is really wrong with widespread and largely unregulated use of CCTV cameras by the state, and what is wrong more generally with the ever-expanding surveillance state? I submit that the correct answer has little to do with privacy or privacy rights. It also has little to do with any danger that the state may mistakenly construe noncriminal behavior as criminal and, as a result, take action against innocent people. Nor does it have much to do with the fact that subjects of surveillance may feel compelled to change their behavior out of fear that the state may make a mistake of this kind. Finally, it has little to do with the fact that such surveillance treats us all as potential criminals (after all, in a sufficiently broad sense of "potential" we are all potential criminals).

Instead, the best answer to this question is to be found in traditional liberal concerns about unfettered state power, which predate liberalism's relatively recent incorporation of what was essentially a romantic (and therefore nonliberal and even illiberal) concern with privacy as a (or even the) central political value. The problem with both sides of the *Res Publica* debate is the implicit assumption that government can be trusted to be well-intentioned (this is the assumption we saw Sunstein and Vermeule (2009) making explicitly in Chapter 5). Ryberg just assumes that CCTV cameras will not be used for purposes other than crime prevention (2007, 128–9), and neither of his critics challenge this assumption.[5] But it is an assumption that is anathema to the most fundamental tradition of liberalism, that is, unwillingness to trust the motives of the state. Traditional liberalism stressed the importance of limiting the power of the state, to prevent it from engaging in persecution, and especially to prevent it from persecuting opponents of the government of the day. The intimate connection between power and knowledge, recognized by Francis Bacon, means that realistic attempts to limit the state's power to this end must include significant limitations on its power to gather information on its citizens. The guiding principle is (roughly) that the state should not be allowed to gather information about its citizens without their consent unless it can demonstrate that they are reasonably suspected of criminal activity.[6]

Unregulated and/or widespread use of CCTV is objectionable, because it makes it much easier for governments and government agencies to gather information about people who are not reasonably suspected of criminal activity. It is objectionable for governments or government agencies to gather such information, not (or at least not principally) because it is a violation of the privacy rights of the people in question, but rather because it makes it more likely that they will be persecuted. When this happens, it is of course a violation of their rights (including, very often, their privacy rights), but it is also a significant harm to society as a whole. It should not be necessary for me to dwell on the value of dissent to any society, or on the history of states (including many of the most liberal ones) using information they have gathered on dissidents to violate their most fundamental rights and suppress dissent.

In contemporary Western societies, most citizens are neither criminals nor dissidents, nor are they members of any group that is likely to be persecuted by the state. As such, many of them adopt the attitude that since they have nothing to hide they have nothing to fear. In response, a number of critics of surveillance have argued in effect that the act of surveillance is harmful *in itself*. This alleged harm consists in a violation of privacy, which, allegedly, is something they should be concerned about, even when it has no further effect on them. This line of argument seems to me (and I suspect to most citizens of most Western countries) extremely unconvincing. Most citizens are not significantly harmed, at least in the short term, by being constantly surveyed by the state (at least when they are in public). Hence they tend to be indifferent to the issue. In order to get them to care about their noncriminal fellow citizens who are more likely to be harmed by such surveillance we need to appeal to their sense of compassion as well as their sense of justice. Perhaps most importantly, however, we need to appeal to their long-term self-interest. Governments do not last forever, and, as a result, people who are not dissidents today may become dissidents tomorrow without changing their opinions. In 2009, the US Department of Homeland Security issued a report warning local police forces of "growing right-wing extremist activity" and calling for close monitoring of groups opposed to abortion or immigration.[7] This report was immediately denounced by many of the most prominent apologists for the surveillance state during the Bush administration.[8] None of these born-again critics of the surveillance state complained when, in the not too distant past, the Department of Homeland Security issued a report on the dangers of "Leftwing extremists."[9] Nor did they object when the FBI engaged in surveillance of noncriminal groups such as PETA, Greenpeace, and the Catholic Worker Group.[10] Now that the surveillance powers they supported and helped realize are being used to target groups with which they are sympathetic, they are scared and outraged.

Government surveillance, like any surveillance, is by definition an intrusion on privacy. When, if ever, it violates a right to privacy, how severe a violation it is, and how such a violation should be weighed against other considerations, are all matters about which reasonable people may reasonably disagree. But there should be no disagreement among reasonable people about the principal dangers of the surveillance state. These dangers have little to do with privacy or privacy rights. Widespread and largely unregulated government surveillance constitutes a threat to certain noncriminal groups, most obviously dissidents and despised minorities. For this reason, we should all, including those who don't themselves belong to any threatened group, be vigilant against the surveillance state. This is not merely a matter of justice (though it is that); for each of us it is a matter of our own long-term self-interest. By making privacy and privacy rights central to their case, many liberals and civil libertarians have inadvertently obscured and trivialized what is really at stake in the surveillance debate.

Notes

1   This does not mean, of course, that governments shouldn't keep any information about any of their citizens. I will have more to say about principles governing this later. A citizen's right to know what his or her government is doing should be overridden only in circumstances of dire emergency, and then only for as long as the emergency lasts.

2   More and more government activities are classified on grounds of national security, while whistleblowers and those who publish their revelations are often prosecuted (and sometimes threatened with extrajudicial action).

3   Changes in the law, changes in technology, and changes in societal attitudes as a result of the "War on Terror," have vastly increased the scope of government surveillance in Western countries.

4   He does claim that "when an agent of the state enters a private residence without permission, we typically think of this as an invasion of privacy. Yet when an individual does the same, we are more likely to characterize the conduct as a form of trespass and a violation of the owner's property rights" (2008, p. 46). This does not accord with my intuitions, for reasons that should become clear later in this paragraph.

5   Goold (2008) does challenge Ryberg's portrayal of Mrs Aremac as a harmless and benign figure, but he doesn't explicitly challenge Ryberg's assumption that the only purpose of CCTV cameras is crime control.

6   This is only meant to be an approximation. In some circumstances the state should be allowed to gather information about people who are reasonably believed to be in a position to help with criminal investigations, though they are not themselves suspected of criminal behavior. Detailed discussion of the precise limits which should be placed on this kind of information gathering is beyond the scope of this book.

7   This information comes from *The Washington Times*, April 14, 2009, http://www.washingtontimes.com/news/2009/apr/14/federal-agency-warns-of-radicals-on-right. Accessed November 1, 2010.

8   Glenn Greenwald, "The Ultimate Reaping of What One Sows: Right-Wing Edition," April 14, 2009, http://www.salon.com/opinion/greenwald/2009/04/14/surveillance/index.html. Accessed November 1, 2010.

9   "Leftwing Extremists Likely to Increase Use of Cyber Attacks over the Coming Decade," January 26, 2009, http://www.foxnews.com/projects/pdf/Leftwing_Extremist_Threat.pdf. Accessed November 1, 2010.

10 Eric Lichtblau, "F.B.I. Watched Activist Groups, New Files Show," December 20, 2005, http://www.nytimes.com/2005/12/20/politics/20fbi.html?_r=1. Accessed November 1, 2010.

References

Adler, J. E. (2002) *Belief's Own Ethics*. MIT Press, Cambridge, MA.

Adler, J. E. (2007) "Gossip and Truthfulness." In: J. Mecke (ed.), *Cultures of Lying*. Galda & Wilch Verlag, Berlin, pp. 69–78.

Almassi, B. (2007) "Review of *The Philosophy of Expertise.*" *Ethics: An International Journal of Social, Political, and Legal Philosophy*, 117. 2, 377–81.

Allport, G. W. & Postman, L. (1947) *The Psychology of Rumor*. Henry Holt, New York.

Alston, W. P. (1989) *Epistemic Justification: Essays in the Theory of Knowledge*. Cornell University Press, Ithaca, NY.

Anderson, L. R. & Holt, C. A. (1997) "Information Cascades in the Laboratory." *American Economic Review*, 87, 847–62.

Archard, D. (2011) "Why Moral Philosophers Are Not and Should Not Be Experts." *Bioethics*, 25.3, 119–27.

Arendt, H. (1959) *The Human Condition*. Anchor, New York.

Aristotle (1924) *The Works of Aristotle, vol. 8: Metaphysics*, trans. W. D. Ross. Clarendon Press, Oxford.

Audi, R. (2001) "Doxastic Voluntarism and the Ethics of Belief." In: M. Steup (ed.), *Knowledge, Truth, and Duty: Essays on Epistemic Justification, Responsibility, and Virtue*. Oxford University Press, New York, pp. 93–111.

Ayto, J. (1999) *Twentieth Century Words*. Oxford University Press, Oxford.

Bambrough, R. (ed.) (1967) *Plato, Popper and Politics*. Heffer, Cambridge, UK.

Bartels, L. M. (1996) "Uninformed Votes: Information Effects in Presidential Elections." *American Journal of Political Science*, 40, 194–230.

Basham, L. (2006a) "Living with the Conspiracy." In: D. Coady (ed.), *Conspiracy Theories: The Philosophical Debate*. Ashgate, Aldershot, UK, pp. 61–76.

Basham, L. (2006b) "Malevolent Global Conspiracy." In: D. Coady (ed.), *Conspiracy Theories: The Philosophical Debate*. Ashgate, Aldershot, UK, pp. 93–106.

Bauer, R. A. & Gleicher, D. B. (1953) "Word-of-Mouth Communication in the Soviet Union." *Public Opinion Quarterly*, 17, 297–310.

Berkeley, G. (1962/1710) *The Principles of Human Knowledge*, ed. G. J. Warnock. Collins, London.

Berlin, I. (1978) "The Hedgehog and the Fox." In: H. Hardy & A. Kelly (eds.), *Russian Thinkers*. Viking Press, New York, pp. 22–81.

Bernstein, M. H. (1986) "Moral and Epistemic Saints." *Metaphilosophy*, 17.2–3, 102–8.

Bonjour, L. (1985) *The Structure of Empirical Knowledge*. Harvard University Press, Cambridge, MA.

Brewer, S. (1998) "Scientific Expert Testimony and Intellectual Due Process." *Yale Law Journal*, 107, 1535–1681.

Broad, C. D. (1925) *The Mind and its Place in Nature*. Routledge & Kegan Paul, London.

Broad, C. D. (1952) *Ethics and the History of Philosophy*. Routledge & Kegan Paul, London.

Broughton, J. (2008) *Wikipedia: The Missing Manual*. O'Reilly, Sebastopol, CA.

Brunvand, J. H. (1981) *The Vanishing Hitchhiker: American Urban Legends and Their Meaning*. Norton, New York.

Brunvand, J. H. (1999) *Too Good To Be True: The Colossal Book of Urban Legends*. Norton, New York.

Buchanan, J. & Tullock, G. (1962) *The Calculus of Consent*. University of Michigan Press, Ann Arbor.

Caplow, T. (1947) "Rumors in War." *Social Forces*, 25, 298–302.

Chadwick, P. (1996) "Ethics and Journalism." In: M. Coady & S. Bloch (eds.), *Codes of Ethics and the Professions*. Melbourne University Press, Melbourne, pp. 244–66.

Chomsky, N. (1980) *Rules and Representations*. Basil Blackwell, Oxford.

Christiano, T. (1995) "Voting and Democracy." *Canadian Journal of Philosophy*, 25.3, 395–414.

Clarke, S. (2006) "Conspiracy Theories and Conspiracy Theorizing." In: D. Coady (ed.), *Conspiracy Theories: The Philosophical Debate*. Ashgate, Aldershot, UK, pp. 77–92.

Clarke, S. (2007) "Conspiracy Theories and the Internet: Controlled Demolition and Arrested Development." *Episteme: A Journal of Social Epistemology*, 4.2, 167–80.

References

Clifford, W. K. (1947/1877) "The Ethics of Belief." In: L. Stephen & F. Pollock (eds.), *The Ethics of Belief and Other Essays by W.K. Clifford*. Watts, London, pp. 70–96.

Coady, C. A. J. (1992) *Testimony: A Philosophical Study*. Clarendon Press, Oxford.

Coady, C. A. J. (2006) "Pathologies of Testimony." In: J. Lackey & E. Sosa (eds.), *The Epistemology of Testimony*. Oxford University Press, Oxford, pp. 253–71.

Coady, D. (ed.) (2006a) *Conspiracy Theories: The Philosophical Debate*. Ashgate, Aldershot, UK.

Coady, D. (2006b) "Conspiracy Theories and Official Stories." In: D. Coady (ed.), *Conspiracy Theories: The Philosophical Debate*. Ashgate, Aldershot, UK, pp. 115–29.

Coady, D. (2006c) "Rumour Has It." *International Journal of Applied Philosophy*, 20.1, 41–53.

Coady, D. (2006d) "When Experts Disagree." *Episteme: A Journal of Social Epistemology*, 3.1–2, 68–79.

Coady, D. (ed.) (2007a) *Conspiracy Theories*. Special issue of *Episteme: A Journal of Social Epistemology*, 4.2.

Coady, D. (2007b) "Are Conspiracy Theorists Irrational?" *Episteme: A Journal of Social Epistemology*, 4.2, 193–204.

Coady, D. (2010) "Two Concepts of Epistemic Injustice." *Episteme: A Journal of Social Epistemology*, 7.2, 101–13.

Coady, D. (2011) "An Epistemic Defence of the Blogosphere." *Journal of Applied Philosophy*, 28.3, 277–94.

Condorcet, Marquis de (1994/1785) "An Essay on the Application of Probability Theory to Plurality Decision Making." In: I. McLean & F. Hewitt (eds. & trans.), *Condorcet: Foundations of Social Choice and Political Theory*. Edward Elgar, Brookfield, VT, pp. 120–38.

Conquest, R. (1992) "The Purge Expurgated." In: F. Mount (ed.), *Communism*. Harvill, London, pp. 244–51.

Crease, R. & Selinger, E. (eds.) (2006) *The Philosophy of Expertise*. Columbia University Press, New York.

Dadge, D. (2006) *The War in Iraq and Why the Media Failed Us*. Praeger, Westport, CT.

Davies. N. (2008) *Flat Earth News*. Random House, London.

Davis, F. (1959) "What Do We Mean by 'Right to Privacy'?" *South Dakota Law Review*, 4, 1–24.

Dawkins, R. (1976) *The Selfish Gene*. Oxford University Press, Oxford.

Dean, J. (1998) *Aliens in America: Conspiracy Cultures from Outerspace to Cyberspace*. Cornell University Press, Ithaca, NY.

Dershowitz, A. (2002) *Why Terrorism Works*. Yale University Press, New Haven, CT.

Dewey, J. (1997/1916) *Democracy and Education*. Free Press, New York.

DiFonzo, N. & Bordia, P. (2007) *Rumor Psychology: Social and Organizational Approaches*. American Psychological Association, Washington, DC.

DuCann, C. D. L. (1960) *Miscarriages of Justice*. Frederic Muller, London.

References

Dummett, M. (1984) *Voting Procedures*. Oxford University Press, Oxford.
Dworkin, R. (1977) *Taking Rights Seriously*. Harvard University Press, Cambridge, MA.
Edel, A., Flower, E., & O'Connor, F. W. (1994) *Critique of Applied Ethics: Reflections and Recommendations*. Temple University Press, Philadelphia.
Eisenstein, E. I. (1983) *The Printing Revolution in Early Modern Europe*. Cambridge University Press, Cambridge.
Elga, A. (2010) "How to Disagree About How to Disagree." In: R. Feldman & T. A. Warfield (eds.), *Disagreement*. Oxford University Press, Oxford, pp. 175–86.
Ellsberg, D. (2002) *Secrets: A Memoir of Vietnam and the Pentagon Papers*. Viking, New York.
Elster, J. (ed.) (1998) *Deliberative Democracy*. Cambridge University Press, Cambridge, UK.
Estlund, D. M. (1990) "Democracy Without Preference." *Philosophical Review* 99.3, 397–423.
Feldman, R. (2001) "Voluntary Belief and Epistemic Evaluation." In: M. Steup (ed.), *Knowledge, Truth, and Duty: Essays on Epistemic Justification*, Responsibility and Virtue. Oxford University Press, New York, pp. 77–92.
Figdor, C. (2010) "Is Objective News Possible?" In: C. Meyers (ed.), *Journalism Ethics: A Philosophical Approach*. Oxford University Press, Oxford, pp. 153–64.
Frankfurt, H. (2006) *On Bullshit*. Princeton University Press, Princeton, NJ.
Fricker, E. (1994) "Against Gullibility." In: B. K. Matilal & A. Chakrabarti (eds.), *Knowing from Words*. Kluwer, Boston, pp. 125–61.
Fricker, E. (1995) "Critical Notice: Telling and Trusting: Reductionism and Anti-Reductionism in the Epistemology of Testimony." *Mind*, 104, 393–411.
Gerber, D. E. (ed. & trans.) (1991) *Greek Iambic Poetry: From the Seventh to the Fifth Centuries BC*. Harvard University Press, Cambridge, MA.
Gettier, E. (1963) "Is Justified True Belief Knowledge?" *Analysis*, 23, 121–3.
Getty, J. A. (1985) *Origins of the Great Purges*. Cambridge University Press, Cambridge, UK.
Giles, J. (2005) "Internet Encyclopaedias Go Head to Head." *Nature*, 438, 900–1.
Goldman, A. I. (1999a) "Internalism Exposed." *The Journal of Philosophy*, 96.6, 271–93.
Goldman, A. I. (1999b) *Knowledge in a Social World*. Oxford University Press, Oxford.
Goldman, A. I. (2001) "Experts: Which Ones Should You Trust?" *Philosophy and Phenomenological Research*, 63, 85–110.
Goldman, A. I. (2002) "The Unity of the Epistemic Virtues." In: *Pathways to Knowledge: Private and Public*. Oxford University Press, Oxford, pp. 51–72.

References

Goldman, A. I. (2008) "The Social Epistemology of Blogging." In: J. Van Den Hoven & J. Weckert (eds.), *Information Technology and Moral Philosophy*. Cambridge University Press, Cambridge, UK, pp. 111–22.

Goodin, R. E. (1995) *Utilitarianism as a Public Philosophy*. Cambridge University Press, Cambridge, UK.

Goodin, R. E. (2002) "The Paradox of Persisting Opposition." *Politics, Philosophy and Economics*, 1.1, 109–46.

Goold, B. J. (2002) "Privacy Rights and Public Spaces: CCTV and the Problem of the 'Unobservable Observer.'" *Criminal Justice Ethics*, 21, 21–7.

Goold, B. J. (2006) "Open to All? Regulating Open Street CCTV and the Case for 'Symmetrical Surveillance.'" *Criminal Justice Ethics*, 25, 3–17.

Goold, B. J. (2008) "The Difference Between Lonely Old Ladies and CCTV Cameras: A Response to Jesper Ryberg." *Res Publica*, 14, 43–7.

Grice, P. (1989) *Studies in the Ways of Words*. Harvard University Press, Cambridge, MA.

Grofman, B. & Feld, S. (1988) "Rousseau's General Will: A Condorcetian Perspective." *American Political Science Review*, 82, 567–76.

Haight, R. M. (1980) *A Study of Self-Deception*. Harvester Press, Brighton, UK.

Hardwig, J. (1991) "The Role of Trust in Knowledge." *Journal of Philosophy*, 88.12, 693–708.

Heil, J. (1983) "Doxastic Agency." *Philosophical Studies*, 43, 355–64.

Herman, E. S. & Chomsky, N. (1989) *Manufacturing Consent*. Pantheon Books, New York.

Hersh, S. (1972) *Cover-Up*. Random House, New York.

Hume, D. (1966/1748) *An Enquiry Concerning Human Understanding*, ed. L. A. Selby-Bigge, 2nd edn. Clarendon Press, Oxford.

Hume, D. (1967/1740) *A Treatise of Human Nature*, ed. L. A. Selby-Bigge. Clarendon Press, Oxford.

Huntington, S. P. (1991) *The Third Wave: Democratization in the Late Twentieth Century*. University of Oklahoma Press, Norman.

James, W. (2007/1897) *The Will to Believe and Other Essays in Popular Philosophy*. Cosimo, New York.

Kapferer, J.-N. (1990) *Rumors: Uses, Interpretations, and Images*. Transaction, Brunswick, NJ.

Keeley, B. L. (2006) "Of Conspiracy Theories." In: D. Coady (ed.), *Conspiracy Theories: The Philosophical Debate*. Ashgate, Aldershot, UK, pp. 45–60.

Kelly, T. (2010) "Peer Disagreement and Higher-Order Evidence." In: R. Feldman & T. A. Warfield (eds.), *Disagreement*. Oxford University Press, Oxford, pp. 111–74.

Kinder, D. R. & Kiewiet, D. R. (1981) "Sociotropic Politics: The American Case." *British Journal of Political Science*, 11.2, 129–61.

Klaidman, S. & Beauchamp, T. L. (1987) *The Virtuous Journalist*. Oxford University Press, Oxford.

Knapp, R. H. (1944) "A Psychology of Rumor." *Public Opinion Quarterly*, 8.1, 22–37.
Koppl, R. (2005) "Epistemic Systems." *Episteme: A Journal of Social Epistemology*, 2.2, 91–106.
Kymlicka, W. (1990) *Contemporary Political Philosophy*. Clarendon Press, Oxford.
LeBlanc, J. (1998) *Thinking Clearly: A Guide to Critical Thinking*. W. W. Norton, New York.
Lemann, N. (1989) "White House Watch." *The New Republic*, January 2–16, 34–8.
Lever, A. (2008) "Mrs. Aremac and the Camera: A Response to Ryberg." *Res Publica*, 14, 35–42.
Levy, N. (2007a) "Doxastic Responsibility." *Synthese*, 155.1, 127–55.
Levy, N. (2007b) "Radically Socialized Knowledge and Conspiracy Theories." *Episteme: A Journal of Social Epistemology*, 4.2, 181–92.
Lewis, D. (2000) "Academic Appointments: Why Ignore the Advantage of Being Right?" In: *Papers in Ethics and Social Philosophy*. Cambridge University Press, Cambridge, UK, pp. 187–200.
Lifton, R. (1986) *The Nazi Doctors: Medical Killing and the Psychology of Genocide*. Basic Books, New York.
List, C. & Goodin, R. (2001) "Epistemic Democracy: Generalizing the Condorcet Jury Theorem." *Journal of Political Philosophy*, 9.3, 277–306.
Locke, J. (1961/1690) *An Essay Concerning Human Understanding*, ed. J. W. Youlton. Dent, London.
Locke, J. (1999/1689) *A Letter Concerning Toleration*. Prometheus Books, Buffalo, NY.
Loewenstein, A. (2008) *The Blogging Revolution*. Melbourne University Press, Melbourne.
Machiavelli, N. (1979/1532) *The Prince*, ed. & trans. P. Bondanella & M. Musa. Oxford University Press, Oxford.
Mackie, J. L. (1970) "The Possibility of Innate Knowledge." *Proceedings of the Aristotelian Society*, 70, 245–57.
MacKinnon, C. (1987) *Feminism Unmodified: Discourses on Life and Law*. Duckworth, London.
Magnus, P. D. (2009) "On Trusting Wikipedia." *Episteme: A Journal of Social Epistemology*, 6.1, 74–90.
Mandik, P. (2007) "Shit Happens." *Episteme: A Journal of Social Epistemology*, 4.2, 205–18.
Massing, M. (2004) "Now They Tell Us." *New York Review of Books*, February 26, 43–9.
Massing, M. (2009) "The News About the Internet." *New York Review of Books*, August 13, 29–32.
Matheson, D. (2005) "Conflicting Experts and Dialectical Performance: Adjudication Heuristics for the Layperson." *Argumentation*, 19, 145–58.

References

Meyers, C. (ed.) (2010) *Journalism Ethics: A Philosophical Approach.* Oxford University Press, Oxford.

Milgram, S. (1974) *Obedience to Authority: An Experimental View.* Harper and Row, New York.

Mill, J. S. (2008/1859) *On Liberty.* The Folio Society, London

Miller, D. (1992) "Deliberative Democracy and Social Choice." *Political Studies,* 40, 54–67.

Mitchell, G. (2008) *So Wrong for So Long.* Union Square Press, New York.

Morgenthau, H. J. (1967) *Politics Among Nations: The Struggle for Power and Peace.* Knopf, New York.

Nottelmann, N. (2006) "The Analogy Argument for Doxastic Voluntarism." *Philosophical Studies,* 131, 559–82.

Nozick, R. (1974) *Anarchy State and Utopia.* Basic Books, New York.

Olson, M. (1965) *The Logic of Collective Action: Public Goods and the Theory of Groups.* Harvard University Press, Cambridge, MA.

Orwell, G. (1961) "Charles Dickens." In: *George Orwell: Collected Essays.* Secker and Warburg, London, pp. 31–87.

Paluch, S. (1967) "Self-Deception." *Inquiry* 10, 268–78.

Patterson, T. (1993) *Out of Order.* Knopf, New York.

Pigden, C. (2006a) "Complots of Mischief." In: D. Coady (ed.), *Conspiracy Theories: The Philosophical Debate.* Ashgate, Aldershot, UK, pp. 139–66.

Pigden, C. (2006b) "Popper Revisited, or What is Wrong with Conspiracy Theories." In: D. Coady (ed.), *Conspiracy Theories: The Philosophical Debate.* Ashgate, Aldershot, UK, pp. 17–44.

Pigden, C. (2007) "Conspiracy Theories and the Conventional Wisdom." *Episteme: A Journal of Social Epistemology,* 4.2, 219–32.

Pipes, D. (1997) *Conspiracy: How the Paranoid Style Flourishes and Where it Came From.* Free Press, New York.

Plato (1997) *Complete Works,* ed. J. M. Cooper. Hackett, Indianapolis, IN.

Plutarch (1999) *Roman Lives,* R. Waterfield (trans.). Oxford University Press, Oxford.

Pollock, J. (1986) *Contemporary Theories of Knowledge.* Rowman and Littlefield, Lanham, MD.

Popper, K. R. (1962) *The Open Society and its Enemies, vol. 2, The High Tide of Prophecy: Hegel, Marx and the Aftermath,* 4th edn. Routledge & Kegan Paul, London.

Popper, K. R. (1972) *Conjectures and Refutations,* 4th edn. Routledge & Kegan Paul, London.

Posner, R. A. (2003) *Law, Pragmatism and Democracy.* Harvard University Press, Cambridge, MA.

Posner, R. A. (2005) "Bad News." Book review, *New York Times,* July 31, 1–11.

Poundstone, W. (2008) *Gaming the Vote: Why Elections Aren't Fair and What Can be Done About It.* Hill and Wang, New York.

Räikkä, J. (2009) "On Political Conspiracy Theories." *The Journal of Political Philosophy*, 17.2, 185–201.

Rawls, J. (1971) *A Theory of Justice.* Oxford University Press, Oxford.

Reid, T. (1970/1764) *Inquiry Into the Human Mind*, ed. T. Duggan. University of Chicago Press, Chicago.

Reid, T. (2006/1785) *Essays on the Intellectual Powers of Man.* Kessinger, Whitefish, MT.

Rosenblum, N. L. (1987) *Another Liberalism: Romanticism and the Reconstruction of Liberal Thought.* Harvard University Press, Cambridge, MA.

Rosnow, R. L. & Fine, G. A. (1976) *Rumor and Gossip: The Social Psychology of Hearsay.* Elsevier, New York.

Rousseau, J. (1967/1762) *The Social Contract and Other Later Political Writings*, ed. & trans V. Gourevitch. Cambridge University Press, Cambridge, UK.

Runciman, D. (2009) "Like Boiling a Frog." *London Review of Books, May* 28, 14–16.

Russell, B. (1928) *Sceptical Essays.* George Allen & Unwin, London.

Ryberg, J. (2007) "Privacy Rights, Crime Prevention, CCTV, and the Life of Mrs. Aremac." *Res Publica*, 13, 127–43.

Ryberg, J. (2008) "Moral Rights and the Problem of Privacy in Public: A Reply to Lever and Goold." *Res Publica*, 14, 49–56.

Sahdra, B. & Thagard, P. (2003) "Self-Deception and Emotional Coherence." *Minds and Machines* 13, 213–31.

Scholz, O. R. (2009) "Experts: What They Are And How We Recognize Them – A Discussion of Alvin Goldman's Views." *Grazer Philosophiscke Studien*, 79, 187–205.

Schumpeter, J. (1992) *Capitalism, Socialism and Democracy.* Routledge, London.

Sen, A. (2009) *The Idea of Justice.* Allen Lane, London.

Shibutani, T. (1966) *Improvised News: A Sociological Study of Rumor.* Bobbs-Merrill, Indianapolis, IN.

Singer, J. B. (2010) "Norms and the Network: Journalistic Ethics in a Shared Media Space." In: C. Meyers (ed.), *Journalism Ethics: A Philosophical Approach.* Oxford University Press, Oxford, pp. 117–30.

Singer, P. (1972) "Moral Experts." *Analysis*, 32.4, 115–17.

Slobogin, C. (2002) "Public Privacy: Camera Surveillance of Public Places and the Right to Anonymity." *Mississippi Law Journal*, 72, 213–99.

Smith, A. (1910/1776) *The Wealth of Nations.* Dent, London.

Sosa, E. (1991) *Knowledge in Perspective.* Cambridge University Press, Cambridge, UK.

Stone, I. F. (1973) *The Best of I. F. Stone's Weekly*, ed. N. Middleton. Penguin, Harmondsworth, UK.

References

Sunstein, C. R. (2009) *On Rumors: How Falsehoods Spread, Why We Believe Them, What Can Be Done.* Farrar, Straus & Giroux, New York.

Sunstein, C. R. & Vermeule, A. (2009) "Conspiracy Theories: Causes and Cures." *Journal of Political Philosophy*, 17, 202–27.

Surowiecki, J. (2004) *The Wisdom of Crowds.* Doubleday, New York.

Taylor, C. (1993) *Reconciling the Solitudes: Essays on Canadian Federalism and Nationalism.* McGill-Queen's University Press, Quebec City.

Thompson, A. C. & Paglen, T. (2006) *Torture Taxi.* Melville House, Hoboken, NJ.

Thomson, J. J. (1975) "The Right to Privacy." *Philosophy and Public Affairs*, 4, 295–314.

Thoreau, H. D. (1958/1849) "Civil Disobedience." In: L. Leary (ed.), *Henry David Thoreau: Selected Writings.* Appleton-Century-Crofts, New York, pp. 9–32.

Tollefson, C. (2000) "Journalism and the Social Good." *Public Affairs Quarterly*, 14.4, 293–308.

Tuck, R. (2008) *Free Riding.* Harvard University Press, Cambridge, MA.

von Hirsch, A. (2000) "The Ethics of Public Television Surveillance." In: A. Von Hirsch, A. Garland, & A. Wakefield (eds.), *Ethical and Social Perspectives on Situational Crime Prevention.* Hart Publishing, Oregon, pp. 59–76.

Weiner, T. (2007) *Legacy of Ashes: The History of the CIA.* Doubleday, New York.

West, H. G. & Sanders, S. (eds.) (2003) *Transparency and Conspiracy: Ethnographies of Suspicion in the New World Order.* Duke University Press, Durham, NC.

Whately, R. (1985/1819) *Historic Doubts Relative to Napoleon Bonaparte.* Scholar Press, Berkeley, CA.

Williams, B. (1973) "Deciding to Believe." In: *Problems of the Self: Philosophical Papers 1956–72.* Cambridge University Press, Cambridge, UK, pp. 136–51.

Wilson, R. A. (1998) *Everything is Under Control: Conspiracies, Cults and Cover-ups.* Harper, New York.

Wollheim, R. (1969) "A Paradox in the Theory of Democracy." In: P. Laslett & W. G. Runciman (eds.), *Philosophy, Politics and Society.* Basil Blackwell, Oxford, pp. 71–87.

Zagzebski L. T. (1996) *Virtues of the Mind.* Cambridge University Press, Cambridge, UK.

Index

What To Believe Now: Applying Epistemology to Contemporary Issues,
First Edition. David Coady.
© 2012 David Coady. Published 2012 by Blackwell Publishing Ltd.

Index

propaganda 102, 105, 109n25, 123–5,
129, 136n17

Räikkä, Juha 130, 134
Rawls, John 21–2
Reid, Thomas 34, 53
Rousseau, Jean-Jacques 61, 64, 73,
83n8
rumor(s) 86–109, 110, 122, 123, 138,
160, 170
and gossip *see* gossip
and history 96, 106
-mongers 86, 87, 90–2, 95, 100,
104–6, 108n10, 110, 123, 138,
170
and natural selection 92–5, 103,
108n
spread of 87–96, 100, 103–4,
108n15
as unofficial communications
96–9, 102–3, 105–7
and urban legends *see* urban
legends
workplace 104
Russell, Bertrand 85n27, 173
Ryberg, Jesper 179–80, 182, 183–4,
187n5

Schumpeter, Joseph 67–9, 84n15,
85n30
self-deception 50–1, 57n27
Sen, Amartya 78–9, 82, 85n24
Shibutani, Tamotsu 90, 92–4, 99,
109n24
Singer, Jane 151, 163–4
Singer, Peter 2, 24n5, 53–5, 57n27
skepticism 173
about experts 30–3
about government assertions 124
about morality 52, 57n31

about politics 172–3
about rumors 89, 94, 96, 97, 107n8,
about testimony *see* testimony
Smith, Adam 129, 137n26
social epistemology iv, 20, 172
veritistic (VSE) 20–3, 26n35, 76,
171–2
social policy 20–3, 26n34, 125,
168n43, 175–87
Sosa, Ernest 18
Stewart, Jon *see Daily Show, The*
Stone, I.F. (Izzy) 156, 167n33
Sunstein, Cass R. 96, 101–2, 105,
109n26, 110, 120, 123–5,
135nn17&18, 184
Surowiecki, James 66, 70, 83n6
surveillance 175–87

Taylor, Charles 71
testimony
expert 31–6, 38, 39, 48, 50–1, 56n13
pathological 87
reductionism about 33–5
skepticism about 31–3
theories 130–1
conspiracy *see* conspiracy theories
of normative epistemology *see*
normative epistemology
Thoreau, Henry David 85n28
torture 112, 119, 120, 121, 149,
166n19, 171–2, 174n2, 176

urban legends 103–4
utilitarianism 4–5, 7, 17, 18–19, 20–1

veritism *see* normative epistemology
veritistic social epistemology (VSE)
see social epistemology
Vermeule, Adrian 110, 120, 123–5,
136nn17&18, 184

201

Printed and bound by CPI Group (UK) Ltd, Croydon, CR0 4YY

09/06/2025

14686114-0001